about the authors

David Renton is currently a Senior Research Fellow at the University of Sunderland.

David Seddon is Professor of Politics and Sociology at the School of Development Studies, University of East Anglia.

Leo Zeilig is a researcher at the Centre for Sociological Research at the University of Johannesburg.

the congo: plunder and resistance

David Renton, David Seddon & Leo Zeilig

ZED BOOKS
London & New York

The Congo: Plunder and Resistance was published in 2007 by Zed Books Ltd,
7 Cynthia Street, London N1 9JF, UK, and Room 400, 175 Fifth Avenue,
New York, NY 10010, USA

www.zedbooks.co.uk

Designed and typeset in Monotype Van Dijck
by illuminati, Grosmont, www.illuminatibooks.co.uk
Cover designed by Andrew Corbett
Printed and bound in the EU by Biddles Ltd, King's Lynn

Distributed in the USA exclusively by Palgrave Macmillan, a division of
St Martin's Press, LLC, 175 Fifth Avenue, New York, NY 10010

A catalogue record for this book is available from the British Library
Library of Congress Cataloging-in-Publication Data available
Library and Archives Canada Cataloguing in Publication Data available

ISBN 1 84277 484 0 Hb
ISBN 1 84277 485 9 Pb
ISBN 978 1 84277 484 7 Hb
ISBN 978 1 84277 485 4 Pb

contents

Lubumbashi = Élisabethville	Isiro = Paulis
Katanga = Shaba	Kisangani = Stanleyville
Kalemie = Albertville	Kinshasa = Léopoldville
Kananga = Luluabourg	Mbandaka = Coquilhatville

map   Democratic Republic of the Congo

introduction

The subject of this book is the relationship between the Democratic Republic of the Congo and the West. The country possesses vast reserves of gold, copper, diamonds and uranium, as well as oil, cadmium, cobalt, manganese, silver, tin and zinc. Cocoa, coffee, cotton, tea, palm oil, rubber and timber are all exported from the country today. Under any consideration, its people should be rich. Yet these resources have been stolen. Western intervention started with the colonisation of the country by the Belgian King Léopold in the 1870s, and continues to the present. While the diamond traders have prospered, the benefits have not been shared. Instead, the conflict between different interests has fuelled a civil war in which millions have died. At one point in the early 1960s there was a real attempt to wrest power from the external forces. But a civil war was fomented and the elected prime minister, Patrice Lumumba, was killed. The Western powers were implicated in his murder. This episode was the first serious attempt to create a democratic government of the Congo by the Congolese, but it failed. Nothing on the same scale has been attempted since. Over a period of 130 years, the wealth of the Congo has been exported, its people starved and enslaved. For the past decade, especially since the death of the country's long-standing dictator General Joseph-Désiré Mobutu, the country has been involved in terrible wars, which have also involved several of the surrounding states. The Congo is perhaps the prime example of what happens to a territory that owns minerals wanted by the capitalist West. The story of the country shows what can happen to countries rich in minerals. Its story has been repeated across the continent, in Angola, Nigeria, Algeria and elsewhere.

Writing about the Congo for a British audience is a chastening experience. Two celebrated books stand in the way: Joseph Conrad's *Heart of Darkness* and Adam Hochschild's *King Leopold's Ghost*. Many readers, we anticipate, will be familiar with the rough outlines of the Congo's history, at least between 1870 and 1900. They will know that the country was once the personal possession of a single ruler, King Léopold of the Belgians. They will know also that his dominion was a time of particular brutality. More readers, we anticipate, will be unfamiliar with the middle and later sections of our book: the account of the fifty years' rule of the Congo after Léopold; the events of independence from Belgium and of Mobutu's rule; the demise of the latter and the civil war that has followed. An American audience might be more familiar with the events of the last ten years. A Belgian audience would be more familiar with events surrounding the murder of the Congolese prime minister Patrice Lumumba. As for Congolese narratives of their country's history, they have a tendency to confound all expectations. For example, André Yav's *Vocabulary of Élisabethville*, the first written history of the Congo to have been produced in today's Lubumbashi (it was written in 1965), and described more fully in our second chapter, treats Léopold as a sort of benevolent sage, a man with a white beard who was planning only to bring resources to Africa. 'If King Léopold II had not died we would not have remained in slavery as we did under King Albert the First.' By contrast, we follow Hochschild in arguing that Léopold was a tyrant. He established habits of private theft and absolute rule that have cursed the country since.

Many people have heard the heroic story of the anti-slavery campaigners, who fought in Britain, America and Belgium against the tyranny of 'red rubber'. There is much less knowledge of the way in which that same campaign looked two ways at once. Unusually among British protest movements, for example, it had more than a hundred supporters in the House of Lords. It was able to draw such backing because of a strong feeling among the rulers of Britain that the Congo should never have been Belgian. Having been discovered by British explorers, the country was properly 'ours'.

Another way in which a British perspective threatens to distort is by focusing on the extraordinary tragedy of Léopold's era; previous writers almost seem to have forgotten that a tragedy of similar dimensions has been unfolding right in front of our eyes. The conflict that began in the Congo in 1998, and that still smoulders on, especially in the north and east of the country, has resulted in several million deaths. The United Nations has estimated that 2.5 million lives have been lost. Amnesty puts the figure at over 3 million. The International Rescue Committee has its own figures of deaths between January 1998 and the end of April 2004: 3.8 million.[1] It is extraordinary how little discussion there has been in Britain of these killings: they are the much larger product of the much smaller Rwandan genocide; but events in Rwanda, by contrast, are much better known in the West. The last two chapters of our book build towards this recent history, explaining why the conflict began, and showing how other historical possibilities were missed.

The chapters follow a chronological sequence. The first main chapter, 'Missionaries and Traders', addresses the period between 1870 and 1908. This was a moment of land-grab and plunder. Western rulers and businessmen saw their roles as being those of missionaries or explorers. Yet the purpose of Stanley, Livingstone and King Léopold of Belgium was as much to spread trade as Christianity. Léopold in particular instituted a system of effective slavery in the production of rubber, which both guaranteed profits to his circle and held back the chances of any healthy development in the region. Vast profits were made. Léopold used the proceeds to build palaces and monuments. Around half the population, meanwhile, or some 10 million people, may have died. Reports of the brutal treatment of Africans in the Congo led to a popular campaign for self-government. The demand for reform of the Belgian Congo was raised in America, where politicians threatened to investigate King Léopold, and above all in Britain, where the opponents of this private empire included the writers E.D. Morel, Roger Casement and Arthur Conan Doyle. The Belgian deputy Émile Vandervelde toured the region and in one famous case defended the critics of the empire in the Congo's courts. The future of the country was determined by a shift in the demands of the Belgian opposition. Once the Socialists had accepted the need for a reformed colony, then the conditions for the next period were in place.

The second chapter, 'Miners and Planters', examines the era from 1908 to 1945. Following the formal annexation of the Congo by Belgium in 1908, the relationship between the West and the Congo altered. In a new period, the emphasis was supposed to be on reforming away the excess of empire. The rubber merchants remarketed themselves as industrialists. In order to support the manufacture of heavy industrial products, the state was obliged to begin spending on schools, hospitals, trains and roads. By the end of the 1914–18 war, mining, and especially copper mining, had become the mainstay of the economy. Yet the conditions of forced labour in the mines continued, with large numbers dying as they were dragooned to work. Anger against colonialism was never long concealed. One of the first forms it took was the religious movement of Simon Kimbangu. As the economy grew, significant workers' strikes took place, including a miners' strike in 1941 and a dockers' strike in 1945. The country possessed a large and stable working class, but, as a result of the legacy of forced labour, it was one with a low rate of unionisation. Meanwhile uranium for the first atomic bombs dropped on Japan came from the Congo, and so the country became of vital national interest to America.

The third chapter, 'Rebels and Generals', looks at the period after 1945, when the most important players were not the West, but the people of the Congo. Through mass protests they showed that they were no longer willing to be governed in the old way. In an era of decolonisation, serious discussions began as to how the African state might be used to build up a strong, democratic society, governing in the interests of its own people. This moment was brought to an end in 1961, by direct foreign intervention. Patrice Lumumba, the figure who best expressed the demand for radical democratic rule, was accused of being a Soviet stooge. He was murdered, on the orders of America and Belgium, and with the connivance of the United Nations. The defeat of this movement for an African democracy led immediately to civil war.

The fourth chapter, 'The Great Dictator', examines the West's return, from 1965 onwards, as the champions of the most regressive, militarised rule under President Mobutu. The West assisted General Mobutu to power as the strong man who would protect American interests in the Congo and across central Africa. With the backing of America, Belgium, France and other Western countries, Mobutu destroyed the economy using the mining companies and the central bank as his personal wealth. Meanwhile, the regime justified itself using an ideology of 'authenticity'. In 1971 the country was renamed Zaïre. In 1972, Katanga was renamed Shaba, in an attempt to destroy the region's long association with campaigns for secession. With Western backing for repression, Mobutu was able to remain in power for over thirty years. Yet even now, an opposition movement continued, based in the cities, and with the support of student groups and others. In the early 1990s, it seemed to have the support needed to topple Mobutu by parliamentary means and without war.

The fifth chapter, 'The Failed "Transition"', addresses a second moment of hope, not on the grand scale of 1960, but something more modest: the idea that in the aftermath of the revolutions in Eastern Europe of 1989, President Mobutu might peacefully be persuaded to concede power or resign. Between 1990 and 1992, a protest movement was born, taking root in every city among workers, the young and the poor. Students at the University of Kinshasa sparked the protests. Food riots followed. Under considerable pressure, Mobutu accepted a certain liberalisation: rival political parties were tolerated, and an all-party National Conference convened. Yet, in a pattern that has been repeated elsewhere in the continent, the protest movement was unable to replace the leader. Instead, the enduring poverty of the country, in a context of declining trade and production, served fatally to undermine the opposition, making it a movement of people with anger but no confidence in their own ability to affect change. Mobutu survived. The failure of the protests eased the way for the later wars.

The sixth chapter, 'Speculators and Thieves,' describes how over the last dozen years an older model of military state capitalism has given way to private capitalism. Not just in the Democratic Republic of the Congo but globally, the demands of the West have become more urgent. Structural adjustment has diminished the central authority. A weakened state has been unable to defend itself against civil war. Following the genocide in Rwanda, widespread clashes took place between Zaïre's Tutsi minority and newly arrived Hutu militants. The conflicts continued, spiralled, and drew in other players. In the words of one recent UN report, foreign companies 'were ready to do business regardless of elements of unlawfulness ... Companies trading minerals which the [UN] considered to be "the engine of the conflict in the Congo" have prepared the field for illegal mining activities in the country.' It was at this moment and with Rwandan backing that Laurent Kabila began his successful bid for power. Mobutu gave way to Kabila, Kabila to his son. Yet the most important changes have been systemic, in the general nature of the relationship between the West and the South post-1989. In the Congo, this has meant a return to features common of nineteenth-century capitalism: naked plunder, theft and greed. Other features of the war have included the presence of America as an arbiter behind the scenes, the military and economic rivalry of the Congo's neighbours, and a change in the nature of economic activity, in war conditions: the break-up of large units of capital, in favour of smaller units, privately owned. In the early 1980s, state-owned Gécamines produced 90 per cent of the country's copper output and a large share of world output. Production has fallen sharply, partly because of lower copper prices, partly because of the changing global context, partly because of domestic Congolese crises. During the recent wars, large-scale copper production came to a halt. The most profitable sectors of the Congolese economy are now the trades in coltan and diamonds: goods that can be produced by artisans, working with their hands. The state raises just $5 in taxes per person per year. What is there to distribute? The entire country has been stripped bare.

I

missionaries and traders

The history of the Congo long precedes contact with those Europeans who claimed to have first 'discovered' the country. The archaeological evidence has allowed some writers to describe a Sangoan people, who inhabited the region of central Africa some 50,000 years ago. They worked with choppers and scrapers and travelled between caves lit by fire.[1] The first known inhabitants, however, were pygmies, hunters and gatherers living in the forests of the north and north-east. The Egyptians knew of pygmies in Africa probably from the time of the fifth dynasty (c. 2500 BCE) when an expedition brought back 'a dwarf' from the land of Punt. Pharaoh Pepi II of the sixth dynasty (around 2300 BCE) had images of pygmies drawn on his tomb. By the last centuries BCE, small numbers of Bantu-speaking people had migrated into Congo from the north and west (today's Nigeria and Cameroon) and settled in the south. The Bantu were agriculturalists who employed Iron Age technology.

The linguist David Lee Schoenbrun suggests that the population of the Eastern Congo was part of a trading bloc that extended from present-day Katanga to Lake Victoria. The peoples of the Great Lakes 'represented an enormous variety of historical traditions in ancient Africa'. They included hunters and gatherers, fishermen and settled farmers, potters and ironworkers, merchants and traders. The evidence of their settlement includes Stone Age sites on Lake Kivu, as well as ceramic 'Urewe ware', from around 700 BCE. Many different languages were spoken. Farmers used pottery and metal, settling on lands with good soil and rainfall. Deposits of charcoal have been found from smelting furnaces, dating back to around 200 CE. 'Forests were larders where communities could trap animals, collect medicines, produce lumber and find fibres for clothing from sources like the bark cloth-bearing *Ficus* tree. The dense, wet landscape provided people with a rich diet, and useful tools.[2]

Although the first settled farmers may already have been working the land, agriculture only took off after the use of iron became widespread. Later farmers used pottery and metal, settling on lands with good soil and rainfall. Agricultural innovation took place: around 500 CE we have evidence of local peoples eating millet and cowpeas. People also learned to keep cattle for their milk and blood. Cattle herding encouraged the creation and appropriation of surpluses, and the rise of hierarchical societies. So too did control of the trade in valuable minerals.

The Mongo, who remain in the Great Forest area of the Congo today, inhabited the forest regions east of Mbandaka from at least the first century CE, when they left traces of their life as hunters and yam farmers. Their main strategies for gathering food included gathering, trapping and hunting. Their diet included fruit, palm kernels, mushrooms, caterpillars, snails, termites, spices, root drinks, monkeys, antelopes, boars, elephants, fish, maize, groundnuts, beans, yams, bananas and oil palms.[3] The dense, wet landscape provided people with a rich diet, and useful tools. 'Forests were larders where communities could trap animals, collect medicines, produce lumber and find fibres for clothing from sources like the bark cloth-bearing *Ficus* tree.[4] Bananas were especially important in the central Congo: they thrived in wet, dense rainforests, where the main alternative crops (yams) often rotted. By around 700 CE copper was being traded on a 1,500-mile journey between the Katanga region and the northern lakes. Its use was a badge of leadership. Cattle herding encouraged the rise of monarchies and even empires.

Relatively little is known about the development of the more complex societies but a more complex division of labour, into chiefs, diviners, doctors and mediums had evolved in the region by around

1000 CE.[5] Early kingdoms included the empire of the Luba, founded in the early sixteenth century and based around lakes Kisale and Upemba in central Shaba. The empire of the Bakongo was founded around the fourteenth century at the mouth of the river and included parts of today's Angola as well as today's Congo. This empire came about as the Bakongo migrated south across the Congo river. Their main commerce was in ivory and hides.

After the fifteenth century, food crops, such as manioc, increased the range of agricultural products, but population densities were never high and agriculture remained based, for the most part, on shifting cultivation rather than settled agriculture. Even today, population density in the Congo is relatively low, about 22 people per square kilometre, and unevenly distributed. Population density in the Great Forest is only about half of the national average, with stretches of several tens of thousands of square kilometres virtually empty because of the dense forest cover. It is here that the pygmies still mainly live, although other groups also inhabit the forest areas. At the edges of the forests, where the trees have been cleared for settlement, population densities are often higher than the national average. At the northern edge of the Great Forest population densities increase up to twenty people per square kilometre and then drop to one or two per square kilometre only in the extreme north of the country towards the Central African Republic. The extreme south is also sparsely populated, with between one and three people per square kilometre.

The land upon which the Bakongo settled was at the western tip of a vast country, little of which they claimed. Its geography included savannas, high plateaus, volcanoes, lakes, rivers and rainforest. The most important feature was the River Congo itself. Its waters are drained from a plateau deep in the African interior. From the edge of this plateau, the river descends 1,000 feet in 220 miles of falls, rapids and cascades. So powerful is the river that on joining the ocean, it carves a canyon in the ocean bed, 100 miles long, and up to 4,000 feet deep. We can understand, then, why the Bakongo held mainly to the west, and knew little of the interior. It was simply impossible to travel upstream by canoe. The land that locals knew was remarkable enough. Even now, the diminished wildlife of the Congo still includes numerous varieties of birds and insects, along with, lions, elephants, okapi, chimpanzees, hippos, gorillas, bonobos, antelope, bushrat and crocodile – a diversity of species. The Congo also holds, of course, a vast mineral wealth.

For the history of the Congo, we have to rely on written sources, and for earlier periods these are rare. We are forced to depend on accounts produced from the outside. Our problem is that Europeans in particular knew little of Africa's historical development. Trying to use these sources is like peering into a shallow river: images come back to us, but they are vague and distorted, and we struggle to make sense of the real history beneath them. In the fifth century BCE, Herodotus reports a story told of 'a group of wild young fellows' who travelled south from Libya into the African interior and, after crossing the desert and travelling far to the west, came to a 'vast tract of marshy country' inhabited by 'little men, of less than middle height', and to 'a town, all the inhabitants of which were of the same small stature, and all black. A great river with crocodiles in it flowed past the town from west to east'. The description may refer to the Niger river or to the Bodele Depression northeast of Lake Chad, now dry. Herodotus also reports Phoenician sailors circumnavigating the continent in a clockwise direction around the end of the seventh century or beginning of the sixth century BCE, and another voyage in the fifth century BCE down the west coast of Africa by Sataspes the Achaemenian, who reported to the Persian king Xerxes that, 'at the most southerly point they had reached, they found the coast occupied by small men, wearing palm leaves'.[6] Although Herodotus and his contemporaries usually named the whole continent 'Libya', the name 'Africa' is usually said to derive from the Greek word *aphrike*, meaning without cold.[7]

The Romans were familiar with the Mediterranean regions of North Africa, and with the trans-Saharan trade, which brought valuable goods from beyond the desert; but they knew little of the lands to the south. In the period after the decline of the Roman Empire, European knowledge of the continent remained limited, in part as a result of the Christian preoccupation with the Scriptures and with a world centred on Jerusalem and the Holy Land, and in part by force of political geography. Hostile Muslim rulers occupied the north of Africa and in any case European ships were incapable of travelling far to the south. Rumours filled the void. Sailors spoke of a Sea of Darkness, breathing with giant serpents. Other stories hinted of lands where gold, spices and precious stones might easily be found. One powerful tale was the twelfth-century legend of Prester John, a fabulously wealthy Christian ruler living on the east side of the Islamic empire. Stories of his empire were used to justify the Second and Third Crusades. Marco Polo even reported Prester John's death.[8] The destruction of the Mongol empire, and the rise of the Ming dynasty put a temporary end to these stories, as trading links between Europe and China were broken.

Africa was not unknown to Europeans at this time, particularly the coastal regions of the Maghreb and of Egypt, but there was virtually no knowledge of the vast regions south of the Sahara. Beyond the familiar world of the Mediterranean coastal areas and the Near East, few ventured to go. Rumours abounded, however, and the trans-Saharan trade revealed to the European merchants established in the cities of North Africa the wealth (in gold and ivory) of 'black' Africa, far to the south. Books described the incredible wealth of lands beyond the seas, the extraordinary challenges that awaited explorers and the strange people and monsters lying in wait to attack them. The storytellers usually had little first-hand knowledge of these exotic regions. Typical were the descriptions given by Mandeville's *Travels*, fanciful accounts of travels in strange lands by an English squire who had never visited any of them. The legend of Prester John was also relocated to Africa.

In 1415, a Portuguese invasion captured the Moroccan city of Ceuta. Following this conquest, and increased access to the trans-Saharan trade, stories began to circulate in Europe of kingdoms south of the Sahara, in Mali, Ghana and Songhai, and cities in Timbuktu, Gao and Cantor. Into the middle years of the fifteenth century, Dom Henrique, the Portuguese ruler of Ceuta, still determined to find Prester John's descendants.

As late as the early fifteenth century, the Venetian fleet, probably the most powerful in Europe at the time, consisted of boats dependent on rowers and was effectively confined to the Mediterranean. New developments in shipbuilding by the Portuguese and Spaniards, however, made further exploration into the Atlantic possible. From the 1440s onwards, the development of a 100-foot long ship, the caravel, enabled Portuguese sailors to travel greater distances. In

1482 Diogo Cão became the first European to visit the area of the modern Congo, when he reached the mouth of the Congo river and sailed a few miles upstream. It was the river that drew his interest. The Congo was the greatest river that any European had seen. For 20 leagues it emptied fresh water into the ocean. The waves breaking on the beach were an astonishing yellow colour, and the ocean was muddy-red as far as the eye could see. Cão recognized the importance of the Congo river as a possible source of transport and trade. He set up a stone pillar marking this Portuguese 'discovery'. He claimed the river and lands around it for the Portuguese king.[9]

Cão regarded himself as the man who discovered these territories, yet the empire of the Bakongo already possessed a ruler, Nzinga Nkuwu, who led some 2–3 million people. The population of the capital Banza (later São Salvador) was around 40,000. Its citizens traded shells, sea-salt, fish, pottery, wicker, raffia, copper and lead.[10] Nkuwu's authority was semi-feudal in character. Local lords had the right to control land, in return for which they paid taxes to their king. His people were skilled in iron- and copper-working and especially weaving. They grew bananas, yams, and fruit; they kept goats, pigs and cattle and fished. From palm trees, they manufactured oil, wine, vinegar and a form of bread. The society was prosperous and self-sufficient. Yet the Bakongo were said to lack any concept of seasons, or a calendar, and the wheel had not been discovered. Cão met Nzinga Nkuwu, and encouraged him to send ambassadors to meet the King of Portugal. Cão then continued on his travels, heading south.[11]

In the aftermath of Cão's visit, Nkuwu opened up his kingdom to Portuguese influences, and soon missionaries, soldiers and noblemen could be found at his court. Following further visits in 1491 and 1500, Nzinga Nkuwu even agreed to convert to Catholicism, starting Africa's first Catholic dynasty. In 1506, Nzinga Mbemba Affonso succeeded him to the throne. Affonso was an intelligent, literate man, who understood that his country might gain from certain forms of European learning, their science, woodworking and om masonry, their weapons and their goods.[12] The challenge was to allow selective modernisation, to take the best parts of Western knowledge, while declining the worst parts, the cruelty and the greed.

Over time, the actions of the Portuguese began to alarm the Bakongo. Their worries grew as the Portuguese extended and professionalised the slave trade. Prior to then, slaves had been part of the domestic economy, and were even sometimes exchanged, but the trade had never been central to the economy of the region. Under Portuguese rule, the number of slaves increased, and their economic role grew. As well as holding lands in today's Morocco, the Portuguese were also settled in today's Brazil, where they set Africans to work, digging and working mines, and harvesting coffee. Slaves were also sent to the plantations of the Caribbean. In order to work these lands at their full capacity, a regular supply of new labour was needed. In the land of the Bakongo, Portuguese traders began to promote feuds between neighbours, knowing that any conflict would result in greater numbers of slaves. Young men set out to work as masons, teachers or priests; but then, faced with the actual dynamics of the existing Portuguese economy, they soon realised that their fortune would be made more quickly if they learned to trade in slaves instead.

Nzinga Affonso was a remarkable, learned man. In 1518 his son was consecrated as a Roman Catholic bishop, the last black man to hold such a position for four centuries. Affonso became a great witness to the horror of sixteenth century Portuguese colonialism. Many of his letters survive, including one sent to King João III of Portugal in 1526:

> Each day the traders are kidnapping our people ... children of this country, sons of our nobles and vassals, even people of our own family.... We need in this kingdom only priests and schoolteachers, and no merchandise, unless it is wine and flour for Mass.... It is our wish that this kingdom not be a place for the trade or transport of slaves.[13]

The ruler of the Bakongo understood that many of the richest of his people were complicit in the slave trade. So taken were they by these new Western goods that they were willing to sell even their relatives. The only way to stop his people from doing this was to limit their access to the West. Of course, Affonso was no better than his times. He did not argue that all slavery should be abolished. He felt rather that it should be regulated, and conducted with respect to the society in which it took place. The Portuguese system horrified him because it was incapable of recognising any limit. In 1526, Affonso reported that the Portuguese were inciting his nobles to rise against the throne. By the mid-1530s, 5,000 Bakongo slaves were being sent west each year. Some used the passage to rise up against the traders.[14] In their absence, the society from which the slaves had been taken was reduced almost to penury. It was no longer able to defend itself from its rivals, descending from lands to the east.

One particular group, the Yakas, or Gagas, or Jagas, attacked the Bakongo from the mid-1500s onwards. Andrew Battell, a sailor originally from Leigh in Essex, observed these fierce warriors at close quarter. He came to Africa having been captured by the Portuguese. Battell described the Yakas as a bellicose people, harvesting palms for wine, pillaging and raiding, quite unlike the urbanised and more peaceful Bakongo. Battell lived among the Yakas for two years as a prisoner, before escaping, and later publishing his memoirs. He reported:

> The Yakas spoile the Countrie. They stay no longer in a place, than it will afford them maintenance. And then in Harvest time they arise, and settle themselves in the fruitfullest place they can find; and doe reape their Enemies Corne, and take their Cattell. For they will not sowe, nor plant, nor bring up any Cattell, more then they take by Warres.[15]

In 1571, the Bakongo, perhaps by virtue of their more productive economic base and better-organised state system, or possibly as a result of access via the Portuguese traders to muskets and gunpowder, finally defeated the Yakas. In the years that followed, a number of attempts were made to rebuild their society and to establish a new relationship with the West, based on fairer relations of trade. Western rugs, beads, mirrors, knives, swords, muskets, gunpowder, copper, tin and alcohol have all been found in the ruins of the towns.[16] Yet the series of wars between the Bakongo and their neighbours served to undermine the older, more urban civilisation of the Bakongo. Soon the Bakongo were neither secure nor free.

One legacy of the Portuguese conquests was a diminution of the power of the Bakongo kings in relation to other regional rulers, who had previously recognised their sovereignty. The seventeenth century saw many wars between the different peoples of the region. Lisbon made a series of attempts to re-establish a base at the capital São Salvador, which failed. The city itself was destroyed in 1678. Another Capuchin mission was expelled in 1717. In 1857 the German traveller Dr. Bastian found São Salvador 'an ordinary native town', with few monuments of its past.[17] New societies flourished on the ruins of the Kongo and Yaka societies. The kingdom of Kuba was founded in the sixteenth century by a federation of immigrants, the Bushong. They settled in the area along the Kasai and Sankuru rivers. Beside the Bushong groups, the Kuba federation incorporated among its members the previous inhabitants of the region, the Twa and the Kete, who continued to live alongside the new arrivals. The Kuba monarch was elected for a limited, four-year term. Women were eligible to stand for office. The kingdom lasted till 1910.[18] Further south, there were several large civilisations, based in present-day Katanga. A Luba state was formed by clan fusion perhaps before 1500, a Lunda state before 1450. The Luba had four kingdoms by the seventeenth century: Kikonja, Kaniok, Kalundwe and Kasongo. The Lunda state arose to Luba's south-west, covering about 400 by 800 miles with two tributary states by 1760, Yaka and Kazembe, each with a capital so named. A Bemba empire began to form towards the end of the eighteenth century under Lunda pressure. These civilisations traded with the Portuguese but were not conquered. The Luba empire broke into Yeke and Swahili–Arab spheres in the 1870s and 1880s, while Yeke and Chokwe broke up the Kazembe and Lunda states.[19]

Despite the destruction of their main allies and their own defeat, the Portuguese retained an interest in the region. In the late eighteenth century, Lisbon-backed African and mulatto traders (*pombeiros*) traded with the kingdom of the Kazembe to the south. In the middle of the nineteenth century, Arab, Swahili and Nyamwezi traders from present-day Tanzania also penetrated the highlands of the Congo from the east, and began a trade there in slaves and ivory. A lively Arabic literature began, describing travels through northern and central Africa.[20] Some traders established their own states. One merchant, Muhammad bin Hamad, or Tippu Tip, from Zanzibar ruled much of eastern Congo, into the 1890s.[21]

As late as the 1870s, the region remained a patchwork of disparate tribes and rulers with no political coherence. This last point is of great importance. For while the British and the French empires in Africa were secured at the cost of great battles, in several of which the colonisers were defeated, the later Belgian empire of the Congo seems to have been achieved without the same military costs. The future rulers of the country were able to capture it without significant conflict, or, more accurately, without their wars ending in the sorts of defeats that would have been noticed in the West. Indeed, in doing so, the new Belgian rulers of the Congo convinced many people that theirs was a new, different and consensual empire. Outside the Congo, it took many years before the true horrors of the conquest became known.

Livingstone and Stanley

By the start of the nineteenth century, Portuguese power had long been in decline. New imperial nations had come to the fore, including Britain, France and Germany. America held its own African colony, the semi-independent state of Liberia. The greatest of all these powers were the British, for they not only possessed the territorial advantage of established naval bases in many regions, they were also the most important industrial power of their day. As the British explorers finally made headway into the interior of Africa, they searched for river routes. Mungo Park travelled through Gambia and Niger seeking the origins of the Nile.[22] Other explorers developed an idea that the Niger river flowed south into the sea. One claim was even that it ended at the mouth of the Congo. Attempts were made to prove this theory. In 1816, Captain J.K. Tuckey lost seventeen men upstream of Boma on an ill-fated expedition. The survivors succeeded in mapping just 150 miles of new territory. Further exploration was discouraged. Public interest was renewed, however, following the successful exploration of the Niger. A new goal was needed, and dreams of discovering the White Nile's source encouraged a new fever of exploration. Some geographers argued that Lake Victoria was its source, while others spoke up for Lake Tanganyika. Richard Burton advanced as far as Matadi in 1863. The explorer Dr David Livingstone set out to resolve the dispute.

Livingstone had been born to a poor family in Lanarkshire, Scotland. A prospector, missionary and occasional British consul,

Livingstone made his name by exploring southern Africa, from the early 1840s onwards. As he progressed with missionary work he developed a desire to travel further and deeper into the continent. Livingstone's mission was driven by a complex series of motives: philanthropy, a belief in the civilising work of commerce, the idea also that Africa was some new space with its history waiting to begin.[23] The Ministry of Foreign Affairs sponsored his expedition. The government's hope was that any discovery would make vast new tracts of land available to religion and trade. Although Livingstone never saw Africans as his equal, he loved them with the Christian charity of a true Victorian. 'We do not believe in any incapacity of the African in either mind or heart', he wrote. 'Reverence for royalty sometimes leads the mass of the people to submit to great cruelty, and even murder, at the hands of a depot or a madman; but on the whole, their rule is mild, and the same remark applies in a degree to the religion.'[24]

Livingstone portrayed his work as a great civilising mission: to rescue the peoples of central and eastern African from being held as slaves by Arab traders. This mission resonated with the children of those who had supported previous campaigns against the British slave trade. For different reasons, the message also had an appeal to the propertied classes, the former slave-traders and their descendants. As may happen, the leading industrial power in the world, on reaching its position of sovereignty, had come to the conclusion that all trade should now take place on a footing of complete freedom. There should be as few tariffs as possible; the exploitation of slave labour was immoral and commercially unfair. From 1811 onwards, British agents had opposed the international trade in slaves, and the last slave market was closed in Zanzibar in 1873.[25] The British project was to demonstrate that there were other ways of relating to the continent. Considerable attention therefore focused on the Arab slavers of East Africa, a visible target, in contrast to the allied Spanish and Portuguese traders, who were tolerated even as they still sent slaves to Brazil.[26] Many Arab traders were of African descent. They were most active in the Swahili-speaking territories of modern Kenya and Tanzania. Having captured people there, the slavers sold them on in Persia or Madagascar, or in the Arabian Peninsula, or compelled them to work plantations in Africa itself.

In 1866, Livingstone set off on one further voyage of discovery. In the course of his travels, he discovered the Lualaba river, located in the south-east of modern-day Congo. Yet he had no means to report his find to the West. Three years passed, and there was no news. Rumours suggested that Livingstone had been killed. It was at this stage that James Gordon Bennett, the owner of the *New York Herald* saw the opportunity for a major scoop. He instructed a 28-year-old reporter, Henry Morton Stanley, to search for Livingstone. Stanley's expedition would kindle a lifelong need for expedition in its author. Over the course of the next twenty years, this journalist did as much as anyone to found the later Belgian Empire in the Congo.

Stanley's origins, like those of Livingstone, were obscure. One of five illegitimate children of a housemaid, Stanley had the name John Rowlands when he entered the workhouse, aged 6. At 18, he left Britain for America, where he served both sides and without distinction in the American Civil War. Certain traits of Stanley's character were now evident: a pathological fear of women, an inability to work with talented co-workers, and an obsequious love of the aristocratic rich. In 1867, he reported the Indian wars for the Northern press. The following year, he was sent by the *Herald* to report on a British war with Abyssinia. Stanley had the foresight to bribe the clerks in Suez, ensuring that only his reports were sent back. Within days, he had converted a temporary posting into a permanent career.

Stanley's claim was that his editor met him in Paris in 1869, where he was told, 'Do what you think best, but find Livingstone!' In fact, he spent the next twelve months dawdling, before taking 190 men with him into Africa. His book *How I Found Livingstone* records that Stanley picked up the track of Livingstone at Lake Tanganyika and followed them into unknown territory. His following narrative records the peril of swamps, crocodiles, disease and Arab slavers. Stanley was the only journalist to cover his own adventure. His two white companions both died on the journey. So did an uncounted number of black porters and guides, starved and whipped by their leader, or victims of the hostile environment. Stanley finally caught up with Livingstone at Ujiji on the eastern shore of Lake Tanganyika in 1871. When found, Livingstone was suffering from acute pneumonia and coughing blood. Stanley's first apocryphal words were 'Dr Livingstone, I presume?'

David Livingstone died in Zambia in 1873 without solving the mystery of the Nile. Yet his failure had produced a greater discovery. The Lualaba river led Europeans to the source of the Congo, the best road to central Africa. In 1874, Stanley returned, exploring the Congo from its upper reaches. He worked his followers at an extraordinary rate, as they trekked through the jungle. It was a hostile and unforgiving world. 'The trees kept shedding their dew upon us like rain in great round drops', Stanley wrote;

Every leaf seemed to be weeping. Down the boles and branches, creepers and vegetable cords, the moisture trickled and fell on us. Overhead the widespread branches in many interlaced strata, each branch heavy with broad thick leaves, absolutely shut out the daylight. We knew not whether it was a sunshine day or a dull, foggy, gloomy day, for we marched in a feeble, solemn twilight.[27]

Stanley ordered deaths recklessly. He boasted of the nickname that the frightened Congolese gave him, *Bula Matari*, or the Breaker of Rocks.[28]

Stanley finished his 11,000-kilometre journey in 1877. What astonished him was the realisation that the Lualaba, a north-flowing river, then turned west and became the Congo. Stanley told the readers of the *Daily Telegraph*, 'This river is and will be the grand highway of commerce to West Central Africa.'[29] Despite the bluster, Stanley was inconsistent in his attitude. Sometimes he described the region of the Congo to his readers as an empty territory. At other times he wrote as if the problem was not the emptiness of the land, but the inability of the locals to work it fruitfully:

A five-mile march across that intervening stretch of plain between Kinshasa and Kintamo may cause our Europeans to reflect upon the prodigious waste which this madcap population by whom they are surrounded is guilty of. Eight hundred muscular slaves, retainers, followers of the nine Kintamo chiefs, absolutely doing nothing. Nay, they are almost starving, only one day from it at least, and here, round about them, are nearly 50,000 square acres of the richest alluvium it would be possible to find in any part of the world! At Kinshasa there are some five hundred stalwart bodies just as lazy. Mikungu, Kimbangu, Kindolo, Lema and other places, can show over fifteen hundred more, whose most industrious employment is sitting down, while they are being rubbed all over with palm-oil and ochre by their females, or having their beautiful chignons or hair top-knots dressed.[30]

Stanley described even the land as glutted:

> there exists on this immense waste of fat earth, enough virtue, if solicited, to raise half a million tons of rice annually, and wheat, sugar, yams, potatoes, millet, Indian corn *ad infinitum*. The lower slopes, too, of those ridges, which lovingly shield the plain from the cold winds of the South Atlantic, would permit the remunerative growth of tea, coffee, sago and other spices.

His dream was to convert of the people of the Congo into wage labourers.

> In every cordial-faced aborigine whom I meet I see a promise of assistance to me in the redemption of himself from the state of unproductiveness in which he at present lives. I look upon him with much of the same regard that an agriculturalist views his strong-limbed child; he is a future recruit to the ranks of soldier-labourers. The Congo basin, could I have but enough of his class, would become a vast productive garden.[31]

Some parts of the Congo were ill developed, of course. In the rainforests, paths had to be cut through thick and fast-growing foliage. Semi-nomadic peoples kept the white traveller at a distance. Yet in the savannah, by contrast, there were large towns and established kingdoms. To these areas, Stanley brought the eye of a commercial surveyor.

> Among the many items available which commercial intercourse would teach the natives to employ profitably, are monkey, goat, antelope, buffalo, lion and leopard skins; the gorgeous feathers of the tropic birds, hippopotamus teeth, bees-wax, frankincense, myrrh, tortoise-shell, *Cannabis sativa*, and lastly ivory, which to-day is considered the most valuable product.[32]

At times, Stanley's eye for profit was extraordinary:

> It may be presumed that there are about 200,000 elephants in about 15,000 herds in the Congo basin, each carrying, let us say, on an average 50 lbs. weight of ivory in his head, which would represent, when collected and sold in Europe, £5,000,000.

He even acknowledged the skills of the Congolese, in order to count them on his balance sheet:

> In minerals this section is by no means poor. Iron is abundant. The Yalulima, Iboko, Irebu and Ubangi are famous for their swordsmiths. The Yakusu and Basoko are pre-eminent for their spears. In the museum of the [International African] Association at Brussels are spear-blades six feet long and four inches broad, which I collected among those tribes.[33]

Stanley attempted to interest the British government in the commercial exploitation of the region, without great success. Indeed he was not alone in this failure. Another rival explorer, Lieutenant Cameron, had followed Livingstone's route. He signed treaties with various chiefs, and had in 1875 declared that the lands of the Congo Basin now belonged to the British Crown. The obstacle facing both Cameron and Stanley was the hegemony of Gladstone's Liberals in Parliament.[34] These were the middle years of the nineteenth century, a period before empires or trusts. The ruling class of Britain remained converted to a policy of expansion by trade, without tariffs, annexations or slavery. It was a moment of peace. The idea that the European powers could achieve progress without conquest was still dominant.

'The king with ten million murders on his soul'[35]

Searching for a patron, Stanley turned his attention to another rich and powerful man, King Léopold II of the Belgians. Léopold's title, with its emphasis on the peoples he ruled rather than the land of his dominion, pointed to a basic insecurity in his state. Belgium had only acquired independence as recently as 1830, and its society contained two distinct linguistic groups, speakers of French and of Flemish. In the period of Léopold's reign, the mood of the majority was also notably secular and republican. There was no natural bond of loyalty between the people and their king. In a position of weakness, Léopold's strategy was to build up his own private power. He was clever enough to see that progress could be achieved most quickly outside Belgium, even outside Europe. Long before he claimed the Belgian throne, Léopold had been an adventurer.

As Duke of Brabant, Léopold had studied the Dutch Empire in Java, a system of government that produced a strong surplus to the exchequer. Another of his schemes was for the purchase of islands off the coast of Argentina.

In 1876, Léopold used the occasion of a geographical conference in Belgium to found an International African Association (AIA). This would be an international organisation of explorers and philanthropists. Supported by grants from Brussels, the Association would propagandise for the abolition of the Arab slave trade. Local committees would be established in each country, electing upwards to an international committee. Léopold volunteered to act as the Association's first chair. His address made much of the philanthropic motives behind African exploration:

> The subject which brings us together today is one of the most important facing humanity. To open up to civilisation the only part of the world which has not been discovered, to pierce the shadows which envelope entire peoples.... Do I need to remind you that in bringing you all to Brussels, I have not been guided by any egotistic purpose? No, Gentlemen, if Belgium is small, she is happy and satisfied with her lot. I have no ambition other than to serve her well. But I will insist on the pride it brings me to think that a progress essential to our age has begun in Brussels. I hope that in this way Brussels may become the headquarters of a civilising mission.[36]

In the resolutions that followed, the Association pledged itself to a programme of discovery, education and trade. Its leading figures included aristocrats, geographers, humanitarians and a number of Léopold's fellow royals. Britain's Anti-Slavery Society and the Church Missionary Society sent delegates to the conference; the Rothschilds gave a generous donation to its funds. Few of these famous names were actually involved in the series of Léopold's later projects. Yet the king never hesitated to blur the boundaries between his projects, using the good name of the International Association later to confer legitimacy on other schemes.

On Stanley's next return to Europe, Léopold succeeded in recruiting the American explorer. Stanley's ambition was vast, and while other backers had greater military or financial power, none demonstrated Léopold's manic urge to acquire new territories. Stanley

met Léopold for the first time in June 1878. By the end of the year
he was employed on a contract worth up to 50,000 francs a year
(around £125,000 in today's money). Stanley returned to Africa, this
time to found an empire.

The main part of Stanley's 1879 expedition was spent hacking
through hostile jungle, while the people of the Congo kept their
distance, as best they could. Jules Marchal records that thirty-three
white men serving under Stanley died in the course of this journey. We should set this death toll against Stanley's argument that
colonialism would improve the European racial stock, 'Hundreds
of raw European youths have been launched into the heart of the
"murderous continent", and the further we sent them the more
they improved in physique.'[37] It was not just Africans, then, whose
manifold destiny was to die if they were yet going to be saved.

Meanwhile, Léopold set out to win the backing of the powers
for his Association. America was the first to accept, persuaded that
Belgium would leave the territory open for free trade. The British
felt that they possessed enough territories already. The French were
persuaded that if Léopold's adventures succeeded in bankrupting the
entire Belgian state, then they could purchase the lands at knock-
down prices. The veteran Prince Bismarck saw through Léopold in
an instant. Yet his banker Gerson Bleichröder was sufficiently enthusiastic to force a deal. Unknown to the European powers, Stanley
was already on the ground, persuading the various Congolese kings
to sign treaties giving Léopold sovereign power over their territory.
Adam Hochschild places these agreements in context:

> Many chiefs had no idea what they were signing. Few had seen the
> written word before, and they were being asked to mark their X's
> to documents in a foreign language and in legalese. The idea of a
> treaty of friendship between two clans or villages was familiar; the
> idea of signing over one's land to someone on the other side of the
> world was inconceivable. Did the chiefs of Ngombi and Mafela, for
> example, have any idea of what they agreed to on April 1, 1884?
> In return for 'one piece of cloth per month to each of the under-
> signed chiefs, besides present of cloth in hand,' they promised to
> 'freely of their own accord, for themselves, and their heirs and
> successors for ever give up to the said Association the sovereignty
> and all sovereign and governing rights to all their territories ...
> and to assist by labour or otherwise, any works, improvements or

expeditions which the said Association shall cause at any time to have carried out in any part of these territories.[38]

On Stanley's return to Europe in 1884, he produced nearly five hundred treaties signed with local chieftains. Stanley could also boast of having founded Vivi, the first capital of Congo (opposite Matadi) and the town of Léopoldville (today Kinshasa). The 1884–85 Congress of Berlin, called to settle disputes between the European powers, recognised Léopold as the lawful head of the International Association of the Congo, soon to be known as the Congo Free State. In return for achieving such recognition, this 'Congo' committed itself to the abolition of slavery, free trade and neutrality in war. France took the north bank of the river.

It is striking that Léopold's private empire should declare itself a 'state'. Few African nations were then recognised as sovereign for the purposes of international law. The Congo Free State was even recognised as independent by the majority of the powers present at Berlin. The naming of the country was a nuanced decision. The Congo could not be a colony, for that would call into question the relationship of the new 'state' not just to King Léopold but, behind him, to Belgium. But in giving this society the form of a judicially sovereign independent state, we could say that Léopold, was quite despite himself, placing a marker before history. At some future point, he seemed to be saying, the Congo would be both independent and free.[39]

For all of King Léopold's evident success, certain obstacles remained. One problem the Belgian administration faced was the challenge of occupying the hinterlands. The declared boundaries of the state were roughly the same as those of the present-day country, but it was not until the mid-1890s that Léopold's control was finally established over the entire region. Successful occupation depended on military campaigns. The most vital instrument was the armed steamboat, from whose protection European troops could blast African villages into submission. In 1891–92, the southern lands of modern Shaba were conquered, and between 1892 and 1894 other territories were wrested from African, Arab and Swahili traders.

The costs of the project soared. Léopold spent around 10 million Belgian francs on the Congo between 1880 and 1890. (For comparison: in 1900, there were 25 Belgian francs to the British pound. The pound sterling, meanwhile, was very roughly worth £60 in today's prices.[40]) In 1890 and 1895, the Belgian parliament was bullied into approving loans to the king totalling some 32 million Belgian francs. This public money, however, was awarded as a loan and for ten years only. Indeed, one of the clauses of the contract gave the Belgian government the power to annexe the Congo, if Léopold could not repay the debt on time. King Léopold had to fight to have this clause withdrawn. He was able to receive slightly more generous terms from the French government, a loan of 80 million Belgian francs, but with the same clause. If Léopold defaulted, Paris would have a claim on 'his' new state.[41]

Red rubber

Although he never visited his private colony, King Léopold held absolute political, judicial and legislative power in the Congo, which he then devolved to a governor-general and a vice-governor. All 'unoccupied' land was claimed as property of his Association, both unexplored lands and fields lying fallow. Even settled farm lands were subject to his orders. Léopold also claimed a large private estate in the region of Lake Léopold II (north-east of Kinshasa). Meanwhile, Léopold also set about confusing the question of legitimacy. In place of the old International African Association, which was now moribund, Léopold constructed a new International Association of the Congo. Holding power always in his own hands, but often in the name of this distinct corporation, with its own flag, Léopold was also able to mask his private empire with some of the veneer of his former 'humanitarian' promises.

In order to fund the project of colonisation, the Association took control of the rubber and ivory trades. Much of the land was given to concessionary businesses, which in return were expected to build railroads or simply to occupy a specific, disputed region. Concessions were granted the power to tax Congolese villages at rates of between 6 and 24 francs annually per head, an almost meaningless figure in a country where there were no large stocks of cash in circulation. Africans then had to work to produce crops in kind. Companies were also set up to exploit the mineral resources, as well as human labour. The Union Minière du Haut-Katanga, established in 1905, was soon joined by the Compagnie de Fer du Congo, the Compagnie du Katanga, the Compagnie des Magasins Généraux, the Compagnie des Produits du Congo, the Syndicat Commercial du Katanga, and so on. Many of these were owned directly by Léopold, or indirectly, through his appointed proxies.

European officers and administrators were recruited to manage the logistics of running a large country as an empire. By 1906 there were 1,500 civil servants, and established transport routes between the coast and the interior. Missionaries were sent, with the explicit blessing of a Vatican keen to counteract earlier Protestant missions. Local troops were organised into a nascent army, the Force Publique. Although this detachment claimed 19,000 troops in 1888, such high numbers could only be maintained through the conscription of unwilling local people. In 1892 one judge wrote to the governor-general asking why it was that three-quarters of his soldiers died between conscription and arrival in the cities?

Similar patterns of forced labour were employed to recruit porters, carriers and other workers. In 1896, the surviving members of the Force Publique were sent out to capture 10,000 unskilled labourers, who were then set to work on the building of the Congo's first railway. We do not know how many survived. Yet we do know that by the time it was finished the track was little more than a short tramline. One critic pointed out that just a few miles of rail had cost 40 million francs; but no one counted the human cost. The waste of people and resources was typical of Léopold's rule. Bill Berkeley observes that for all the kleptocratic dictators of the Congo, there has been one model, Léopold.[42] According to historian Neal Ascherson:

> Like one of those last dinosaurs at the end of the saurian age whose very size or length of fang or desperate elaboration of armour sought to postpone the general decline of their race, Léopold developed in his own person into a most formidable type of King, designed for the environments of the late nineteenth century, which used the new forms of economic growth to strengthen and extend royal authority. Other monarchs watched the growth of modern trust capitalism with mixed feelings of suspicion, incomprehension and contempt. Léopold understood that the private fortunes of a King remained as much a measure of his power to act freely as they had been in the Middle Ages.[43]

Léopold would not even allow the Belgian state any authority over his kingdom. His concern was precisely the limits to his power that existed in free, constitutional Belgium. Private ownership of a giant colony allowed him to escape from the limitations of his situation and live out long-buried fantasies of holding great power. The second striking feature of this period was Léopold's dependence on a small range of strategies for the accumulation of wealth. In its first years, the colony proved to be extremely costly. It did possess one enormously valuable 'crop', ivory, a versatile material that could be worked to make piano keys, carvings and the like. It was a profitable business. In the late 1890s, Congolese ivory exports reached 1,000 tons per year.[44] The only problem with ivory was that the product's future was limited. Contrary to Stanley's calculation, no ruler could kill the entire herd in one stroke, without bringing the entire trade to a sudden end. The herd had to be managed. The resource could not be exhausted too fast. In his colony's first decade, Léopold was compelled to adopt cost-cutting measures in his own court, and at his own table. Léopold's adventure threatened to bankrupt him and undermine the future of his rule.

What changed everything was William Dunlop's 1890 discovery that cheap inflatable bicycle tyres could be manufactured from rubber. Other uses of rubber were soon patented, in tubing, insulation and wiring. Eventually, the greatest use for rubber would be found in car tyres. The sources of Léopold's wealth were more modest, a Dunlop-inspired cycling boom. Forests of cultivated rubber were eventually to be planted in Southeast Asia, but in the years before these came to maturity, the greatest source of rubber was equatorial Africa, where rubber grew wild.

In March 1890 Léopold quadrupled the export duty on ivory.[45] Eighteen months later, he announced that his representatives in the Congo would now enjoy a monopoly of the trade in rubber and ivory.[46] An 1891 decree compelled the Congolese to supply these goods to Léopold's representatives. No trade was required. 'Labour' was accumulated along perceived family and tribal lines.[47] Villages were presented with terrible demands, which could only be paid if the men of the village gave themselves over to forced labour. Where villages refused, Léopold's army, the Force Publique, was employed.

Homes were burned and the hands of the victims were taken for payment, as evidence of successful kills.[48]

Karl Marx famously described the importance of economic production for social organisation. 'The hand-loom gives you a society with the feudal lord; the steam mill, with the industrial capitalist.'[49] In the context of the Congo, we might rather say that rubber production created a slave society, dependent on the mass levy of village labour, under the auspices of an authoritarian colonial administration; later, copper would be the source of independently run state growth, depending as it did on a network of mines, transport, machinery and a thriving state apparatus. Eventually, as we shall see, the production of diamonds for export would be able to continue profitably whether under regular government or in conditions of extreme deprivation, in malign anarchy, through the collapse of the state and civil war.

Conan Doyle provided a vivid account of the conditions under which the rubber was taken. White agents were paid 150 to 300 francs per month, a lower salary than many European workers. But the greater the rubber harvest in their area, the more money they received by way of bonuses, and the greater was their own chance of securing enough money to buy their own passage home. The agents employed black foremen, 'Capitas', to live among villagers, imposing discipline on them. These newly appointed 'local officials' were often former members of the Force Publique. They had been trained to commit acts of the most extreme brutality:

> Imagine the nightmare which lay upon each village while this barbarian squatted in the middle of it. Day or night they could never get away from him. He called for palm wine. He called for women. He beat them, mutilated them, and shot them down at his pleasure. He enforced public incest in order to amuse himself by the sight.... The more terror the Capita inspired, the more useful he was, the more eagerly the villagers obeyed him, and the more rubber yielded its commission to the agent.

Not surprisingly, the Capitas were extremely unpopular: in one period, various rebellions killed some 142 of them in just seven months. But resistance was often fatal. Learning of the death of one of their representatives, white agents would only come with arms and destroy the village. Black people managed the tyranny, but they did so under white orders. 'Often too the white man pushed the black aside, and acted himself as torturer and executioner.'[50] Other critics dubbed this system 'red rubber', as if the trees grew on the blood of Léopold's dead. This economic system contained something of the feudal system. There was a military power. The structure of authority was like a pyramid, with King Léopold at the top, appointing subordinates downwards. As in conditions of feudal breakdown, little thought was given to the feeding of the people, but force was everything. Yet to see this system as a reversion to the 'backward' conditions of past times, or of some pre-European pre-industrial system, would be quite mistaken. The rubber and ivory taken in this fashion was all exported, for exchange purposes, on the global market. Subsistence agriculture was not recognised in this system, lest this encourage the people of the Congo to concentrate on feeding themselves. The extracted 'surplus' was everything they could harvest. Few goods were traded within the local economy. The people were forced to live at a subsistence minimum; many starved to death.

Along with theft and hierarchy, a third striking feature of this period is the similarity between the Belgian colony and other imperial conquests of the same time in their adoption of various forms of what Marx referred to as 'primitive accumulation'. Under direct European or American rule, forced labour became widespread throughout the continent, and an 'economy of pillage' became the norm.

> The term *chibalo* (or *chibaro*) was used commonly in central and southern Africa from the late nineteenth century onwards to describe a variety of oppressive forms of labour introduced by the Europeans. The Portuguese in Mozambique stipulated that all adult males had to perform *chibalo* for six months a year. Commonly used for compulsory labour services on large colonial plantations in Mozambique, it stipulated that all adult males had to perform *chibalo*.[51]

In 1900, French Equatorial Africa (today Chad, Gabon, Central African Republic and the Republic of the Congo) was divided up between forty French concession companies. Coquery-Vidrovitch has described the result as 'an economy of pillage'. The companies were parasitical on African life and labour. They did not provide machinery or investment. Even the state was dependent on such private profits.[52] A web of loans and debts tied these competing empires together. King Léopold invested in the French scheme. French bankers invested back in the Belgian empire. Concessions were held by and in British firms.

Many commentators have studied the economic processes that drove the conquest of Africa. In his book *Imperialism: The Hightest Stage of Capitalism*, the Russian Marxist Vladimir Lenin maintained that the conquests were linked to an internal, economic process, the centralisation of capital, the merging of banks and industry.[53] Colonialism was simply another expression, in a grander form, of the general tendency towards competition between businesses that was typical of a capitalist system. The British historian Eric Hobsbawm has argued that Léopold was motivated rather by a search for consumers, to purchase excess Belgian goods. With bitter irony, Hobsbawm records that Léopold's 'favourite methods of exploitation by forced labour was not designed to encourage high *per capita* purchases, even when it did not actually diminish the number of customers by torture and massacre'.[54] It is possible that such explanations are in fact too complex. Hobsbawm's model fits the system that Livingstone desired to create, not the one that Léopold actually made. Meanwhile Lenin argued that under capitalism the colonial powers would tend to export capital. This process did happen in the Congo, but only systematically after 1908. All production was for the market, but in the early years the most striking feature of Léopold's conquest was its similarity to an older form of accumulation, simple theft.

Resistance

'The most potent symbol of colonialism's brutality', writes Charlie Kimber, 'was the severed hands.'

> African soldiers in the pay of their Belgian masters were sent out to smash opposition. To demonstrate that they had not wasted their bullets they hacked the hands from their victims, alive or dead. The novelist Joseph Conrad wrote that it was extraordinary that a world that no longer tolerated the slave trade could blithely ignore the Congo. It was, he said, 'as if the moral clock had been put back'.[55]

According to the British philosopher and humanitarian Bertrand Russell,

Each village was ordered by the authorities to collect and bring in a certain amount of rubber, as much as the men could collect and bring in by neglecting all work for their own maintenance. If they failed to bring the required amount, their women were taken away and kept as hostages in compounds or in the harems of government employees. If this method failed, native troops ... were sent into the village to spread terror, if necessary by killing some of the men; but in order to prevent a waste of cartridges, they were ordered to bring one right hand for every cartridge used. If they missed, or used cartridges on big game, they cut off the hands of living people to make up the necessary number.[56]

For the historian Peter Forbath,

The baskets of severed hands, set down at the feet of the European post commanders, became the symbol of the Congo Free State. The collection of hands became an end in itself. Force Publique soldiers brought them to the stations in place of rubber; they even went out to harvest them instead of rubber.... They became a sort of currency. They came to be used to make up for shortfalls in rubber quotas, to replace ... the people who were demanded for the forced labour gangs; and the Force Publique soldiers were paid their bonuses on the basis of how many hands they collected.[57]

In 1906, the Belgian anti-slavery activist Alphonse Jacques warned of the 'complete extinction' of the Congolese people. Such language may seem extreme, yet there is no doubt that the advent of Léopold's colonialism was a disaster for the local population. Famine combined with disease and the introduction of forced labour. The demographic evidence shows an extraordinary rate of killing. Citing Belgian sources, Adam Hochschild writes that the population of the region fell from over 20 million people in 1891 to 8.5 million in 1911, only to recover somewhat over the next decade to 10 million in 1924.[58] As a proportion of the total population (the numbers that could have been killed) such a number is comparable to the well-known genocides of the twentieth century, the Nazi Holocaust, the murders in Rwanda. As an absolute number of deaths, the figure in the Congo may be higher than each.

Yet Léopold's capture of the Congo had been based on the most fair-sounding of promises. In 1889–90, for example, Brussels hosted eight months of humanitarian meetings, culminating in an Anti-

Slavery Conference of the major powers. Under Belgian direction, Léopold indicated, the Congolese were proceeding quickly in the direction of prosperity, public education and eventual self-government. Such a language was required if the other European powers (and indeed the Belgian public) were to acquiesce in his schemes. As late as 1898, in a widely circulated letter from 'the King-Sovereign of the Congo Free State to the State agents', Léopold encouraged his admirers to regard the project as both a moral crusade and a programme of economic and social development. 'The task which the State agents have to accomplish in the Congo is noble and elevated', he wrote. 'It is incumbent upon them to carry on the work of the civilisation of Equatorial Africa, guided by the principles set forth in the Berlin and Brussels resolutions.' (The Berlin resolution was the final document of the 1884–85 Berlin congress; the Brussels resolution was the founding document of Léopold's previous International Association).

> The aim of all of us, I desire to repeat it here with you, is to
> regenerate, materially and morally, races whose degradation and
> misfortune it is hard to realise. The fearful scourges of which, in
> the eyes of our humanity, these races seemed the victims, are al-
> ready lessening, little by little, through our intervention. Each step
> forward made by our people should make an improvement in the
> condition of the natives. In those vast tracts, mostly uncultivated
> and many unproductive, where the natives hardly knew how to get
> their daily food, European experience, knowledge, resource and
> enterprise, have brought to light unthought-of-wealth. If wants
> are created they are satisfied even more liberally. Exploration of
> virgin lands goes on, communications are established, highways are
> opened, the soil yields produce in exchange for our varied manufac-
> tured articles. Legitimate trade and industry are established. As the
> economic state is formed, property assumes an intrinsic character,
> private and public ownership, the basis of all social development,
> is founded and respected instead of being left to the law of change
> and of the strongest. Upon this material prosperity, in which the
> whites and blacks have evidently a common interest, will follow a
> desire on the part of the blacks to elevate themselves.[59]

Beneath the high-flowing rhetoric, financial calculations were evidently being made. Yet to see only this side of Léopold would be to misunderstand the public impression that he gave. By loudly trumpeting the glorious future facing the black Africans, by holding out the distant possibility of tutelage leading to self-government, by declaring his new country a 'Free State', Léopold successfully presented himself as the inheritor of the liberal ideal. From empire would come freedom. Stanley made a similar point in response to published scepticism of Léopold's motives:

> He is a dreamer, like his *confrères* in the work, because the sentiment is applied to the neglected millions of the Dark Continent. [The critics] cannot appreciate rightly, because there are no dividends attaching to it, this ardent, vivifying and expansive sentiment, which seeks to extend civilising influences among the dark races, and to brighten up with the glow of civilisation the dark places of sad-browed Africa.[60]

The problem both men faced was that the promises always threatened to prove empty. All that was required was that witnesses should come forward.

The greatest victims of Léopold's actions were the people of the Congo. They were also the first to criticise and to resist. A number of Congolese peoples responded with war to Belgian incursions. They included Msiri's Garenganze, the Zande federation of King Gbudwe and the people of the Swahili-speaking region under Tippu Tip. The most developed, settled populations were least likely to rebel: towns always fall first to an invader. The initiative passed to smaller, more martial kingdoms, often those that had accumulated resources in the aftermath of the Portuguese slave trade. The most famous such rebellion was that led by King Msiri in the Katanga region. Msiri refused to recognise Belgian sovereignty. His people were then crushed in 1891. There were also rebellions of troops from Léopold's army, including an uprising at Kananga garrison in July 1895, the Ndirfi mutiny of February 1897 and the Shinkakasa mutiny at Boma in April 1890. The first of these was a guerrilla movement triggered by the state's failure to pay bonuses owed. Drawing on alliances made with other Congolese people living between the Lulua and Lualaba rivers, the Kananga mutineers were able to hold out for several years.

The 1895 rebellion coincided with the end of a previous bout of fighting between Léopold's army and his Arab rivals in the east of the country. Employing Congolese auxiliaries, and to much fanfare in the West about the defeat of the slave trade, Léopold's supporters declared victory in 1894. Yet this victory led almost immediately to further challenges. 'After the Arab campaign', records the official *Encylopedia of Belgian Congo*, 'Batetela soldiers were concentrated in Luluabourg. Already angry at being paid late', they then learned that General Duchesne, following what the *Encylopedia* termed 'an unfortunate error', had executed Gongo Lutete, their leader.

The Batetela rose and took control of their camp, killing on 4 January 1895 Captain Peltzer. Lieutenants Lassaux and Cassart could preserve their lives only by fleeing. The mutiny became a revolt and soon covered the whole region of Lomami. Officers Gillain, Lothaire and Michaux confronted the rebels, with mixed success.

In October 1896, some 4–5,000 Batetela took arms and headed towards Gandu. General Michaux harried them. Eighteen Batetela were captured in April 1900 and executed. A thousand escaped and took to the mountains around Lake Kisale, living 'as brigands'. Major Malfey is described as successfully 'pacifying' the region in April 1902, but the last of the rebels were captured only in 1908. Colonial accounts such as these, with their soothing assurances of European invincibility, tend to obscure the fact that this revolt lasted thirteen years, securing large areas of land and the temporary freedom of several thousand people.[61]

The Ndirfi revolt began after a 150-day forced march through the north-east regions; 2,500 troops were involved. These rebels held out for 'only' three years. They eventually gave themselves up, not to Léopold or his allies, but to German troops on the other side of Lake Tanganyika.[62] Several uprisings were able to take large areas of land. Another revolt from 1905 broke out with the desperate words, 'The rubber is finished. You have no more to do here.'[63]

The great problem in making sense of these movements is that few Congolese voices were heard outside the country, and few others have been recorded for posterity. In recent decades, historians and anthropologists have tried to get round this absence of written sources by consulting the oral traditions of different Congolese peoples. We are forced to depend on scraps of writing, stories passed down between generations, and sometimes the evidence of songs.

Many of the people living in the eastern jungles had a culture that emphasised the continuity between generations, and the link between the people and the land where they lived. 'The forest', according to the Mongo peoples, 'is a relic of the ancestors. It stays with the family.' Equivalent sayings in the Lower Congo included: 'Those who decide to act alone, must live in the same house.' 'Don't think of the planter when you touch his trees, but of his successor.' Proverbs such as these, or 'It is better to hunger than to steal', acted in place of legal precedents. In a society based on limited agriculture, notions of authority depended on ideas of earned rule, rather than inherited status. 'Before the Belgians, we had no chiefs as they later became. Our villages used to be led by famous warriors.'[64] In 1904, one missionary went about the people of this region, and recorded their contemporary feelings about the dispossession that was under way:

> It is interesting to hear the Bongandanga people tell of the begin-
> ning of the rubber trade. How wonderful they thought it was that
> the white man should want rubber, and be willing to pay for it.
> How they almost fought for baskets in order to bring them in and
> obtain the offered riches. But they say, 'We did not know, we never
> understood what it would become in the future.' Now it is looked
> upon as the equivalent of death; they do not complain so much of
> want of payment, as there is no rest from the work, and no end to
> it except death.[65]

Occasionally a more substantial memory has come down to us, and with an individual's name attached. A white functionary recorded Ilanga's story:

> Our village is called Waniendo, after our chief Niendo.... It is a
> large village near a small stream, and is surrounded by large fields
> of *mohago* (cassava) and *muhindu* (maize) and other foods.... Soon
> after the sun rose over the hill, a large band of soldiers came into
> the village, and we all went into the houses and sat down. We
> were not long seated when the soldiers came rushing in shouting,
> and threatening Niendo with their guns. They came to my house
> and dragged the people out. Three or four came to our house and
> caught hold of me, also my husband Oleka and my sister Katinga.
> We were dragged into the road and were tied together with cords
> about our necks, so that we could not escape.... On the sixth
> day we became very weak from lack of food and from constant

marching and sleeping in the damp grass, and my husband, who marched behind us with the goat, could not stand up longer, and so he sat down beside the path and refused to walk more. The soldiers beat him on the head with the end of his gun, and he fell upon the ground. One of the soldiers caught the goat, while two or three others stuck the long knives they put on the ends of their guns into my husband ... Many of the young men were killed the same way, and many babies thrown on the grass to die ... After marching ten days we came to the great water ... and were taken in canoes across to the white man's town at Nyangwe.[66]

For every person such as Ilanga, whose history was recorded, there were millions more whose suffering left no written record for posterity.

In the absence of sustained Congolese voices, we have to make do with Western sources. The first significant protest to find its way into the newspapers came in 1890, when George Washington Williams, significantly a black American lawyer, historian and missionary, dedicated an *Open Letter to His Serene Majesty Léopold II*. The contents were less flattering than the title. Williams had actually travelled to the region, initially believing that the Congo was an area of human advance. On his expected return to America, he hoped to establish a movement of black people to travel back to Africa. What Williams actually found in the Congo dismayed him. He learned from the people he met that Stanley had cheated his way into acquiring these territories, with gin, threats and fake magic tricks. Prisoners were jailed. White traders had kidnapped black women for concubines. Good government and public services were non-existent. Far from bringing an end to slavery, Léopold's agents had made the system endemic.[67] Williams' *Open Letter* was printed widely discussed by the press in Europe and America. Only its author's death, in England in 1891 of tuberculosis, prevented the furore from engulfing the entire colony.

Another early critic, the Swedish missionary Edward Wilhelm Sjöblom arrived in the Congo on 31 July 1892. Within days, he had witnessed a terrible beating, on the steamer in which he travelled. The instrument employed was the *chicotte*, a whip of trimmed hippo hide with edges like knife blades. The captain of the steamer was under orders to catch 300 boys, who might serve in the Force Publique. One boy was indeed found, and then bound to the steam engine, the hottest part of the boat. Sjöblom took up the story of what happened to the child.

The captain showed the boy the *chicotte*, but made him wait all day before letting him taste it. However, the moment of suffering came. I tried to count the lashes and think they were about sixty, apart from the kicks to the head and back. The captain smiled with satisfaction when he saw the boy's thin garb soaked with blood.... I had to witness all this in silence. At dinner, they talked of their exploits concerning the treatment of the blacks. They mentioned one of their equals who had flogged three of his men so mercilessly that he had died as a result. This was reckoned to be valour. One of them said, 'The best of them is too good to die like a pig.'[68]

Sjöblom's reports were published in his home country of Sweden. By 1897, he was speaking at meetings of the Aborigines Protection Society in London.

Who gained?

The stated purpose of intervention was that the Congolese would prosper under European rule. It is even possible that some young Congolese welcomed the arrival of Stanley, hoping that the people of the region too would benefit from the evident wealth of the Europeans. There was, however, no process by which wealth or skills were allowed to 'trickle down'.[69] The exploitation of the local population intensified; the misery increased. The population declined sharply, as a result of disease, massacre and the toll of forced labour. Some of the winners were more obvious: Léopold's family, the share owners and the banks. Exports from the Congo Free State rose from 11.5 million francs in 1895 to 47.5 million in 1900. Exports of rubber rose from 580 tons to 3,740 in the same years. Between 1896 and 1905, just one concession the *Domaine de la Couronne*, earned Léopold 70 million Belgian francs in profit.[70]

King Léopold's private empire soon established links with other blocs of mining capital. The American mining groups Ryan and Guggenheim also had interests in the region. The most important firm in the mineral-rich region of Katanga was the Union Minière du Haut-Katanga. This giant business was itself an alliance between Léopold and a consortium of British mining interests, represented by Robert Williams, owner of Tanganyika Concessions Limited (TCL). At different times, between one-seventh and one-half of the Union Minière shares were owned by TCL, itself financed by such British-based banks as Barclays, Midlands, Barings and Rothschilds. Tanganyika Concessions controlled one of the main export routes, the rail-link west through Angola. It was a conduit to existing mining and engineering works, including the copper mines of Zambia, and a source of revenues in its own right.[71]

Beyond Léopold, there stood a network of acolytes, allies and place-keepers, all of whom received shares in the great enterprise. Vast profits were made. Company Abir, one concession in the Belgian Congo, possessed capital of just one million Belgian francs, yet in 1897 it returned an annual profit of 1,247,455 francs: more than a 100 per cent turnover on the initial stake.[72] Léopold also used the vast profits he made to build palaces at Laeken, the Arch of the Cinquantenaire, and a colonial museum at Tervuren. He even succeeded in cooking the books, to make the rich empire look like a money-loser. Eventually, in 1908, the Belgian government agreed to pay Léopold the sum of 110 million francs to release him from his 'debt'. Even this vast sum does not convey the extraordinary profits that Léopold was able to make, as a result of his conquest. In November 1909, a month before his death, Léopold bought fifty-eight large properties worth at least 12 million francs. Another front company, the Fondation de Niederfüllbach possessed assets worth 45 million francs, including jewels. Yet Léopold's estate was worth just 15 million francs.[73] The rest had been spent on parks, mistresses and other extraordinary, personal greed.

Further critics

The Belgian parliament did not originally plan to annex the Congo, but reports of the brutal treatment of Africans in the Congo, especially those forced to collect rubber for the companies, led to a popular campaign for Belgium either to allow the people of the Congo to reclaim self-government or to take over the ruling of the colony from Léopold. By the late 1890s, a new generation of Western travellers had finally learned to treat Africa with fraternity, not as a place where the people deserved pity, nor as a commercial property waiting for the market, but as a region that was fruitful, interesting and good in itself. Mary Kingsley's account of her *Travels in West Africa* described a visitor living in harmony with the social and natural environment that she found. Although Kingsley did not describe the Belgian Congo, her travels helped to change people's ideas of the relationships that were possible. One group of people among whom Kingsley lived were the Krumen:

> I have always admired men for their strength, their courage, their unceasing struggle for the beyond, the something else, but not until I had to deal with the Krumen did I realise the vastness to which this latter characteristic of theirs could attain.

The ideal remained benign imperialism: 'Would not a very hopeful future for West Africa regarding the labour question be possible, if a *régime* of common sense were substituted for our present one?' Yet compared to the awful present, such words were read as a call for reform.[74] The demand for reform of the Belgian Congo was raised in America, where politicians threatened to investigate King Léopold. Other critics included the novelist Mark Twain and the black activists Booker T. Washington and W.E.B. DuBois. British opponents of the private empire included E.D. Morel, Roger Casement, Arthur Conan Doyle and Joseph Conrad. The Belgian deputy Émile Vandervelde toured the region and defended the critics of the empire in the Congo's courts.[75]

The most surprising of these dissidents was perhaps Morel. A successful trader of French extraction, Morel's full name was Georges Edmond Pierre Achille Morel-de-Ville. He was employed from 1891 at Elder Dempster, the Liverpool shipping company that controlled the trade between Britain and the Congo.[76] An occasional visitor to Belgium, Morel also worked as a freelance journalist. He started to write about Africa from 1893. One early article, published in the *Pall Mall Gazette* on 16 July 1897, defended King Léopold's Free State. Contrary to the accounts that were then coming out in other British papers, Morel insisted that there was no slavery in Léopold's colony. Black workers were paid the equivalent of 30 s per month, more than many unskilled workers in Britain. Some 4,000 tonnes of goods were sent out from the Congo each year. The colony was evidently not bankrupt. If there were problems with the Congo, this was because the people were still degenerate, ignorant and backward. The Belgian experiment deserved 'fair play'.

So far, there was nothing untypical about Morel. But one day in 1897 or 1898, a strange thought occurred to him. Morel took to studying the goods loaded and unloaded from the Congo ships. He saw vast quantities of rubber and ivory being unloaded in Antwerp, but nothing of any substance was sent out, beyond officers and firearms. What did that mean? The realisation then dawned on him that there could only be one answer. For all the wealth produced in Africa, the people of the country must receive nothing in return. Their wealth was simply being stolen from them.

On 24 March 1900, Morel penned his first critical article, 'Belgium and the Congo State', in *The Speaker*. He described the Free State as a system of private theft. Morel left his post with Elder Dempster, devoting his energies full-time to the anti-Belgian cause. He established a paper, the *West African Mail*, which filled its columns with exposés of Léopold's 'system'.[77] Morel made contact with Roger Casement, the British consul to the region. They met for the first time on 10 December 1903, with Casement recording in his diary: 'Grattan Guinness called on me in afternoon and then Ed. Morel. First time I met him. The man is honest as day. Dined at Comedy together late and then to chat till 2 am. Morel sleeping in study.' It was an eventful meeting. Casement persuaded Morel to launch a new public campaign, the Congo Reform Association. Through the next ten years, Morel's Association campaigned for reform. Hundreds of meetings were held each year.

The campaign grew in size. It also suffered many setbacks. One of Morel's best sources was a Nigerian trader, Hezekiah Andrew Shanu, an independent-minded person, with strong business links across the region. Shanu's letters of criticism had to be shipped out from the Congo in great secrecy. They were then published in the British press, but always under a pseudonym. In 1904, Léopold's agents revealed that Shanu was the source. Facing ruin, Shanu killed himself.

From 1903 onwards, Morel did not campaign just for the reform of the Belgian Congo, but also for the transformation of the French Congo. He argued that the French rulers of the neighbouring territory had witnessed the success of Léopold's empire, and were now determined to copy it themselves. The intensive competition between

French and British traders had been to the detriment of British interests: 'The factories of British merchants are broken into; native traders in British employ are flogged; produce paid for by British merchants is openly appropriated.'[78] This last observation highlights an important contradiction within the reform movement. Morel and his closest friends closest to the reality of European colonialism were radicalised by the campaign. They also learned of widespread abuses in British Africa, and realised that more was wrong than simply the Belgian ownership of the Congo Free State and the actions of French traders. From being simply a middle-of-the-road businessman, Morel became a critic of all imperial adventures. Yet, even while Morel and Casement were pushed leftwards, their campaign still received considerable support from Liverpool businessmen and Conservative bishops. In May 1903, the House of Lords unanimously passed a motion accusing the Belgian rulers of the Congo of ill-treating the black population.[79] The message was directed towards the rulers of imperial Britain. Morel described his cause as 'the British Case'. Only after 1908 did Morel's full radicalism become evident. Following the success of this campaign, his next cause would be the struggle to expose the secret treaties, and the pernicious role they played in the outbreak of the Great War. After 1914, Morel blamed European colonial adventurism for the outbreak of war.[80] By then, however, Morel was taking positions far to the left of the ones that he had held before 1908.[81]

Morel's ally Roger Casement was an Anglo-Irish diplomat. Arriving in Africa in 1885 he briefly worked for Elder Dempster, which also employed Morel. Casement then served as a civil servant on Léopold's project. This experience of the Congo in the 1880s served Casement well. It meant that he possessed vivid memories of the situation before Léopold's empire had been fully established; against which he could then contrast the system at its height. In 1891 Casement was appointed to a post at the Colonial Office, working for the Niger Coast Protectorate. Then in autumn 1900 Casement was sent back to the Congo as British Consul. It was a position of some considerable authority. Sent by the government to answer the colony's critics, Casement found everywhere the signs of a people dying. Fields were deserted. The surviving people complained bitterly of floggings and of the rubber tax. Casement was convinced that Léopold's whole project was unjust. His 'Congo Report' was submitted to the Marquess of Lansdowne on 11 December 1903, the day after his first meeting with Morel. 'The trade in ivory', Casement wrote, 'has entirely passed from the hands of the natives of the Upper Congo, and neither fish nor any other outcome of local industry now changes hands on an extensive scale or at any distance from home'. One Belgian expedition of 1900 had resulted in seventeen deaths and loss of much livestock. Compensation was paid to chiefs at a rate of 1,000 brass rods per head (50 francs), 'not probably an extravagant estimate for human life, seeing that the goats were valued at 400 rods each (20 francs).' The population of Lukolela, he observed, had fallen from 6,000 in January 1891 to 719 in December 1896. Another Town, 'O', had comprised 4,000 people in 1887.

> Scores of men had put off in canoes to greet us with invitations that we should spend the night in their village. On steaming into O [in 1903] … I found that this village had entirely disappeared, and that its place was occupied by a large 'camp d'instruction', where some 800 native recruits, brought from various parts of the Congo State, are drilled into soldier-hood by a Commandant and a staff of seven or eight European officers.

The population of Lake Mantumba had fallen by 60 per cent as a result of forced labour.

> During the period 1893–1902, the Congo State commenced the system of compelling the native to collect rubber and insisted that the inhabitants of the district should not go out of it to sell their produce to traders…. This great decrease in population has been, to a very great extent, caused by the extreme measures resorted to by officers of the State, and the freedom enjoyed by the soldiers to do just as they pleased.

On his return to England, Casement devoted his energies to the Reform Association. It was launched following a meeting in the Philharmonic Hall in Liverpool on 24 March 1904. Earl Beauchamp was elected president, Edmund Morel the honourary secretary. Other early supporters included the Bishops of Durham, Liverpool, Rochester and St Asaph. In June 1905 Casement became a Companion of the Order of St Michael and St George. The award was made in recognition of his services to the reform of the Congo. It raises an awkward point.

Casement was well aware that a part of the campaign's support relied on the reformers' refusal to criticise similar adventures conducted by the British throughout Africa. Indeed, while some supporters of the campaign argued that the best solution would be the full freedom of the Congolese people, others could join it believing that the only alternative to Belgian control was British rule. Casement and Morel were radicalised by their experiences into the adoption of a more fundamental critique of imperialism. Yet they made few efforts initially to distance themselves from mainstream support.

Support for reform eventually led Casement to a position of total and principled opposition to all colonialism. Following his retirement from the British consulate, he became increasingly aware of his own Irish background. 'In those lonely Congo forests where I found Léopold', he wrote, 'I also found myself.' The history of the British occupation of Ireland no longer seemed very different to him from the history of the Belgian Empire in the Congo. In 1916, Casement was discovered in Ireland, leading a mission to recruit soldiers to an Irish Brigade. The courts convicted him of treason, yet a movement led by George Bernard Shaw remembered Casement's role in the Congo and demanded that his life should be spared. The British government was forced to resort to subversion. The cabinet leaked details of Casement's same-sex affairs from his diaries, in order to secure his execution.[82]

The novelist Arthur Conan Doyle joined the campaign relatively late, publishing his book *The Crime of the Congo* in 1909. It was dedicated to E.D. Morel, 'The unselfish champion of the Congo races'. Of Belgium, Conan Doyle wrote: 'Her colony is a scandal before the whole world. The era of murders and mutilations has, as we hope, passed by, but the country is sunk into a state of cowed and hopeless slavery. It is not a new story, but merely another stage of the same.' Was it fair to put so much emphasis on Belgian rule? What about British territories? Conan Doyle, a self-declared patriot, rejected the comparison: 'Where land has so been claimed, it has been worked by free labour for the benefit of the African community itself, and not for the purpose of sending the proceeds and profits to Europe. That is a vital distinction.' The main theme of his pamphlet was Léopold's greed:

> During the independent life on the Congo State all accounts have been kept secret, that no budgets of the last year but only estimates

of the coming one have been published, that the State has made huge gains, in spite of which it has borrowed money, and that the great sums resulting have been laid out in speculations in China and elsewhere, that sums amounting in the aggregate to several million pounds have been traced to the King, and that this money has been spent partly in buildings in Belgium, partly in land in the same country, partly in building on the Riviera, partly in the corruption of our public men, and of the European and American Press ... and finally, in the expense of such a private life as has made King Léopold's name notorious throughout Europe.[83]

Another critic of Belgian rule was the novelist Joseph Conrad. A friend of Roger Casement, Conrad had piloted a Congolese steamboat in his youth, and the experience of the first decades of Belgian rule informs his best-known novel, *Heart of Darkness*.[84] Conrad accepted the myth that colonialism was intended as a form of benign tutelage. He argued, however, that Western intervention could never succeed. The Belgian project was 'a sordid farce acted out against a sinister back-cloth.' His protagonist Marlow observes the motivating force of conquest, which was profit. He describes the company agents as 'a lot of faithless pilgrims bewitched inside a rotten fence. The word "ivory" is in the air, was whispered, was sighed. You would think they were praying for it.' The key figure in *Heart of Darkness* is Kurtz. A trader and anthropologist, half-English, half-French, he represents the pride and conviction of conquest. Kurtz persuades the Congolese to follow him, like a god. In the process, though, he becomes lost. A profound madness infects his soul. 'Exterminate the brutes', Kurtz shouts. He hoards a row of Congolese skulls. His voyage ends in madness, 'the horror, the horror' are his last words. Finding the older man convinces Marlow that the result of colonialism must be disaster.[85]

The subsequent success of Joseph Conrad's novel has given it a special status. Many read Conrad as if he understood better than anyone the horror of the Western colonial system. Yet Conrad's novel 'points in opposite directions'.[86] Its argument against empire is that Africans are incapable of progress. As in the books of Livingstone and Stanley, the black Africans appear as savages, good or bad.[87] Long ago Chinua Achebe indicted Conrad's work for its complicity in racism, and in 'the dehumanisation of Africa and Africans which this age-long attitude has fostered and continues to foster in the world'.[88] Many passages of Conrad's novel confirm this reading. The men and women of the Congo appear mute, degraded, something alien. Yet their otherness is linked to their degradation and subordination. At the beginning of his trip, Marlow sees six black men advancing in a file.

> They walked erect and slow, balancing small baskets of earth on their heads, and the clink kept time with their footsteps ... I could see every rib, the joints of their limbs were like knots in a rope, each had an iron collar on his neck and all were connected together with a chain whose bights sung between them, rhythmically clinking.

Marlow's complex narrative stands in for an authorial voice. He describes the people of the Congo rather as inoffensive. He refers to the 'pure, uncomplicated savagery' of the Africans, 'something that had a right to exist, obviously, in the sunshine'. The people of the region 'still belong to the beginning of time, had no inherited experience to teach them, as it were'. In later passages, the Congolese appear as howling mobs. They do not appear as thinking, speaking and rational people. Other reformers shared both his concern and his distance from the Congolese people.

The end of Léopold's empire

The most important movement against Léopold's rule was the resistance of the Congolese themselves. In December 1899, another Congolese revolt against the agents of the Société Anversoise and the Force Publique began to fuel widespread criticism of the Belgian regime. But if Léopold was ever going to be defeated, some demand for the ending of the empire would also have to emerge within Belgium. The reform campaign in that country was dominated by the figure of Émile Vandervelde. He was a lawyer, a parliamentarian and a leading member of the Socialist International. Born in 1866 to a magistrate and a factory manager, Vandervelde was the first Belgian socialist to campaign against Léopold's empire. In 1895, Vandervelde described Léopold's project as 'the Congolese corpse'. In June of the same year, he led the opposition in parliament to Léopold's loan. 'What remains is a choice between the enterprise of the Congo and workers' pensions', he declared. 'You propose to grant to the king what you refuse to the workers.' Émile Vandervelde began to speak of Africans not as an economic burden but as important potential allies of Belgian labour. In one powerful speech from April 1900 he told the white masses: 'The cause of the blacks is your cause ... not only because you are men, but because you are workers. In the end [Léopold's] politics will threaten you as well.' This was the highpoint of Vandervelde's personal crusade.

After 1900, however, Vandervelde's approach slowly changed. Having previously advocated Belgian withdrawal from the Congo, he now began to argue that it would be better not to desert the people of Africa. Instead, a benign imperialism should remain, under conditions of democratic public ownership. The shifts in Vandervelde's argument were subtle, and it was some time before his comrades in the Socialist Party realised that his position had changed. Yet from July 1901, Vandervelde encouraged a Belgian takeover of the Congo from Léopold and a fundamental reform of the regime there, arguing that 'European civilisation is destined to conquer the world'. On 1 July 1903 Vandervelde attacked existing systems of colonialism as the source of slavery abroad and militarism at home. As long as the empire remained 'in the forms that it takes under the capitalist regime', then such exploitation would continue. Working closely with Morel, Vandervelde told the Belgian parliament on 7 December 1906: 'We cannot be responsible before world opinion without having acted ourselves, without having reformed the institutions of the Congo.' After 1906, he took part in a commission to draft a new treaty for the Congo. Finally, in June 1907, the Socialist Party debated Vandervelde's new position. His critics to the left included Louis de Brouckère, who argued that imperialism of any kind would inevitably lead to further exploitation. Eugène Hins argued Vandervelde's earlier position, that colonialism would reduce the living standards of Belgian workers. Vandervelde lost the vote, and then argued that he would resign unless he was granted the right to vote independently in parliament. This freedom he won. Later that same year, the Belgians were criticised at the Stuttgart Conference of the Second International. Despite backing from socialists in other colonial states, including France, a majority argued for an unconditional anti-imperialist position.[89] Vandervelde was undoubtedly a brave opponent of King Léopold. As late as 1908 Léopold's allies sought to try a black American minister, Sheppard, whose accounts of the horrors had encouraged the reform movement. Morel wired Vandervelde asking for the name of a young lawyer who might be persuaded to voyage out to Africa and defend Léopold's critics. To general surprise, Vandervelde took on the case on a pro bono basis, travelling out to the Congo at his own expense, defending the minister, even risking his own life, but eventually securing Sheppard's release. For all Vandervelde's appealing personal qualities, though, his politics were shaped by the same compromises as those of Morel or Casement. His biographer Janet Polasky presents her subject as standing *Between Reform and Revolution*. This is too generous: Vandervelde's argument that the reform of empire was better than deserting the people to stand alone meant in reality that the Congolese should remain under outside dominance. Such rule may have been reformed, but it was still a form of empire. Had the leaders of Belgian parliamentary socialism clearly demanded self-government for the people of the Congo, such was the crisis, the demand could have been won. In its place, Vandervelde's own scheme was adopted. After 1908, Léopold's private empire was 'nationalised' by the Belgian state.

The end, when it came, was rapid indeed. In the Congo, Léopold had succeeded in establishing absolute rule. The nature of a private empire meant that its security depended ultimately on the personality of its ruler. King Léopold was determined to hold on to his conquests; yet he lacked the means to force Europeans to accept his will. Increasingly threatened by the campaign of Morel and the others, Léopold resorted to bribery and other ruses. In 1905, he set up a handpicked Commission of Inquiry, composed of loyal judges, to prove that his regime was sound. Criticised on all sides, even such a man as the chief judge of the Congo was forced to admit that crimes had been committed. In the words of the final report:

> The Congo Free State is not a colonising state, it is barely a state at all: it is a financial enterprise. The colony has been administered neither in the interests of the natives nor even in the economic interest of Belgium: to obtain for the King-Sovereign a maximum of resources, this has been the objective of government activity.[90]

As Léopold aged, he was ever more despised at home. He was seen as a philanderer and a wastrel. One of his last acts was to give his mistress 6 million francs, plus an even greater fortune in Congolese bonds. The movement for the reform of the Congo grew each year in numbers and support. The feeling was widespread that something had to he done. After a long parliamentary debate, the Belgian parliament annexed the region in 1908. The king died in December of the following year. Surely, people hoped, something *better* would now begin.

2

miners and planters

Belgian parliamentary rule was supposed to bring an end to the worst excesses of the Free State. Its effective architect, the socialist parliamentarian Émile Vandervelde, justified the new system of government in 1911, arguing that a brief period of Belgian parliamentary rule would be followed necessarily by a different period of 'free consort' between the peoples. The future would be one in which goods and ideas were shared freely. The old days of one-man rule belonged now to the past.

> The workers understand that against the politics of capitalist colonialism, a politics of domination and exploitation, they most oppose no sterile negations but a politics of indigenous socialism, a politics of emancipation and of the defence of the oppressed.... This politics will aspire to make men free. It will 'educate towards independence'. It will tend to substitute for the subordination of the colonisers to the colonised the simple relationships of exchange between people equal before the law.[1]

Vandervelde was well versed in the art of concealing privilege in an elaborate appeal to the most heroic of instincts. The goal of Congolese freedom was dismissed as 'sterile', all prospect of change transformed into something unrealisable, an 'aspiration', and the 'simple' practice of foreign white domination tolerated for the indefinite future. As we saw in the previous chapter, before 1907 other Belgian socialists had resisted Vandervelde's policy, but after 1907 it became the position and certainly the practice of his party.

Overt slavery may have diminished, but the Congo was still seen in Belgium as a source of revenue, and little was done to give Africans a significant role in the running of their own country. Instead, the previous regional and administrative divisions remained in place. The greatest difference was that at the top of the structure was a colonial secretary, reporting to the democratic Belgian cabinet, rather than to the private officials of Léopold's rule. This was not because the politics of empire had changed, but because the world was moving in new directions, towards industry and armaments, and in order to obtain the most amounts of profits from the colony, some economic and social progress was allowed. Rail lines were laid, copper mines dug and plantations set out. Africans were still labourers, and Europeans always managers.

The annexation of Léopold's private empire by the Belgians led quickly to one important but rarely mentioned 'reform'. While the trade between the private empire and Europe had been a monopoly business, after 1913 the Congo was opened up to 'free trade' with Europe. In 1913, for reasons of commerce, and with the likelihood of war against Germany in mind, Britain recognised the colony for the first time.[2] Almost overnight, the previous establishment support died away from Morel's anti-slavery campaign. More positively, the Congo was now opened up to world trade. It was in this context that trade increased, the economy diversified, and the work on the Congo's infrastructure was begun. In the years that followed, many Africans moved from the countryside to urban areas, looking for work. Rubber declined in importance: in 1901 it had constituted a staggering 90 per cent of the country's exports, but over the next thirty years its significance declined almost to nothing. New products, including copper, took rubber's place, and implied a different set of relationships. Instead of slaves and masters, the Congo became a society of bosses and workers. Settled industrial employees required training. Missionaries brought European-style schools, and encouraged the demand for learning, even if only very few Africans were educated beyond the primary level. Hospitals were built. Slowly, a small class of educated Congolese began to emerge. The sort of modern urban and transport infrastructure was established which it was hoped could meld the Congo into a single integrated state. Expectations were raised, without being fulfilled. The remaining injustices of a colonial system created the conditions for further protest.[3]

Élisabethville

At the end of this period, there were 14 million people living in the Congo.[4] As a legacy of the genocide of the 1890s, this was still a small population compared to the enormous territory. Nearly a quarter of the population lived in cities, and this proportion tended to grow over time. The population of the capital Léopoldville (today's Kinshasa) rose from 25,622 in 1935 to 388,961 in 1958.[5] Stanleyville (now Kisangani) grew at a similar rate, from 23,000 in 1935 to 185,000 in 1957. Yet of all the cities of the Congo, the one that imbibed most of the spirit of the period was Élisabethville (today's Lubumbashi). The source of its success lay in the finding of copper in Katanga. In 1898, Robert Williams of Tanganyika Concessions received authorisation to explore some 60,000 square miles in the border region between Northern Rhodesia (today Zambia) and the Congo. Williams chose this area precisely because Africans had long worked it for copper. During his travels, he found a hundred old mines, several of which could be reopened. It was on his return to Belgium that Williams founded Union Minière de Haut-Katanga.[6]

King Léopold had granted control over the Katanga region to a joint-stock company, the Comité Spécial du Katanga, part owned by Union Minière. Other regions were given to courtiers; only in Katanga did business play this dominant role. Copper production began in 1909 and grew rapidly, especially with the high demand for metals during the First World War. Early extraction techniques were little more sophisticated than those practised before the advent of colonialism. Only the highest grade of ore was removed, and all operations were carried out manually. It was a process that relied on abundant cheap labour. Copper became the most important sector of the Congo's economy, and would remain so for many years.

Élisabethville became a major hub of industry in central Africa. Union Minière built up the town, as its capital and private fiefdom. A Special Committee accountable to the copper concern administered the region. In 1910, the administration of Katanga was placed in the hands of a vice governor general, separate from the rest of the Belgian Congo. Union Minière developed, meanwhile, as an alliance between Belgian and British interests. The latter provided many of the early foremen and managers and a large share of the initial capital. As Élisabethville grew, the most important rail and transport links were never with the Congolese capital Léopoldville to the north, but with Lusaka and with the various British colonies to the south.

The most pressing concern in 1910 was the need to recruit workers. While it was accepted after 1908 that the Belgian authorities could hardly condone slavery, they had not yet found any other means to recruit sufficient labour. Different strategies were employed. On the one hand, all Congolese were still required by law to work for the state, without pay, for sixty days a year. In mixed agricultural and industrial areas, as in the rural hinterland of cities, it was possible to recruit some labour by making use of this requirement. But for expanding mines, the rule was insufficient. Private companies were therefore charged with recruiting labour, which they tended to bring in from outside, from today's Zambia, and soon from as far away as today's Rwanda and Uganda. Workers were persuaded to travel to Katanga by means of the most extraordinary false claims. In the region of Shabunda, one historian records, the recruiting agents of Union Minière came up with the ingenious idea of dressing up a man (Mwenyemali Mupanga) and woman (Bitondo) with the clothing that was promised to all those men and their wives who would work for the company. These two mannequins went from village to village explaining to all onlookers that anyone who wanted these clothes and anything else (cooking pots, blankets, children's clothes and the like) had nothing more to do than to present themselves to the whites who would bring them to the territory.[7] Such tactics became less successful over time as news spread of the real conditions on offer. Other workers soon had to be captured and forced at gunpoint to travel south. They were then marched for hundreds of miles, with many dying on the way. Union Minière lost as many as 6,000 men to hunger and disease in 1920 alone.

One of the few Congolese sources for this period is a text titled the *Vocabulary of Élisabethville*, which was collected in Katanga by

André Yav in 1965. Yav seems to have been a domestic servant, and the text is based on his own memories and those of his fellow workers, some who had begun work in the city as far back as 1885. The text is surprisingly positive about the reign of King Léopold, which is contrasted with the harsh times in Élisabethville after 1910. Yav writes of the later period:

> There was not a single worker who was able to open his mouth, even a little bit. They were big trouble, those many whites when they lived in Termite Hills. They thought [it good] to build for the black man just a one-room house. [But] this man had his wife and children, some of them male, some of them female.[8]

Slowly, a compromise was adopted. Prospective workers would still be rounded up in levies. Yet, having been captured, they would now be paid. Similar methods spread to other sectors of the economy, including the army. Some 10,000 labourers were requisitioned in the first three months of 1917 in just one eastern district, Tanganyika-Moero alone. But, having been rounded up like slaves, these employees did at least receive a wage. On the mines, as the most easily accessible deposits were exhausted, the first investment in machinery was made.

One historian of this process, Donatien Dibwe dia Mwembu, argues that in the absence of a state spending money to house, educate and care for all its people, Union Minière was forced to fill the gap, providing elementary welfare services to its workers. The company provided food, mainly beans, flour and some vegetables. The allocation was reviewed in 1933, 1937, 1939 and 1948, each time with the idea of improving its quality. Doctors and hospitals were established, including the first antenatal clinic in 1925. Workers' camps were built, with high standards of hygiene. Within each camp, there was a chief or Tshanga-Tshanga charged with maintaining order. Ideas of common interest did take a certain hold among the workers, as Binyangie Kalunga recalls:

> We were like the children of the same family. Tshanga-Tshanga was like our father. He was the one who considered our words while we women quarrelled among ourselves. Sometimes also he sanctioned extra rations for us. When a woman learned she was pregnant, and we wanted to celebrate the news, he would bring us *bukali* and chicken, sometimes rice or beans. It was a feast.[9]

Between 1914 and 1918, Union Minière produced 85,000 tonnes of copper, worth 37.5 million francs, of which 7.5 million francs was returned to the colonial administration through taxes. The expansion of the business in these years undoubtedly made it easier to retain experienced workers. Between 1918 and 1920, the wages of black labourers rose by 78 per cent.[10] After 1908, writes David Gibbs, 'living conditions did improve somewhat'.[11] Bruno de Melder describes what he terms Union Minière's 'doctrine of stability'.[12] By 1921, all machinists on the copper mines were black. There was a white industrial class, comparable to the skilled workers of South Africa. Yet in the Congo, such employees were normally foremen or supervisors, not workers. In 1922, Union Minière opened a training school for miners. In October 1927, workers were placed on three-year contracts.[13] Attempts were made at reform. The aspect of compulsion reduced, the degree of bribery rose. The forced recruitment of 747 miners in Lulua in 1926 resulted in 'only' 122 deaths. By 1927, Union Minière believed that it had reduced its fatality rate to just 4.3 per cent a year. The depression of the early 1930s may even have achieved some good. It reduced the demand for production, and therefore for more labour.

We should not exaggerate the difference of the new system from the old. The planning of giant camps was no act of disinterested charity. It was intended rather to result in greater labour stability. It was also accompanied by much more intense supervision of the Congolese worker. Wage levels still discriminated against African labour. Even in the industrialised areas, there was no equality between the races. 'In 1929, it was estimated that a worker for the Union Minière might be worth some Fr. 50,000 to the company each year, while earning a mere Fr. 27 to Fr. 30 a day.'[14] Wage rates fell again in the 1930s, under the pressure of the global recession. In 1929 the copper price was £113 per tonne. Three years later, it was just £28 per tonne.[15]

Conditions were little better in the rest of the country. In 1931 a major revolt broke out in the Kwilu region, controlled by another Belgian company, HCB. Over 500 rebels were eventually killed. In 1936, the head of Stanleyville province observed that tax collection rates had fallen below 90 per cent. To make up the deficit, he instructed that all the city's unemployed labourers should be compelled by force to take unpaid work in the army or as porters. Those who refused were jailed.[16] As late as 1956, the average annual income per capita was estimated at $41 for the Congolese, falling to just $29 among the inhabitants of rural areas.[17]

While many workers responded to the conditions in the camps with feelings of gratitude, others were less enthusiastic. It was clear that companies such as Union Minière profited handsomely from the sweat of their workers. But how far down were the rewards actually being shared? Raphaël Makombo was one of the sceptics:

> You must remember that wages remained low. In fact, they were truly derisory. One or two francs a day, it was absolutely miserable. One day, I returned to the works to see a few friends during my rest hours. I found them with a boss, a white. As they were chatting, one of the workers asked him about salaries. This is how the white man replied, 'A black needs money? But what can he do with it? We give you food rations and you eat as much as you can. When you fall ill, there are chemists and hospitals until you recover. Why do you always demand a rise in your wages?' That was the white man's response. In the mind of the whites, the black man did not need to be paid.[18]

Makombo described having to save for months to be able to afford even very modest goods like a bicycle or a sewing machine. If Union Minière was just one family, then its workers were being treated not as full adults, but more like small children.

Strict racial segregation was practised in Stanleyville. Workers were kept in compounds and denied access to white areas. When whites kept blacks as domestic servants they would not even let them have a room in their house, but kept them in huts outside, which they locked at night.[19] Education was restricted. Social centres, including restaurants, theatre and the cinema, closed their doors to Africans, even those who could pay. The use of their own African languages by workers was discouraged. In April 1918, the compound managers were instructed that all managers had to learn to speak one African language. The majority of whites chose Swahili, not because many locals spoke it, but because it was the language employed by similar white-owned businesses in the lands to the south and east.[20] Eventually, Swahili would become the regional language of Katanga. Not for the first time, an 'African' tradition was invented for the sake of a white manager class.

The church

Another new tradition to take root was the Catholic Church. Centuries before, the Portuguese had achieved religious conquests on the coast. Their missions, however, left few traces. The English, too, had included missionaries among their number, although here as elsewhere Livingstone seems to have had surprisingly little success in making converts. The advantage faced by the Belgian monks and nuns who settled in the Congo in large numbers from the last decades of the nineteenth century onwards was the preferential treatment given them by the state. Religious bodies received generous financial grants, priests were paid to emigrate from Belgium to the Congo, the education of children was handed over to the Catholic schools. Trappists appeared in the Congo in 1895, to be followed by Lazarities, Passionites, Picpus and Scheutists. In the period of Léopold's rule, the missionaries acted as his main domestic shield, deflecting criticism, and exaggerating the virtues of his system. One 1905 report of the Belgian parliament into Léopold's system denounced the monks in sharp language: 'Whatever the reason for their attitude, whatever the interests which have put a gag in their mouth … posterity will say that never did the Catholic church betray more openly its own mission and the morality of its founder.'[21]

After 1908, Catholics took control of the Belgian Colonial Ministry. Between 1908 and 1945, three of the nineteen ministers were liberals and sixteen were representatives of the Catholic parties. The Socialist Party took almost no interest in colonial affairs, leaving the issue to the centre and right even when they were in coalition with them. Other figures are equally revealing. In 1936, there were 18,683 whites in Congo, of whom 12,654 were Belgian. The other 6,000 came from all over Europe and southern Africa. By 1958, this figure had risen to 113,671 non-Africans (88,913 Belgians), of whom an extraordinary 7,557 were missionaries. Slowly, a number of Africans began to receive a religious education and to qualify as priests. There were 93 black African priests in the Congo in 1945, and some 369 fourteen years later.[22]

The most important projects conducted by the Church concerned the recording of indigenous culture. A small minority of monks realised that in order to convert the local people, it would be necessary to learn their languages and habits. One instance of the latter activity was the work of Gustaff Hulstaert and Edmond Boelart at Bokuma. Hulstaert produced grammars in the Lomongo language. Boelart translated *Nsong'a Lianja*, a body of Mongo legends. In 1960, UNIMO was formed, a party agitating for Mongo independence. Its early programme thanked the work of these missionaries for encouraging them to feel that they could be free. Yet here, as elsewhere, we should not exaggerate the extent to which reform was possible in the colonial period. Different missions seem to have taken very different approaches towards proselytising among the Congolese. Many priests insisted on conducting services in Latin and education in French. Other monks simply quit the seminaries rather than work with people of the calibre of Hulstaert or Boelart.[23]

Catholicism shaped life in the Congo. One of its unintended consequences was the slow promotion of an African generation that embraced European culture. Clerks, teachers and nurses were called *évolués*, the 'evolved'. They often acted as intermediaries between the Belgians and the Congolese. African clergy had a distinctive status, being the only Africans in colonial society who were considered on a plane close to approaching social equality with the Europeans.

The social wage

As early as 1908, Congolese exports were already worth some 43.4 million Belgian francs, with 36.7 million francs generated by sales of rubber and ivory alone.[24] In a short period, much of rural Congo was transformed. Palm oil production began in 1911, controlled by Lever Brothers. The same year also saw the founding of a rail link between Katanga and Johannesburg. Wages were introduced, as a prerequisite for taxation in money. By the 1930s, the Congo produced half the world's industrial diamonds. As well as industry, Belgium also invested in agriculture. 'Native farming settlements' were established to enable the cultivation of export crops. Cotton production began in 1917. By 1933, the country had 700,000 planters. Cocoa production rose dramatically, from 340 kilos per year in 1923 to 427,000 kilos in 1937.

In Europe and America, the middle decades of the twentieth century were a period of state capitalism. The small private companies of previous decades were amalgamated to form giant trusts and combines. These huge firms were greedy to annex the materials for new production and new markets. States were charged with building up the domestic economy, above all during times of slump. The competition between businesses encouraged military competition between nations. One politics that thrived in this atmosphere was that of military conquest. While France, Belgium or Britain might claim colonies in Africa or Asia, Germany and Russia could grow only through annexations in mainland Europe. The state's growing involvement in military production facilitated the trends towards war, culminating in 1914 and 1939. Ironically, the emphasis on production for war purposes also served to increase the bargaining position of labour. Giant factories were established, the working-class citadels of Clydeside, North Italy and the Ruhr. Workers had a certain power. Some accepted the limits of the system, others wished to create something very different. The idea became established that the state was needed to pass reforms. The second major feature of this period was therefore the rise of the welfare state.

The Congo was partly integrated into both aspects of these global developments. Its mineral economy in particular grew quickly as Europe pondered war. Many of its natural resources were needed for the manufacture of munitions. Meanwhile, the development of industry hastened the need for social reform. A settled labour force was required. New generations of workers were imported from central Africa. A modest system of welfare was introduced, for the benefit of the miners. Gains spread to other areas of life. The pregnant wives of male workers were given greater food allowances. It was in Stanleyville that Union Minière provided the first schools and hospitals for Congolese workers. By the late 1940s, this model had become general throughout the country, as an aspiration, at least, if not yet a reality. In 1949 a statutory minimum wage was introduced.

The limits of reform

André Gide was a visitor to the Congo in 1925. He reported the case of an official sent out at a young age. 'He needed a strength of character that he was without. When these are lacking, a man tries to make the natives obey and respect him by the spasmodic, outrageous and precarious use of brute force.' Aggression was widespread. The official, Gide wrote,

> gets frightened, he loses his head; having no natural authority, he tries to reign by terror. He feels his hold slipping from him and soon it becomes impossible to quell the discontent of the natives, who notwithstanding that they are often perfectly amenable, are goaded to fury by injustice, violent reprisals, and cruelty of all sorts.[25]

The supporters of empire, in Belgium and throughout Africa, refused to acknowledge the basic cruelty and lack of democracy on which their empires were based. They emphasised instead the supposed justice of their cause. In January 1930, for example, the cartoonist Hergé began a series, *Tintin in the Congo*. Although he had never visited the Congo, Hergé belonged to a circle of patriotic Catholics, including Leon Degrelle, a leading figure in Belgium's later collaborationist wartime regime. Similar values infected Hergé's understanding of African life. The world that Tintin encountered was set safely in the tribal past, a society of witch doctors and leopard-men. At one point, Tintin stands in for a sick teacher, and addresses the class of young Congolese children: 'My dear friends, I am going to speak to you today about your motherland, Belgium.' The African characters are 'infantile, ignorant, idle and superstitious'.[26] The cartoon was dishonest in its treatment of the Congolese people, and wrong also in its assumption that the Belgian colony remained the same as it always had been.

By the middle years of the twentieth century, Congolese society had entered on a path towards a certain 'modernisation'. An education system existed. There was widespread employment, especially in the great cities, and for the workers fortunate enough to secure stable employment there were systems emerging of subsidised housing and health care. Roads and rail had begun the process of uniting the country. Goods were certainly traded across vast distances. Compared to the living hell of the early 1900s, we might judge that a certain progress had taken place. Yet this improvement was as nothing compared to the growing sense of greater class equality that could be found in the West, where opposition groups and trade unions operated relatively freely under the shelter of parliamentary democracy.

Still, the rulers of the Congo saw no prospect of having to under-
take major reforms. According to Marvin Markovitz,

> During the interwar period Belgium was concerned mainly with
> internal problems and paid scant attention to the Congo.... In the
> other nations of Europe which had colonial possessions in Africa,
> especially in Britain and France, criticism of colonial policy was
> nearly continuous. But in Belgium there was almost none. Almost
> to the end the Socialist Party remained virtually mute on colonial
> issues. Such criticism as there was came from a small circle of mis-
> sionaries, financiers, politicians, *colons* (white settlers) and colonial
> administrators. It was a case of experts talking among themselves.[27]

Thirty years after Gide's visit, inequality was still endemic. Before
1950, no African child was allowed to attend any European school.
After 1950, African children could be accepted at the school's dis-
cretion, but only following an inspection of the pupil's family. As
late as 1955, all Congolese men were still obliged to provide many
days' unpaid service to the state, and while this practice had been
allowed to lapse in the cities, it remained widespread in rural areas.
By 1958, less than 10 per cent of the intake to European schools was
composed of indigenous children.[28] There were some 10,000 white
European administrators in the Congo at the end of the 1950s. The
salaries they earned were comparable to the wages of civil servants
in Belgium. They lived in large houses and owned their own cars.
In 1958 the average white salary was still thirty-three times higher
than the African average.[29]

In 1953, one civil servant gave the following account of the need
for separate punishment between the races:

> If Whites and Blacks ever appear before the same tribunal to
> answer similar facts, any difference either in the nature or the
> seriousness of the penalty will be even more obvious. For, whether
> we like it or not, the same penalty used against a native and a
> White undoubtedly produces very different effects. The native has a
> different conception of the penal offence than the White, and most
> importantly, he reacts differently towards the inflicted penalty.[30]

Marie-Bénédicte Dembour recently published a number of interviews with former officials of the Belgian Congo. When Dembour
spoke to them, many had been retired for thirty years or more. The

former officials were open in their support for the old system, in their identification with the colonial project, and in the belief that the colony had been ruled in the best possible way. Yet reading their accounts now, the astonishing aspect of their testimony is their unblinking enthusiasm for the violence on which imperial rule was based. 'Peters' arrived in Congo in 1948, worked as a territorial officer in the Sankuru district where the main crop was cotton. It was harvested to pay a tax system whose structure had not changed in fifty years:

> It was out of the question to register a lower return compared to that of the previous years. Quantitative results had to be good. Thus, we could not afford to be lax and to let someone go through the meshes of the net. Each HAV [able-bodied man] had to clear thirty-six *ares* a year. The agricultural monitors determined where the good places were. We used a system of rotation, which differed from region to region, according to the ground and the climate. Where I was, it was as follows: manioc in the first year, rice in the second, cotton in the third, nuts in the fourth, manioc again in the fifth, and then back to the forest. Agronomists acted as judicial police officers and could send me those who had not been work-ing well with a statement to this effect … I preferred to send the defaulter to jail rather than to impose a fine. There was no point in taking away from them their last penny (*sou*). Moreover, other members of the clan would have paid for the culprit who would then have failed to draw any moral lesson from the condemnation. The punishment would have affected the wrong persons. With imprisonment, it was a different matter. This was especially so since, with me, seven days of jail meant seven times four strokes of the whip. I always managed to find a [legal] excuse to give the whip to the prisoners. Maybe you find this shocking, but it was like that. At the beginning one is shocked, but then you get used to it.[31]

Away from the cities

Any attempt to understand the dynamics of the colonial enterprise in the Congo needs to be aware of the ways in which the local societies were transformed by European intervention. Prior to 1900, the region had been divided between a multiplicity of structures. There were lesser and greater kingdoms. There were also smaller units of people, often organised around village structures, or united in loose federations of people bound together not by acknowledged leaders but rather by language or ethnicity. The classic structure of the Congolese kingdom involved a paramount chief, numerous chiefs at different levels, and village heads. Authority was a matter of transmitted precepts. Family ties were often matrilineal. Under the political system of the Bushong, for example, authority was decentralised from the paramount chief, or Nyimi, to minor chiefs, and from these to regional heads, and from these to village heads. About 70,000 people were ruled in this way.[32]

Under colonialism, most chieftaincies were kept under white supervision. The Belgian administration generally intervened in customary criteria of succession. Chiefs were salaried and given police powers, but the administrative divisions bore little connection to the pre-colonial reality, and even the powers of the kings were limited. Some existing chiefs were formally recognised, including the Yaka sovereign, who was regarded as a stabilising force in the Kwaango. The Lunda paramount titleholder of the upper Kwaango, by contrast, was ignored for decades, although his traditional status was higher than that of his Yaka vassal. Only when a new Lunda monarch, Ditende, pledged loyalty to the Belgians was this situation reversed.[33]

In the north-east, where Sudanic-speaking peoples with broadly acephalous (chiefless) societies and groups predominated, the colonial administration established the basis for new hierarchical structures and new divisions between people. This is what happened to the Lugbara, members of the Eastern Sudanic-speaking group of peoples, who extend over the area of the Nile–Congo divide, from the Azande in the north-west to the Lugbara and Madi in the south-east. The administration had relatively little knowledge and still less under-standing of the indigenous Congolese societies which they now formally ruled.

The sources we have for life outside the cities are often mediated through a language of anthropology, which tends to treat African villages as something static and timeless, the holders of a set of tradi-tions that have not changed in centuries. Sometimes, almost despite themselves, the sources give a sense of how rapidly these worlds were changing under the enormous pressure of Belgian occupation. In the late 1940s and early 1950s, for example, the British anthropologist

Mary Douglas undertook fieldwork in the Kasai region of the Belgian Congo. The Lele, on whom Douglas concentrated her fieldwork, were a group of people on the western border of the Bakuba Empire (as she put it) in Basongo territory. The population was divided into three chiefdoms, of which she studied only the westernmost. These were sparse settlements. The staple foods were maize and manioc, vegetables, meat, fish and palm wine. Men worked as hunters, women in agriculture and fishing. It was a society that only became fully monetarised at the time of the 1939–45 war. European administration was felt mainly in terms of the building of roads. Belgian laws 'appeared as a multitude of arbitrary infringements'.[34] The Catholic religion was spreading, with the benefit of Belgian assistance, and served often to enforce divisions between younger Europeanised Lele and their parents. But, despite her recognition of the impact of colonial rule on the Lele and the Bushong, Douglas focused her study almost exclusively on local-level structures and her analysis is very much in the 'structural-functional' tradition of the times among British anthropologists, set in a timeless 'ethnographic present' and concentrating on the persistence of structures rather than on the dynamics of their transformation.[35]

Early independence struggles

For those who were more attuned to the wider social realities, however, there were visible tensions in the colonial structures of the Belgian Congo. Even before 1939, a number of Congolese movements had begun to campaign for some sort of change, although such phrases as 'self-government' or 'independence' were still rare. In 1908, reports described a series of raid by Mbole people from Yaotike against company factories in Lokilo. The raids became so frequent that they were treated as routine. At about the same time, peasants from the Ilanga villages were attacking neighbouring Ilipa. The Mbole even developed a term for the Belgian agents, *atama-atama*, meaning slave traders. They refused to distinguish between previous generations of Arab slavers and these new Belgians, their supposed liberators.[36] Another uprising, meanwhile, took place from 1915 to 1917 in the Upper Ulele. Afterwards, the revolts continued, in Lomami until 1917, in Sankuru, Equateur and around Lake Léopold from 1919 to

1921. In Kivu, rebels held out until 1923 and in Kwango until 1931, when some 500 deaths were recorded.[37] Yet none of these revolts showed the potential to spread. A common language of grievances and rights was missing. There were no agreed political figures around which the dispossessed could rally. Few of these rebellions left any sort of trace. Yav's *Vocabulary of Élisabethville* mentions one revolt from 1917:

> There was a very dangerous, narrow and deep valley. So when the Whites were laying their rails to get to Kalule-Nord, there was one man, his name was Bwana Kienda-Biela. The man was capable of working very powerful miracles. And he did not like Bwana Jean Jadot's railroad passing there. This Bwana Kienda-Biela was very much opposed to their having the railroad passing there. And, as you know, these people from Europe also have a very tough spirit. So they opposed Bwana Kienda-Biela, and they made war against each other with great force, [Bwana Kienda-Biela] and the Whites. Truly this Bwana Kienda-Biela had muzzle loaders, bows and arrows. Bwana Kienda-Biela had no modern guns or [other] firearms at all. Truly they fought a war for many days. And the Whites, the children of Europe, on their side, put all their strength to it and they beat this Bwana Kienda-Bala ...They brought him here to Élisabethville. He arrived at this place called Drooplans. That is where he arrived and they skinned him alive, without killing him first.[38]

Yet this revolt has not been documented elsewhere.

One of the largest and most effective movements was the millenarian campaign led by Simon Kimbangu, who established himself as a prophet in the area around Nkamba.[39] This region had felt the effects of large numbers of Protestant and especially Baptist missionaries. Kimbangu gathered together a large following, and some of his supporters began to discuss the idea of a Congolese Church. He did not advocate independence. When pressed on this point, in a phrase reminiscent of Jesus' 'render unto Caesar' he told his followers: 'Give the rulers of the country all that they ask of you, but give your heart to God.' The movement rushed ahead of its leader. Soldiers and urban workers left their jobs to join Simon Kimbangu's movement. There were rumours of strikes on the railways. The state felt compelled to act and moved to arrest the prophet in June 1921. Soldiers fired on the crowds defending Kimbangu, and he was forced to go into hiding.

After several weeks without capture, Kimbangu conceded defeat and volunteered himself to the authorities. He was deported to Katanga and sentenced to death. This was later commuted to life imprisonment. Such was the furore surrounding his case that machine guns had to be mounted in Kinshasa in fear against further revolts. In all areas of the country, Kimbangu's movement gave rise to a series of fantastic stories and reports. André Yav records the stories that were put about in Élisabethville, for example.

> Truly this Bwana Simon Kibangiste arrived here in copper capital city in the year 1922, from Léopoldville ... At the Government veterinary's, that is where they put Bwana Simon Kibangiste. Then they made a hole in his crate, for a big military cannon, in order to kill this man. Truly, they put the [muzzle of] a cannon through the hole in the crate. When this cannon went off the crate exploded completely. But Bwana Simon was alive. By one of his miracles he had split into two parts, after which this man got together again and stayed alive.[40]

Even after its leader's capture, the movement continued underground. In the late 1930s, Simon-Pierre Mpadi organised a Kimbanguist revival before being forced by the Belgians to flee. Further attempts continued into the 1950s.[41] Kimbangu himself died in detention in 1951. His Church was eventually recognised by the Belgians in 1959 and would later claim some 4 million members across Africa.[42]

While Kimbangu himself insisted on the apolitical character of his following, no one else could miss the importance of a mass social movement originating among Africans and led entirely by Congolese. When the authorities discussed his movement, they interepreted it as having five key demands:

> (1) the Lord was to come immediately, (2) no gardens need be tilled and no food stored up, (3) the white man would be driven to the land, (4) the land would be returned to the native, (5) no native need work any longer for the European or pay taxes to the government.[43]

Whether or not the movement was reported fairly, we can begin to understand the panic with which the Belgians responded: a programme of boycotting taxes and redistributing land was indeed threatening to the colonial order.

World War II

In many ways, the 1939–45 war advanced the cause of African freedom. The struggle against fascism possessed a moral authority. Its example opened up a space to argue that all systems of racial domination were wrong. A method of guerrilla warfare, modelled on the Resistance movements, would later have an enormous symbolic impact in Africa. More immediately, the fall of Brussels to German troops in 1940 suggested that the coloniser could be defeated. Even in the landlocked cities of the Congo, news began to filter through of the Belgian defeat. The loss of around 75,000 civilian lives drained the coloniser of men and morale. The Belgian royal family was accused of having collaborated with the Germans, and the King was forced to abdicate. The relationship between centre and periphery was reversed, as one Belgian official explained:

> The Congo was able to finance all the expenditures of the Belgian government in London including the diplomatic service as well as the cost of our armed forces in Europe and Africa, a total of some 40 million pounds. In fact, thanks to the resources of the Congo, the Belgian government in London had not to borrow a shilling or a dollar, and the Belgian gold reserve could be left intact.[44]

The war also increased the social power of Congolese workers. There was a greater demand for munitions, and for the raw materials that would enable arms to be made. More workers were needed. For example, between 1938 and 1944 the size of the Union Minière workforce rose from 25,000 to 49,000. Wages rose. The increased orders also led, however, to an intensification of the work-rate, with severe consequences. The number of fatal accidents at Union Minière plants doubled.

The war encouraged workers across the Congo in particular to look at Belgian rule, and to judge it more objectively. It was evident that the wealth existed within their society to fund a much more equal division of power. Union Minière was the third largest copper-producing company in the world, after the vast North American businesses, Kennecoot and Anaconda.[45] Why should black sweat be wasted in the cause of guaranteeing white Belgian civil servants their pensions? Dibwe dia Mwembu's interviews with the miners of Élisabethville give a vivid sense of the conditions in the mines. According to one employee, Jean Féliz Kabeya, 'the working conditions were not at all good. We were exposed to more and more accidents and illnesses. The whites made us work like machines, like slaves.' Léon Kalume describes an anger bordering on mutiny.

One day we were hard at work. One of us was so tired he could barely continue. He started to lie down. A moment later, the boss came in. He jumped on our colleague, and kicked and punched him. We were shocked by this treatment. The head of our team took a risk and advanced on the white boss. 'When are you going to stop hitting a man who is too weak to respond?'[46]

Increasing numbers of workers began to escape at night.

In 1935 and 1940, there had been strikes among copper miners in Northern Rhodesia. Autumn 1941 saw strikes in Élisabethville by white foremen in the Association des Agents de l'Union Minière et Filiales. There was a growing cadre of skilled black workers in the mines. Such workers felt increasingly confident, secure in their own position. Why should they not emulate the whites? From November 1941, miners at Jadotville, Kipushi, Likasi, Luisha and foundrymen in Élisabethville (Lubumbashi) began to plan some sort of general strike. Reports came in of urban factory workers fleeing the cities to live in squatters' areas like Katuba. Reports circulating between mining managers began to warn of an 'air of premeditation' sweeping the African workers.[47] There were attempted strikes at Kikole and Kipushi. On the night of 3 December 1941, workers at the Shituru and Pandotville factories in Jadotville voted to go out on strike, the following morning. Striking workers were sent out to the surrounding areas, to Likasi, Luishia and Kambove, to call for support.

This regional general strike relied on an alliance between factory workers in Élisabethville and Jadotville, and underground workers at Kipushi. As workers, mothers and wives, women played a prominent part. For many factory workers, the key demand was a wage rise to 1.50 francs per hour. The demands of the male factory workers were amended to reflect issues that had been raised by their partners. The women demanded that rations were given to them as well as to their husbands. They also wanted a restoration of the conditions from the 1920s, when wives had been granted incentives, including free sewing machines. On 4 December, the authorities made a first attempt to end the strike with violence. Troops were sent to fire on a demonstration in Jadotville. At least fifteen people were killed. The strike spread. By 9 December, workers at all the main Union Minière sites were out.

At its peak this was an extraordinary movement. Often described wrongly as just a miners' strike, it involved also factory workers, railwaymen, night soilers, watchmen and food peddlers: an alliance of skilled and unskilled workers with 'penny capitalists' engaged in the informal sector. In December, the strike arrived in Élisabethville. The government panicked. Troop reinforcements were summoned. Strikers were promised an average wage rise of 30 per cent. Maron, the governor of Katanga, addressed the strikers. Contrary to his expectations, no promise could induce them back to work. Finally, the company responded with violence. Soldiers shot at crowds of strikers. Georges Lievens, a white trade-union leader who was present at the events, suggested that over one hundred people, many of them women, were killed.[48] Four mineworkers from Élisabethville, Clément Kalenga, Rémy Ilunga, Clément Mwasa and Amédée Kabgangu, recall the events of the strike:

> It was the inadequate level of salaries that caused the 1941 strike.... It is true that we had food in abundance. But could one go in the bar and exchange it for a bottle of beer? Of course not. We needed money to secure some of the basic needs of life … Union Minière made us leave the villages, but don't people eat in the villages? … It was for the money that we came here.
>
> The workers were united under Léonard Mpoyi, originally from Bena Nshimba and a clerk of the works. Léonard Mpoyi told us that we risked dying for nothing, and that Union Minière should increase our wages. 'Why should a white man be paid more than a black, when all the white man does is stand there, giving orders, his arms behind his back, and with a pipe in his mouth? We should take our rights, or we won't work tomorrow.' Mpoyi was a canny one, he had been to school. All of us were with him.
>
> The day came; we stopped work and left the mines. On our return we found soldiers distributed right through the camp. We thought their guns were not armed. A few soldiers toyed with us. They ordered us to give up. They told us that rations would be raised. There was a long discussion between the whites and the black workers. The director of Union Minière tried to convince us, but in vain. Then they asked the workers to reassemble at the

football pitch to find a solution. Everyone was there. Everyone demanded a raise in our salaries. The soldiers, now armed, surrounded us. We did not know if we were going to die. Monsieur Maron, Governor of Katanga, arrived at the strip. He called a short white man, Monsieur Mukambile who worked at the passport office.... These two gentlemen posed the question, why had we left our work? We replied that we wanted the raise. These two people then advised us to return home to choose four representatives who could discuss with the whites. The representatives would return to us that afternoon and report back on what had been discussed. We didn't want representatives, we wanted a raise.

In the negotiations that followed, Léonard Mpoyi found himself face-to-face with the governor.

Maron demanded that the workers return home. Mpoyi responded 'I refuse. You must give us some proof that the company has agreed to raise our salaries.' So Maron said, 'I have already demanded that you go to the office to check.' Then he pulled a gun out of his pocket and shot Léonard.

In the aftermath of this incident Maron ordered the troops to fire on the strikers.[49] On 10 December, the day after the massacre, the majority of strikers returned to work. In industrial terms, standing alone, they had been defeated. The reality of the strike served, however, to transform the conditions in the mines as well as the consciousness of tens of thousands of working Congolese. Never again could the white mine-owners assume that theirs would always be a loyal and acquiescent workforce.

The strike at Élisabethville was by no means the only industrial revolt in this period. Between 1941 and 1947, mining strikes in Katanga were common. Between February and May 1944, there was an attempted soldiers' insurrection in Katanga. Its leaders called for an end to starvation, the abolition of forced cultivation, and the ending of corporal punishment in the prisons, as well as the abolition of racial epithets in the army and at work. Planned to cover the entire length and breadth of the Congo, the revolt was defeated by preemptive arrests. The rebels captured Luluabourg, but were forced to retreat. Mineworkers from Kolwezi and Liushia were among the soldiers' allies, helping to guide them towards safety in Angola. Support also came from the peasants of Kasai and Katanga. Matadi saw dock strikes in 1945. The following year, the laws were changed to allow the formation of (heavily circumscribed) black unions. Wages rose after the general strike. Union Minière was forced to invest in an expensive programme of rural development.[50]

Despite the allied victory in 1945, the old conditions of empire across Africa could no longer be maintained. In 1946, Pierre Ryckmans, the governor-general of the Congo, declared that 'the days of colonialism are over'. The following year, the Belgian Senate sent a mission to the Congo to draw up reforms. Some change was needed, it was agreed, or independence would inevitably follow.[51]

The demand for freedom

'The works of men', writes Helen Winternitz, 'decay with a luxuriant restlessness in the tropics. The equatorial sun bakes their edges brittle. The humidity rots them to the core. Exuberant moulds eat at their foundation and the vegetation riots, overwhelming everything.'[52] So it was with the complex structures of the Belgian empire. Intact for decades, the entire structure collapsed with astonishing speed. In 1955, Antoine van Bilsen, a Belgian professor, published a plan for granting the Congo increased self-government. His document was titled *A Thirty Year Plan for the Political Emancipation of Belgian Africa*. The idea was still that independence could be placed far into the distant future, so far in fact that there was no real point considering it. The following year, the British and the French suffered a humiliating defeat at the hands of Colonel Nasser over Suez. In the following ten years, the British Empire in Africa was rapidly scaled down. The French were reluctant to follow this example, but between 1956 and 1960 most of their territories in Africa, both north and south of the Sahara, were given independence. In the special case of Algeria, it took a murderous seven-year war to convince the French to leave.

Like elsewhere in Europe, the immediate post-war years were a time of intense political turmoil in Belgium. Before 1949, political conflict was a three-way struggle between Socialists, Christian Socialists and Communists. Even after 1949, the centre of political gravity, on all issues save the empire, remained far to the left. In 1950, a referendum was held to discuss whether the royal family would be allowed to return. King Léopold III was believed to have worked too closely with the Germans. His return was only narrowly passed. After Léopold took up residence in the Laeken Palace, he was met with such a wave of protests that he was forced to abdicate in favour of his son Baudouin. A left-wing coalition came to power in 1954, and began to rethink Belgium's commitment to maintaining its overseas territories.

From the early 1950s, civil servants were encouraged to portray the regime no longer as a colony but as a sort of Belgo-Congolese community, in which Africans and Europeans shared the same common interests. A 1952 decree provided that Africans of the appropriate 'state of civilisation' should be judged as being subject not to tribal but to civil law. From 1953, Africans were allowed to own private land; in 1955 they were authorised to buy alcohol. From 1957, they were even granted limited rights to vote for their own candidates in elections to control local administration. Already, however, there were those who could envisage more radical change. Tshilemalema Mukenge recalls a song performed for the first time in 1955: 'Sooner or later the white man will be overthrown/ Sooner or later the world will be purified/ Sooner or later the world will be turned upside down.'[53]

Yet the spread of national consciousness was uneven. Even where people began to feel a sense of common interest, they still lacked any sort of confidence to take on their Belgian masters. Another incident from 1955 conveys the enormous sense of psychological domination that the Belgians still continued to exert in the Congo. In a letter home, Mme Genevieve Ryckmans, the wife of a colonial administrator, described travelling through a village in the Kwango district:

> The instant André [Ryckmans] appears on the horizon, or seated at a table appears ready to get up, the women and children escape with all speed. At Kimpuni and at Kikamba I succeeded, slowly, to hold them back by telling them not to be afraid, but here things are more difficult. Yesterday two small children were dying to come close to [their child] François' baby carriage. I called them over and a man explained to me that they were afraid that André would put them in jail for having looked at his son![54]

The first documented claim for Congolese independence was a statement published in 1956, by a small group of Catholic intellectuals,

Joseph Malula, Jospeh Ileo and Joseph Nagalula.[55] The demand emerged late. The inequalities in education meant that in comparison with the rest of Africa the Congo did not possess a large cohort of Congolese intellectuals. There was no obvious group to place themselves at the head of the struggle for reform or self-government. The country was isolated from other African states by the difficulty of land travel and the high costs of journeys by air. Yet once the struggle for freedom was under way, the idea took hold quickly.

The people who rose to prominence were a new category of Africans, people who had been trained by the Belgians to serve as junior soldiers, clerks or missionaries, and who claimed senior positions as the empire collapsed. For although imperialism discriminated against all Africans, the growth of the Congolese economy did allow a space through which some of the ambitious could squeeze. By 1953, for example, there were already 463 African merchants in Léopoldville, who possessed enough capital to afford their own car. At least one commentator has spoken of a 'new class' to describe this set of men, which included those who would lead the campaign for national liberation, and those who would betray it.[56]

Georges Nzongolo-Ntalaja describes the involvement of *évolués* in the campaign. It 'was basically a continuation of their fight for equality of opportunity in the colonial political economy', he writes, 'where they experienced discrimination with respect to career and other economic opportunities, in addition to the daily humiliations of colonial racism'. The experience of oppression tied this group, at least in the short period between 1958 and 1960, to the wishes of the rural and urban poor.

> For the protest of the peasantry against compulsory cultivation, forced labour and a heavy tax burden; the demands of the working class for higher wages and better working conditions; and the struggle of the lumpen proletariat for a right to earn a decent livelihood in the cities, from which the unemployed or *chômeurs* were frequently deported, had a common denominator with the cause of the *évolués*; they were part of the struggle for a better life socially and economically.[57]

The outstanding representative of this generation was Patrice Lumumba, later the first president of the Congo. Lumumba was born on 2 July 1925 in the Sankuru district of Kasai province. His father was a Batetela kinsman who converted to Roman Catholicism. Young Patrice was educated into the same religion, and believed for many years his father's stories with their 'God will provide' endings. Tidy and studious, he enjoyed school and left with sadness after achieving his high grade school certificate. Between 1943 and 1945, he trained as a nurse, one of the most 'advanced' courses then open to Congolese. He then worked in Kivu as a clerk to a mine. Next employed as a postman, Lumumba taught himself the skills of a writer. His early journalism emphasised social problems, while also arguing for a continuation of foreign rule. Patrice Lumumba joined clubs for his fellow intellectuals and established a Liberal association in Élisabethville. In 1956, he was accused of embezzling funds from the post office where he worked as a clerk and was sent to prison. On release from jail, he played a prominent role in a series of student, liberal and friendship networks, including one Christian Democratic Study Group, which also accounted for such future leaders as Joseph Ileo. Patrice Lumumba's world was dominated by the educated and the trained, people who sensed in themselves the skills to lead, but who were still held back by the dead hand of Belgian rule.

The decision of the state to prosecute Lumumba should not be seen as an isolated action, but rather as one minor expression of a much greater process, a war of manoeuvre that was taking place between young, educated Congolese, and their colonial overlords. The *évolués* were constantly struggling for more power, and constantly being pressed back. Two simple facts express each side of the contradiction. In 1956, there were 313 clubs for *évolués* in the Congo, with a combined membership of some 15,000. Yet as late as 1960, there was only one black Congolese citizen with a Congolese law degree.[58] It was the uneven way in which this new social class emerged that drove its members to the left. Had progress been constant, there might have been larger numbers arguing for Belgium to retain some proprietorial interest in their country: the constant, petty humiliations ensured that even the *évolués*, Belgium's natural partners, turned against the empire.

The post-war boom also contributed to a rising of collective ambition. Between 1950 and 1953, copper prices rose by 26 per cent. American companies began to speculate in Congolese industry. Modern Kinshasa emerged as a wall of concrete and glass. In 1952,

Forbes magazine ran a special issue praising the Congo as an investors' paradise. One survey of several dozen Belgian companies compared the profit rates of European businesses that operated either just in Belgium, or in both Belgium and the Congo. Within the first group, profit rates in 1950–59 stood at between 7.85 and 9.49 per cent. In the second group, profit rates varied between an impressive 15.10 per cent and an extraordinary 21.48 per cent.[59]

Congolese nationalists were impressed by the visit in late 1958 of French President Charles de Gaulle to the neighbouring French Congo. De Gaulle offered Africans the opportunity to chose between continued association with France or for full independence. At much the same time, the Belgians sent Patillon, the former Minister of the Congo, to conduct 'an inquiry concerning the administrative and political evolution of the country'. In the months running up to this visit, Lumumba joined the Mouvement National Congolais (MNC), a moderate nationalist organization created in 1956. In October 1958, Patrice Lumumba declared the foundation of a 'national movement' dedicated to the goal of national liberation. Six weeks later, an All-African People's Conference was held in Accra, hosted by Kwame Nkrumah. The moderate Congolese nationalist Joseph Kasavubu was invited to attend and put the case for Congolese autonomy, but the Belgians refused permission for him to attend. In his absence, Lumumba filled the gap. His militancy became the public face of the campaign for independence.[60] Lumumba and his 'class' were becoming radicalised. He was also rapidly becoming better known.

In January 1959 there were serious riots in Léopoldville, in which at least forty-nine people died. The troubles began with a legal demonstration called by the Abako party, the Association des Bakongo pour l'Unification et la Défense de la Langue Kikongo, led by Joseph Kasavubu. A middle-aged former seminary student, Kasavubu vacillated between forms of regionalism and national organisation. In the 1940s he had argued that the future ownership of the country should not belong to its entire people but primarily to the Bakongo, the descendants of the empire of the Kongo, and the largest ethnic group in the capital Léopoldville. Yet this long-term goal was not designed for rapid implementation. As its name suggests, Abako was for many years an organisation to promote linguistic and cultural activities. Only much later did it become a party in its own right.

Faced with a modest public meeting, called by Abako, the police intervened to disperse a crowd. This action led to fighting between the police and large numbers of rioters, who attacked the symbols of Western occupation: missions, schools and social centres. The army was sent in. While the Belgians satisfied themselves with proving that their troops had killed less than 50 people, most Congolese estimated the actual number to be closer to 500. The white residents began to militate for a military takeover of the civilian government. Yet rather than prepare for a long period of military rule, the Belgian government in Brussels drew the conclusion that their regime now lacked all popular legitimacy. The civil servants prepared to leave.

Hebert Weiss was living in the Kwango-Kilu area when news of the disturbances came in.

> Within three weeks a fundamental change occurred. This was when the first repatriated unemployed youths began to arrive at the territorial headquarters ... The repatriated youths insisted on being transported back to their villages, a request considered to be utterly outlandish. But, breaking all precedent, they very aggressively insisted and showed the administrators none of the usual respect. Eventually they returned to their villages by one means or another, but significantly they had broken the psychological relationship which had heretofore existed between the ordinary Congolese and the Belgian without having had to pay for it in any way.[61]

The story is revealing. All political legitimacy rests on an alliance between national and local power. The individual ruler cannot be present everywhere. Their authority must manifest itself in a series of relationships. If their people cannot dominate locally, they cannot dominate nationally. For the first time since King Léopold, the Belgians were being challenged for control of the Congo.

Lumumba was arrested for a second time in November 1959, and charged with making seditious statements. He was sentenced to six months in jail, but was released when his fellow members of the MNC insisted that they would not negotiate without their leader. His release coincided with an upturn in the struggle. A 'round table' conference in Brussels decided in February 1960 that the Belgian Congo would become fully independent from 30 June of that year. Once the Belgians had agreed to independence they refused to budge on the date for the handover of power. 'Decolonisation' was now a matter of months away. The round-table negotiations were a farce. They were supposed to discuss the nature and timetable of the transition, but did nothing of the sort. The decision had already been made. Although two of the principal leaders of the opposition, Lumumba and Kasavubu, were anxious not to be seen publicly to want to prolong colonisation, both men approached the Belgian authorities and suggested an 'interim provisional government' before full independence. They were turned down. When independence finally came to the Congo it arrived abruptly, there was no transitional stage.

Preparing for power

Most explanations for the speed of the Belgian departure of 1959 portray it as a matter of accident. Before 1958, the colonial power had no plans to leave; the haste with which Belgium then departed was almost indecent. Certainly, groups of Belgians responded with anger to the decision: many settlers packed and left in a great hurry; others, particularly those associated with the military, attempted to challenge or later reverse this defeat. The catastrophic early period of independence has even led some writers to present the Belgian departure as a sort of feint, a 'neo-colonial' venture, hedged rapidly by plans for further involvement. It is true that the departure was attempted quickly and with little sign of any plan. But the motives of the Belgian authorities were simple; all over Africa, other nations with greater resources were removing their citizens, and bowing to the demand for African self-government. In the Congo, the first signs of weakness led very rapidly to a collapse of Belgian morale. Nationally, locally, in every village, the 'rulers' no longer seemed to be just that. Very rapidly, the nationalist movement established itself as the real power in the land.

The events of 1960 were the Congo's revolution. They were accompanied by all the signs of insurrection: crowds taking control of the streets; people talking, thinking, reading; a condition of general euphoria; the withdrawal of the old powers. The greatest change, as in all such processes, took place in the minds of women and men, as they learned for the first time to be free. The revolution was embodied in the figure of Patrice Lumumba. As an *évolué*, trained by the Belgians, and sympathetic to the treasures of European culture, he spent many years as a moderate nationalist, calling for an orderly transition towards self-government. In January 1957, he wrote from Stanleyville to Brussels, to offer a series of suggestions for future cooperation between the two countries. His planned book, *The Congo: Land of the Future*, was not published until after his death. A plea for self-government, it was aimed at a Belgian audience, and made several concessions to its readers. At the time of Léopold II, Lumumba wrote, the Congo had been overrun by ignorance,

> Belgium, moved by a very sincere and humanitarian independence, came to our help, and with the assistance of doughty native fighters, was able rout the enemy, to eradicate disease, to teach us and to eliminate certain barbarous practices from our customs, thus restoring our human dignity and turning us into free, happy, vigorous, civilised men.[62]

Lumumba was not just naive in arguing that colonialism had been of human value; he was repeating instead the common sense of his generation. It took the experience of many personal defeats, the constant lies of the colonial foremen and masters, to teach Lumumba the need for a much more militant critique.

In December 1959, the victim of one period of imprisonment, and a second public trial, Lumumba interrupted his campaign for independence to attend the Accra Conference of African States. His speech there demonstrated a hardening of his position:

> This conference ... makes one thing clear to us: despite the frontiers which separate us, despite our ethnic differences, we have the same consciousness, the same soul, which is steeped, night and day, in anguish, the same earnest wish to make this Continent of Africa a free and happy continent, a continent set free from anxiety, from fear and from colonialist domination. Down with colonialism and tribalism! Long live the Congolese nation![63]

Lumumba campaigned for independence through a party, the MNC, and with a newspaper, *Uhuru*. The paper reported on the progress of liberation struggles throughout Africa. It argued for a conception of Congolese independence that was based not on race, nor on tribal loyalties, but on secular conceptions of universal rights to independence, democracy and freedom.

In the negotiations leading to independence, the MNC quickly acquired a reputation as the major obstacle to continued Belgian rule. The old colonial power attempted to promote rival, moderate forces, such as the Interfédérale des Groupes Ethniques, which in turn gave rise to the Parti de l'Union Congolaise and then the Parti National du Progrès. The latter was a consistent advocate of conciliation with Belgium. On the eve of the first democratic elections, journalists began to report on the distinctions between the different leaders. There was the 'big bellied', 'sedate' Joseph Kasavubu, leader of Abako. The 'smooth' Moïse Tshombe was a rich middle-class *évolué*, leader of Conakat, the party of the Balunda in the south, and a strong advocate of federalism. Against these ethnic politicians, stood the 'man of integrity' Lumumba. But even where party organisation was strongest, voting tended to split down to the most local level. For example, in Katanga, where 80 per cent of the population voted, and there were polarised pro- and anti-Lumumba blocs, out of a total of 325 rural council seats, only 49 were captured by candidates from party lists, the other successful candidates winning from ethnic or local lists.[64]

We can trace something of the contradictions of these elections through the records of the Parti Solidaire Africain, a party that had some base in Léopoldville and its strongest support among the rural Kwango-Kilu districts in the south and west. Although they were outside Lumumba's party, the PSA would later provide some of his staunchest allies, including Antoine Gizenga and Pierre Mulele. The leaders of the PSA were all *évolués*. The twenty members of its National Central Committee and National Political Bureau in January 1960 were all teachers, bank or government clerks, or medical assistants. In early 1960, the PSA, like other Congolese parties, attempted to root itself in the rural areas. They began with the local leaders, people who had been accepted by the Belgians as tribal representatives. These were encouraged to join the PSA, and to persuade a majority of their people. Between December 1959 and March 1960, several of the main PSA leaders were out of the country. They anticipated Belgian military resistance, and a crackdown against Congolese nationalism. They were surprised on their return to find that democratic politics had been tolerated. Something still more important was happening: power was being taken locally. Hebert

Weiss was then living in the areas of PSA support. He saw a people who were used to thinking of themselves as the victims of history, become confident and begin everywhere to challenge their rulers.

Belgian–Congolese relations developed into a sort of game where the Congolese would 'test' Belgian reactions with ambiguous attacks on authority, which if successful constituted a moral victory for the 'assailant', but if resisted would prove difficult to punish or even to define in legal terms.… For instance, people refused to appear for the census, or mothers refused to appear with their children for medical examinations, or they asked that they be paid for bringing their children on the argument that the Belgians would not have insisted on doing this all these years if it did not bring them some advantage. Pregnant women also refused to have themselves examined unless they received payment. There were also more subtle attacks on authority. People would no longer stand at attention when addressing administrators, they would be conspicuously slow in responding to questions put to them, and any incident would be immediately magnified. Thus a quarrel between a mission driver and a local villager which previously would have been stopped by a stern word from a European nun now would mushroom, and on occasion would end with the pelting of the mission truck.[65]

Conflicts between the people and their old rulers were common-place. In the Lower Congo, for example, one colonial source reported that Abako's passive resistance campaign, dismissed initially as 'intimidation', had now become a 'popular movement'. Refusal to pay taxes was widespread. Accused and plaintiffs refused to answer summonses to appear in the tribal courts; tribal judges, too, stayed away. The Abako operated its own system of courts. All administrative measures dealing with land and health were ignored.[66] We might normally describe such a situation as one of dual power: with local structures of power in competition, the rules of colonialism competing with the future institutions of independence. But to use the term 'dual power' in this instance would be to imply that the outcome of the struggle was unknown, when this was not the case. Because Belgium had already announced the decision to leave, there was no threat that the authorities could use to keep hold of their power.

Through May and June, the remaining Belgian authorities insisted on supervising the elections themselves, directing the press to warn against the 'Communist' Lumumba, financing rival parties, doing everything they could to guarantee that relationships between the two countries remained those of the master and slave. With notable exceptions, such as the MNC and PSA, those parties that organised on the basis of region or ethnicity received direct Belgian government funding. They were useful to Brussels because their power structures reflected the links of ethnicity and 'tribal' loyalty that the European power had been strengthening for nearly a century. They represented the best hope for the continuation after 1960 of the previous, dependent relationships. But the MNC won a majority. With 88 seats taken by allies out of a total of 137 members in the new National Assembly, Lumumba was the obvious choice to head the government. The Belgians attempted to stall his appointment, but failed. Lumumba's first real battle had been won.

The second victory also went to Lumumba. The events of the independence ceremony helped to propel the Congo and its prime minster into every living room around the world. The day started according to the official timetable, and the handover was due to take place in the parliament building. There, before members of the Belgian ruling class, including King Baudouin, delegates of the new, independent Congolese government, foreign dignitaries and reporters, an amicable separation was to be announced. The *Guardian* correspondent described the atmosphere leading up to the arrival of the king:

> The crowd around the wide square of the Palais des Nations was as small, and as unenthusiastic as an independence crowd could be. There were only about four thousand there, due, perhaps, to the confusion caused by hasty arrangements. But the shouts of 'Le Roi' from loyal Belgians as the King entered the Parliament Building was the first cheering note for him.[67]

Lumumba had not been scheduled to speak, and the government was to be represented instead by its president, Joseph Kasabuvu. The king rose to announce the official end of Belgium rule in the Congo, but he did much more. His speech turned into a historical justification for the crimes of colonisation, and argued that the last eighty years had seen only development and the fulfilling of the 'white man's burden'. The king pronounced:

The independence of the Congo is the crowning glory of the work
conceived by the genius of King Léopold II, undertaken by him
with firm courage, and continued by Belgium with perseverance.
Independence marks a decisive hour in the destinies not only of
the Congo herself but, dare I say, of the whole of Africa. For eighty
years Belgium has sent to your land the best of her sons, first to
deliver the Congo basin from the odious slave trade which was
decimating her population, later to bring together the different
tribes which, though former enemies, are now preparing to form
the greatest of the independent states of Africa. [These] pioneers
deserve admiration from us and acknowledgement from you. They
built communications, founded a medical service, modernised
agriculture, and built cities and industries and schools.

To compound the insult, King Baudouin continued: 'It is now up to
you, gentlemen, to show that you are worthy of our confidence.'[68]

Lumumba could now be seen desperately scribbling a new speech
to answer that of the king. When the king finished there was the
respectful round of applause before Kasabuvu replied, acknowledging
the 'wisdom' of the Belgian state. Lumumba followed, fully aware of
the significance of the event. The flashguns of the assembled pho-
tographers fired, as Lumumba sorted the pages of his new speech:

Our wounds are too fresh and too painful still for us to drive
them from our memory. We have known harassing work, exacted
in exchange for salaries which did not permit us to eat enough to
drive away our hunger, or to clothe ourselves, or to house ourselves
decently, or to raise our children as creatures dear to us. We have
known ironies, insults, blows that we endured morning, noon and
evening, because we are Negroes. Who will forget that to a black
one said 'tu', certainly not as a friend, but because the more hon-
ourable 'vous' was reserved for whites alone? ... For though this
independence of the Congo is today being proclaimed in a spirit of
accord with Belgium, a friendly country with which we are dealing
as one equal with another, no Congolese worthy of the name can
ever forget that we fought to win it [applause], a fight waged each
and every day, a passionate and idealistic fight, a fight in which
there was not one effort, not one privation, not one suffering, not
one drop of blood that we ever spared ourselves. We are proud of
this struggle amid tears, fire, and blood, down to our very heart of
hearts, for it was a noble and just struggle, an indispensable struggle, if we were to put an end to the humiliating slavery that had
been forced on us.[69]

The transfer of power, presented by the Belgians as a sort of gift or loan, was recast into something quite different, a real declaration of independence.

The speech was transmitted live across the Congo. When Lumumba finally finished the speech, to 'loud and long' applause, and returned to his chair, the king threatened to cancel further engagements and return to Belgian. The programme was interrupted for an hour as the king and members of his entourage threatened to leave. The king, as the personification of Belgian power, had correctly taken the speech as a personal insult.[70] This was an offence that he never forgave, and one that still generated a visceral hatred of Lumumba among members of the Belgian ruling class many years later. The effect of the speech was explosive around the world but particularly in Belgium. The press called for Lumumba's head. Never had the king or the dignity and pride of the Belgium state been so insulted, and by a black man. One academic study notes that 'Lumumba's eloquent denunciation of colonialistion in the Independence Day speech ... caused such consternation in Belgian conservative circles and earned him their undying hatred.'[71] Among opponents of colonialism, opinions were rather different. In New York, Malcolm X told his followers that Lumumba's was the 'greatest speech', and that it had been made by the 'greatest black man who ever walked the African continent'.[72] Belgium was humiliated, and the Congo's freedom properly won.

3

rebels and generals

On 30 June 1960, the Congo finally gained independence from Belgium. Patrice Lumumba became the first prime minister of the country. His party, the Mouvement National Congolais, was committed to unitary national politics, a multi-ethnic state, and policies of redistribution to the rural and urban poor. The MNC's objective was to secure the emancipation of the Congo while encouraging among its supporters 'a consciousness of their national unity and responsibilities'. It was essentially a non-tribal party. This distinguished the MNC from its various rivals, including Abako (the cultural association of the Bakongo, founded in 1950 with the aim of restoring the ancient Kongo empire but later converted to the idea of a federalist Congo), led by the aristocratic Joseph Kasavubu, Conakat (through which the Balunda aimed to exercise power in Katanga either within a federal Congo, or separately), led by the rich middle-class *évolué* Moïse Tshombe, and Balubakat (which eyed the Balunda to the south with considerable suspicion and prevented Conakat from speaking for the whole of Katanga), led by Jason Sendwe. African political organisation was officially forbidden under Belgian rule, and so various 'cultural associations' were formed which had the same force as political parties. Most of these groups favoured a federal state, with a regional structure. The Belgian authorities had long favoured the idea of a unitary state based on a centralized administrative system. It was only with Lumumba's victory that the Belgians were converted to federalism.

The passive revolution

The political parties of the Congo were different from their counterparts elsewhere in Africa, writes Crawford Young; their history was shaped by the speed with which independence had been won. 'They were born in an environment where the nationalist awakening was very belated and had tended to be preceded and accompanied by a reinforcement of ethnic self-consciousness.' The authoritarian nature of Belgian colonialism 'had given less leeway for the acquisition of experience in African associational activity than had been the case in former British or French territories'. In many areas of the country, the leadership of the independence struggle had been captured by forces hostile to Lumumba's MNC. Most were motivated by ideas of ethnicity, rather than nationalism. Young continues,

> The vast size of the country, with its two major poles of modernization at opposite ends and several major regional centres in between, each developing its own distinct African elite until 1958, created a built-in fragmentation problem which was given little time to be overcome. And when the elite did begin to communicate nationally, the dissolution of colonial resistance provided little of the compulsion to unity which has been a vital argument elsewhere for advocates of a single independence movement.[1]

Jean-Paul Sartre, writing in 1972, made much the same point, but more angrily:

> An independence that is conceded is merely slavery in another guise. The Congolese had suffered for almost a century, they had often been beaten, and strikes and uprisings had become more frequent despite cruel repression. Just a short time before, the disturbances of January 1959 had been if not the cause, at least the occasion of the Belgian government's new colonial policy. There is no doubting either the courage of the proletariat and of the peasant warriors, or the profound, the absolute, refusal of each and every colonized Congolese to accept colonization, sometimes despite himself. The fact remains, however, that circumstances neither permitted nor favoured a recourse to *organized* struggle.[2]

Lumumba knew that independence would not be sufficient to free Africa from its colonial past; the continent must also cease to be an economic colony of Europe. An independent Congo should not be compelled to obey Belgium; it should seek its own path of development. He held that the Congolese people could overcome all obstacles and create some sort of just society. He had the ability to articulate the grievances of the majority and the charisma to inspire them. He was undoubtedly the outstanding political figure of his generation. Lumumba wanted a strong centre rather than a diffuse federation, but powerful forces were aligned against him from the start.

Long ago, the Italian Marxist Antonio Gramsci described the two red years of 1918–19 as Italy's passive revolution. He meant that the great struggles of the Italian workers, their protests for control over their workplaces, had failed to reach the possibilities open to them. Despite the war, which had discredited the old powers, despite the vacillations of their enemies, the working class in Italy had failed to seize power. By their weakness, they had created the conditions for a counter-revolutionary struggle that pushed history backwards. The workers' adversary, fascism, had been the revenge of the men who owned the factories and the land.[3]

It is not entirely fanciful to see the possibility of a similar danger weighing on the mind of Patrice Lumumba, even during his moment of triumph on 30 June 1960. The economic situation was dismal:

> On the eve of its independence the Government was faced with large current deficits (£40 million on current account for 1960 alone). The flight of capital and the loss of international confidence, because of the events of 1959, meant the new Government would come to power with no liquid assets at all.[4]

The new government would inevitably be faced with problems of resources, expectation and ability. When Lumumba spoke of 'a fight waged each and every day', he was schooling his people for the period of conflict ahead, the real war for independence. 'Who will ever forget', he asked, 'the shootings which killed so many of our brothers, or the cells into which were mercilessly thrown those who no longer wished to submit to the regime of injustice, oppression and exploitation used by the colonialists as a tool of their domination?'

Belgium had only 'learnt the lesson of the history'. Her promises of friendship could never be fully trusted. 'For our part we shall, while remaining vigilant, try to observe the engagements we have freely made.'[5]

Certainly, even while the Congo was reaching towards independence, there were people working to thwart it. Mahmood Mamdani argues that the nature of colonial rule in the Congo militated against a united national movement. In the colonial period, ethnic authorities were set up by the colonial state, and these 'native authorities' were the only direct relationship most Congolese had with the state. As Mamdani explains, 'Unlike civic power which is the urban-based state of Congo, it is better to think of rural Congo as a giant federation of Bantustans.'[6] With independence, the people of the cities were granted the freedom to become citizens, but the people living in the rural areas remained subject to chiefs. The MNC strategy of seeking to control civil society was flawed, Mamdani argues, because it took no account of the situation of the rural majority; it raised demands which were not their own.

Other obstacles were more apparent even at the time. In July 1959, Lumumba had fallen victim to a first attack when his colleagues Jospeh Ileo, Cyrille Adoula and Albert Kalonji left the MNC to establish their own rival, 'moderate' party, the MNC-Kalonji. The split deprived the main party of some of its most capable leaders, and narrowed its base in the key province of Katanga in the south. A second conflict broke out in this very region, with its copper, cobalt, manganese, uranium, tin, zinc and gold mines, and from spring 1960 Tshombe argued that Katanga should separate from the Congo altogether. He had the support of powerful vested interests.

One observer, Staelens, was reported in the Belgian newspaper *La Relève* as saying,

> Independence was never intended to be anything but 'purely fictitious and nominal'. Financial circles believed, our political circles were more naïve than anything, that it would be enough to give a few Congolese leaders the title of 'Mister' or 'Deputy' with decorations, luxury motor-cars, big salaries and splendid houses in the European quarter, in order to put a definite stop to the emancipation movement which threatened the financial interests concerned.[7]

Such boasts have the ring of authenticity: the Belgians, certainly, had little interest in a genuine departure. The Belgian economy was closely tied to its colonial empire in central Africa, with a third of Belgium's trade involving imports from central Africa. Cobalt extraction in the Congo already represented three-quarters of world production. In the late 1950s, Union Minière alone produced a regular profit to Belgium of 4 billion Belgian francs a year. Following Tshombe's declaration of secession (in 1960), Union Minière had enough spare cash to pay 1.25 billion Belgian francs into Tshombe's private bank account. The Belgian companies that made their fortunes in copper, gold, diamonds and construction would not leave, not without a fight.[8] Nor would Lumumba's rivals, Kasavubu and Tshombe, easily abandon their ethnic view of a future Congo.

The second war of independence

Two days after Lumumba's speech, on 1 July 1960, his army the Force Publique mutinied for the first time. The soldiers seemed to have expected that independence would improve their pay and open the way to officer grades, which were filled by white men. When this radical change did not take place, they decided to oust the whites themselves. The Belgian chief of staff was replaced, and Victor Lundula was appointed commander-in-chief, with Joseph-Désiré Mobutu, a former NCO in the old colonial Force Publique, as his deputy. Touring the country's military bases, playing up his own army experience, Mobutu persuaded the soldiers to return to barracks. But fresh mutinies and violence quickly followed. Following the second, 4 July, mutiny of Congolese troops, Lumumba was forced to ask the Belgians living in Matadi to evacuate the city. They agreed. The women and children were taken away, by boat. The men remained. They proceeded to fire on the Congolese working in the docks. Dockers, the unemployed and students, the people were killed without discrimination. At least nineteen are known to have died, and many more were wounded.[9]

Worse followed. On 11 July, Tshombe began an armed uprising, with French, Belgian and British backing, to secure the independence of copper-producing Katanga. The diamond-rich South Kasai also resolved to secede. The immediate effect was to infuriate Lumumba, who suspected a plot to subvert the autonomy of the newly independent state and disrupt it by detaching its richest provinces. The new state seemed doomed to break apart, as its former colonial masters continued to exercise a nefarious power over events inside the country.

The Katangan secession in the first few weeks of Congo's independence was a formal process, with a precise beginning and a precise end. It was proclaimed by Tshombe on 11 July 1960 and renounced by him on 21 December 1961. Tshombe refused to allow Kasavubu and Lumumba, the federal president and prime minister respectively, to travel to Élisabethville, his capital and his stronghold. Tshombe's campaign always lacked popular legitimacy, even in his home region, where supporters of Lumumba formed themselves into militias to combat the insurgency, and the supporters of the Balubakat under Jason Sendwe also provided a dissident voice. But Tshombe asked Belgium for help; and the Belgians agreed, occupying Léopoldville with parachute troops the very same day.

On the eve of independence, the Congo and Belgium had signed a Treaty of Friendship, Assistance and Technical Aid. Among its many clauses, this agreement ruled that no Belgian troops could be brought to the Congo, except by mutual consent. Despite this, the Belgians now effectively abrogated their recently signed treaty and switched to Tshombe, providing him with an army. They actively collaborated in the break-up of the Congo. There were powerful interests at work. By 1960, the important sections of the Belgian capitalist class had developed a direct stake in the continuation of empire. Ludo de Witte mentions just a few of the snouts in the trough:

> Count d'Aspremont Lynden was Lord Chamberlain at the court. He was also a commissioner of the Société Générale de Belgique, and administrator of the Compagnie Maritime Belge and the Compagnie du Katanga. Together with the Honourary Lord Chamberlain, Prince Amaury de Mérode represented the royal house on the college of twelve commissioners which was the ruling body of the Société Générale.... Deputy Prime Minister Lilar was a former President of Titan anversois et des Ateliers de Léopoldville. The president of the Belgian chamber, Baron Kronacker, and Ministers Sceyven, Wigny and Albert De Vleeschauwer were administrators of a whole series of colonial enterprises.[10]

Even the limited independence that was granted to the Congo was sufficient to spark a major crisis in Belgium. The dramatically reduced access to its wealth brought crises of trade and production. The government announced tax rises of 10 billion francs. It also introduced new laws restricting Belgian trade unions. Strikes by electricity workers, port workers and civil servants fused together so that by December 1960 a general strike had broken out, involving at its height some 600,000 workers. The king returned to Brussels. Belgian troops were brought home from the Congo. Only with difficulty were the massed ranks of Belgian labour forced back to work.[11] We can understand, then, the bitterness with which the representatives of the Belgian business and political classes determined to fight to retain their power in the Congo. At stake was not just the right to control someone else's country, but the fate of their own, as Lumumba recognised: 'Belgium intends to have Katanga, the richest province, because she cannot exist without Katanga and the Congo.'[12]

With just 12 per cent of the Congolese population, Katanga accounted for nearly 60 per cent of the country's resources. Lumumba was determined to resist what looked like a Belgian–Katangan plot to tear the new society apart. He called on the Belgians to withdraw. They refused. He expelled Belgian diplomats. He called on the United Nations for assistance, and hinted that it might be necessary to ask the Soviet Union for help. The Western powers expressed their alarm. Lumumba represented a nationalism of the kind that frightened the Western powers, with its socialist rhetoric and populist politics. He also represented the furthest left tendency within the class of *évolués*. Tshombe, by contrast, had developed closer links with the expatriate bourgeoisie associated with the mining sector in mineral-rich Katanga, and his declaration of secession served to emphasise the regional and ethnic and class divisions that had developed in the Congo during the colonial period.

Kasavubu and Lumumba made three successive appeals to the United Nations, on 10, 12 and 13 July 1960. They appealed first for technical aid. In their second and third messages, they appealed for help against Belgian aggression. United Nations Secretary General Dag Hammarskjöld asked the Security Council to consider immediate technical assistance for the Congo and to respond to the problem of law and order. The Council authorised the sending of military aid to the Congolese government, with the proviso that force should not be used except in self-defence. On 14 July, the day after the second request for assistance against foreign aggression, the UN Security Council voted to send a force to the Congo to help establish order. The first United Nations troops landed in Léopoldville. The permanent members of the Security Council were divided, however, on whether to oblige the Belgians to withdraw. While the Russians pressed for an ultimatum, the Americans were opposed. Britain, France and China abstained.

Even conservative analysts questioned Belgian support for Katanga's war of secession. The *Daily Telegraph*, no friend of Lumumba's, reported the campaign:

> Mr. Tshombe, the self-styled President, is today far more under the domination of Belgian officials than he ever was as an obscure provincial politician before independence.... Mr. Tshombe's principal speeches are being written for him by a Belgian, Mr. Thyssen, a local businessman and politician. Count D'Aspremont Lynden, Chief of Cabinet to the Belgian Prime Minister, who ostensibly heads a technical aid mission, provides a link to Brussels. Colonel Champion is all but Military Commander of Katanga.[13]

For its part, the Katanga regime put the matter a little differently:

> Conscious of the imperious necessity of an economic collaboration with Belgium, the Government of Katanga, to which Belgium, in order to protect human lives, has just granted assistance of its own troops, asks Belgium to join Katanga in a close economic community.... It asks Belgium to continue its technical, financial and military aid. It asks Belgium to re-establish public order and security.[14]

Resistance to secession

Faced with the threat of secession, Lumumba had only two options. He could look without or within. Outside the Congo there were many potential allies: in Ghana, and in the growing ranks of the non-aligned countries that described themselves as the 'Third World'. These states, however, meant well but delivered little. There was little to be gained from America, France or Belgium. They were a hostile camp. The USSR represented a potential source of civilian aid, advice and guns. But to side with the Soviet Union would have required breaking with almost all of Lumumba's domestic supporters. Within the Congo, Lumumba was by no means powerless. He had regional allies in the south, including Jason Sendwe's Balubakat party. He had the prestige of his own authority. Yet his own army had already rebelled once. Nor was it large enough to defeat any insubordination. The ideal of a single Congolese state was not so popular that it could have triumphed easily over ethnic sentiment. Sartre captures the essence of Lumumba's strategy to make Congolese democracy work:

> He would take off in a plane with Kasavubu, who remained silent as a tomb and followed him everywhere; when news of a disturbance, unrest, or hostility reached him, he would land at the trouble spot, and almost the moment he climbed out of the aircraft he would hold a meeting somewhere. The warmth of his voice, his sincerity, his optimism, a sign of naïvete or mysticism, as one prefers, charmed every group he spoke to and often swayed them. When he had overcome their prejudices, calmed their misgivings, answered their objections, and *explained*, above all explained, his plans and his reasons in detail, he would come out on top for one evening; for one evening, in a provincial city, this dictatorship of the spoken word, the only one he exercised, would bring about a Jacobin unity of a few hundred people, the only ones who were politically aware. Amid their acclaim, Patrice would return to the plane, take off, and think: the match is won; and Kasavubu, sitting beside him would think: the match is lost, the spoken word is not that powerful.[15]

The few possibilities remaining to Lumumba closed off fast. The United Nations offered little more than acknowledgement of the Belgian coup. The army was now in the hands of Lumumba's appointee Joseph-Désiré Mobutu, but it was becoming evident that he could not be trusted. Early on, the Western powers had identified Mobutu as a potential ally. He had received payments from the CIA and was in contact with Western military attachés. Many workers were loyal to Lumumba, but their position was weak. As late as 1940, just 536,000 people out of the Congo's adult population of 10.4 million had been classified as workers. The unionisation of African labour was far from complete.[16] Even the power of Lumumba's rhetoric was to prove insufficient. He attempted to land on the airstrip at

Élisabethville, the heart of the secession. The Belgian officers controlling the town turned off the lights to make a landing impossible. If Lumumba had landed, he would have been shot.

Tshombe's fiefdom

Tshombe took advantage of Lumumba's weakness to consolidate his position. While the UN was trying to re-establish order in Léopoldville province, the Belgians did so in Katanga. They also provided Tshombe with administrative services, and they ran the mines and paid royalties to Tshombe directly instead of to the central government. These payments were in direct breach of the pre-independence agreement that had been signed by the Belgian government and accepted by, among others, Tshombe. They enabled Tshombe to recruit and pay an army of foreigners with which to oppose his Congolese adversaries and, if needs be, the UN. Tshombe was an unsuccessful businessman turned politician. He was the son of a more dynamic and popular father. He was also the veteran of Katangan politics, a man who had successfully played different sides. In the words of one historian:

> While both he and his father Joseph served on the Provincial Council of Katanga from 1947 to 1956, Tshombe shrewdly avoided any association with the industrial councils and with an economic and social policy that sanctioned racial discrimination. Tshombe, then, was less a leader of the mineworkers than a spokesman who appeared to be against the implementation of a wage policy based on the South African 'colour bar'. Because of his mother's blood ties to two of the Lunda royal family and his father's entrepreneurial skills, he was able to wear simultaneously the face of an aristocrat and an évolué in his forays among the workers. Until 1957, he kept his connections to the Union Minière administration loose and ambiguous. As far as the miners could see, Tshombe's position in the unfolding political drama in Katanga was one of opposition to the mining company's wage policy.[17]

Observer journalist Colin Legum described him as follows:

> Tshombe, the forty-two-year-old leader of Conakat (the Confederation of the Association of Tribes of Katanga) was never part of the nationalist movement. In the days of colonialism he stuck close to

the Belgians, and had he been as good a businessman as his father (who left him a string of businesses) he would have prospered. But he lost his patrimony and went bankrupt three times. However he never stayed down for long. Like many unsuccessful businessmen he became a leading figure in the politics of commerce: he was President of the African Chamber of Commerce Association.[18]

Outside Katanga, Tshombe's party was known to receive the backing of the Belgians. It was also known to have the support of white-run Rhodesia, whose leaders encouraged Tshombe to join their Federation. Even within Katanga, there were rival parties. Jason Sendwe of the Balubakat was also strong in the region. His party spoke out strongly for independence and a unitary state. But Tshombe was able to play on a strong ethnic and regionalist consciousness.

Rivalry between Kasavubu and Lumumba had grown rapidly in the meanwhile, with Lumumba's 'Communist orientation' increasingly used as an excuse for the schism. The proposed attack on Katanga was called off and Tshombe gained a second breathing space. His Belgian troops took the opportunity to move north and establish a second secessionary state in Kasai, under the short-lived presidency of Albert Kalonji, who had earlier broken away from the MNC. A separate state backed by the Belgians had come into existence in the south. In the north-east, the Russians were beginning to consider the idea of another state, backed by themselves. The Congo appeared to be on the brink of breaking up into three large and warring units, two of which would in effect be foreign bases, and a number of smaller ones.

The play of external forces

A fourth meeting of the Security Council on 21 August 1960 saw a resolution offering support for Hammarskjöld. This in turn, however, was opposed by the Soviet Union, which evidently was beginning to share some of Lumumba's concerns about the partiality of the secretary general and the serious implications of the failure to resist the Katanga breakaway for the viability of the Congo under Lumumba and Kasuvubu. Throughout August, the situation deteriorated, with every prospect of a major clash between the Katangan and the Congolese armies. A conference of thirteen African states convened in Léopoldville failed to give Lumumba the support he wanted and advised against an attack on Katanga. Increasingly isolated, Lumumba turned to the Soviet Union for help, requesting transport planes, trucks and weapons to wipe out breakaway movements in Katanga and Kasai. Larry Devlin, a CIA operative in the Congo, recalled the arrival of the Soviet support:

> I had a little Congolese sitting at the airport counting any white man who came off a Soviet aircraft in batches of five. Roughly 1,000 came in during a period of six weeks.... To my mind it was clearly an effort to take over. It made good sense when you stopped to think about it. All nine countries surrounding the Congo had their problems. If the Soviets could have gotten control of the Congo they could have used it as a base, bringing in Africans, training them in sabotage and military skills and sending them home to do their duty.[19]

The Soviet arrivals ended Lumumba's relations with Kasavubu. The army was also unhappy, particularly when the new Soviet advisers began to lecture the Congolese troops. Mobutu asked Lumumba to keep the Soviet advisers away from the army. The Americans were also, predictably, unhappy with Lumumba's willingness to accept Soviet assistance. In mid-August 1960, US operatives received authorisation for an operation aimed at replacing Lumumba with a pro-Western group. The situation was aggravated when, on the opening of the UN General Assembly in September, President Khrushchev arrived in person to attack the secretary general, and two rival Congolese delegations competed with one another for seats in the Assembly. This session of the UN was also notable for the admission of seventeen new African members. They refused to support the Russian attack on Hammarskjöld and joined with the Western bloc to isolate the 'Communist' states. But they neither agreed with the West nor were united among themselves.

In Britain, France and the United States, the Katangan case, propagated by a lavishly supplied lobby, made many converts in political and business circles, suggesting that Katanga was an oasis of civilisation in an otherwise barbarous and increasingly Communist Congo. This travesty cut less ice with the Africans, who condemned Tshombe and his actions, while still being divided on what to do. One group turned against the UN, and supported Lumumba's earlier plan for a joint African force in Katanga. Another remained attached to the idea of UN action, though dissatisfied with the action proposed. The latter became a pressure group at the UN with the objective of persuading the secretary general and other members that a policy of reducing Katanga by negotiation was hopeless and should be replaced by direct action. A third group, consisting of recently independent ex-French colonies, placed its faith for a time in the Mobutu–Kasavubu alliance and the gradual radiation of law and order from Léopoldville out into all the provinces.

US strategy

The principal players in Lumumba's downfall were Belgium, the United Kingdom and the United States. British Prime Minister Harold Macmillan referred to Lumumba as a 'Communist stooge'. The Western powers used the threat of 'Soviet Communism', arguing that the Congo and its great mineral wealth would inevitably fall to the Soviet Union if Lumumba were allowed to take power. How real was this fear? There is no question that the period was marked by vicious Cold War rivalry, which was played out to devastating effect on the continent, but in the Congo in 1960 it seems to have been more of a cover for Lumumba's immediate removal. A.M. Babu is clear about the extent of Soviet involvement at the time of independence:

> when the Congo stormed into independence in 1960, the only contact the Soviet Union had with that country was through a Czechoslovakian trade representative who was so ill-informed about what was going on in the country that he gave the Kremlin a completely wrong picture of the situation when Lumumba requested Soviet military assistance.[20]

On the other hand, there is no doubt that a wave of Soviet 'technical advisers' did fly into the Congo. Devlin was almost certainly correct to see this as part of a Soviet strategy, admittedly opportunistic, but real nevertheless, to make inroads in central Africa.

All over Africa, previously submerged nations were now claiming their independence. Self-government posed a common challenge to each of the imperial nations; their responses were different. Britain, following defeat at Suez, quickly let go of her former possessions.

France maintained her empire a little longer, granting a whole group of African countries independence in 1960 and only hanging on for the trauma of defeat in the long war in Algeria. Portugal kept her colonies until the death of the dictator Salazar. Belgium had little to lose but the Congo. While European powers were on the retreat in Africa, others were hovering to take their place. Despite the Soviet Union's formal espousal of anti-imperialist rhetoric, it is hard to see it as playing anything other than a similar role. The United States still retained something of the allure of a force for emancipation, given its distant revolutionary origins, and opposition to the French and British adventures in Suez. America's influence in the Congo was growing while that of France and Belgium waned.

The formal reason given for Washington's lack of trust in Lumumba was his 'extreme nationalism', combined with his evident willingness to turn to the Soviet Union. Lumumba was a Soviet asset, the CIA maintained, and the Congo a 'Cuba in the making', as Larry Devlin told his superiors.[21] Yet if Lumumba could be anathematised for accepting foreign military aid, it is striking that no action was taken against his rival Tshombe, a man who openly boasted of his dependence on Belgian guns. Being members of NATO, the Belgians were of course the 'right' kind of foreign power, while the Russians were the 'wrong' kind. The country was caught up in the familiar American binaries: 'their' men in black hats versus 'ours' in white. There was no possibility that the Congo might be left to work out its own future. Its mineral wealth alone was grounds for special interest, let alone the military applications of resources, including uranium. Cobalt was identified in excited memoranda sent back to the USA as the most basic material necessary for success in the space race then occupying the superpowers. The country's other resources received scarcely less attention. Indeed, as early as 1950, a company owned by the Rockefeller family had taken a one-fifth share in Union Minière, which controlled the uranium mines.[22]

The willingness to intervene went very far indeed. Richard Bissell was the head of operations at the CIA in 1960 and 1961. He records that his supervisor Allen Dulles authorised the removal and assassination of Lumumba. Even President Eisenhower was consulted. 'The President would have vastly preferred to have him taken care of some other way than by assassination, but he regarded Lumumba as I did and as a lot of other people did: as a mad dog ... and he wanted the problem dealt with.'[23] The CIA station in Léopoldville under Devlin was provided with a variety of instruments with which to achieve the killing: a high-powered rifle, poisoned toothpaste, and the funds to pay for assassins. In the end, they would achieve the same result, but through the support of local proxies.[24]

The fall of Lumumba

Lumumba and Kasuvubu had begun by working together in reasonable harmony, but in September 1960 their alliance broke apart. Kasavubu dismissed Lumumba and appointed a new government. Parliament supported Lumumba, who maintained that the president's action was illegal. This political deadlock was resolved by the intervention of the armed forces. In mid-September, Joseph Mobutu assumed control, neutralising both Kasavubu and Lumumba in what he described as 'a peaceful revolution', involving an army takeover aimed at giving the civilian politicians a chance to calm down and settle their differences. Soviet bloc diplomatic personnel were given forty-eight hours to leave. But it was as much a putsch as an effort to maintain law and order. According to Lumumba:

> The capital of the republic is a scene of disorder, where a handful of hired military men are ceaselessly violating law and order. The citizens of Léopoldville now live under a reign of terror. Arbitrary arrests, followed by deportation, are a daily and nightly occurrence ... The majority parties in Parliament are forbidden to publish newspapers. All loyal army personnel and government officials, who wanted to have no truck with the unlawful activities and the policy of national demolition pursued by the head of state and his handful of supporters at Léopoldville, have been dismissed from their posts, maltreated and turned out into the streets. Hundreds of loyal soldiers who oppose Mobutu are sent back daily to the villages: others are now in the Bina concentration camp.[25]

Dag Hammarskjöld's UN representative in Léopoldville, Andrew Cordier, closed the airport and shut off the radio, thereby giving an advantage first to Kasavubu and then to Mobutu by denying Lumumba the opportunity to state his case in different parts of the country or make his voice heard on the air. This action was bitterly resented within the Congo and beyond. It led to fierce Congolese attacks on the UN, with Russian support. As at every previous stage in the crisis, once again it seemed that the United Nations was working actively to promote the interests of the secessionists and Belgium. The Congo crisis was the first of the UN's peacekeeping missions. The intervention established the pattern for future UN activity throughout the world: vacillation before dictatorship, obedience when faced with US power.[26] From the American perspective, the important thing was that this great African domino had not fallen: the Congo had been kept safely out of Soviet hands and 'their man' had taken control. It was exactly what Washington wanted.

Patrice Lumumba, deprived of Soviet support from outside and prevented from communicating with his own constituencies, remained in Léopoldville in his official residence. He must by now have realised the threat to his political leadership and to his life. On 6 October, the Belgian Minister for African Affairs, Count d'Aspremont Lynden, sent a cable to Élisabethville, stating clearly that Belgian policy was now directed at the 'definitive elimination' of Lumumba. The new head of the UN mission in Léopoldville and successor to Andrew Cordier, Rayeshwar Dayal, refused to assist him, and Lumumba became in effect a prisoner, until he fled from the city at the end of November, hoping to reach Stanleyville by car. Stanleyville was the centre of nationalist agitation. It represented Lumumba's last chance, not for asylum, but to regain the initiative in the struggle for independence.[27] He was overtaken a few days later by Mobutu's troops and trapped at the Sankuru river. He appealed to the United Nations to save him, but their troops refused to do so, on orders from New York. He was then flown to Léopoldville, where Brigadier Indarjit Rikhye, the head of the UN military mission, saw him bleeding, his hair dishevelled and his glasses broken. 'We could not intervene', says Rikhye, without further explanation. Further humiliation followed at Mobutu's villa, where Lumumba was beaten in front of television cameras. He was then despatched to Thysville military barracks, more than a hundred miles from Léopoldville. The Belgians insisted that Lumumba be handed over to Tshombe. Aware that after his arrest in December, torture and death were almost certain, Patrice Lumumba managed to record a final farewell to his wife:

My beloved companion, I write you these words not knowing
whether you will receive them, when you will receive them, and
whether I will still be alive when you read them ... They have
corrupted some of our countrymen; they have bought others; they
have done their part to distort the truth and defile our independence. What else can I say? That whether dead or alive, free or
in prison by order of the colonialists, it is not my person that is
important. What is important is the Congo, our poor people whose
independence has turned us into a cage, with a people looking
at us from outside the bars, sometimes in charitable compassion,
sometimes with glee and delight. But my faith will remain unshak-
able. I know and feel in my very heart of hearts that sooner or
later my people will rid themselves of all their enemies, foreign
and domestic, that they will rise up and say *no* to the shame and
degradation of colonialism and regain their dignity.... We are
not alone. Africa, Asia and the free and liberated people from
every corner of the world will always be found at the side of the
Congolese. They will not abandon the light until the day comes
when there are no more colonisers and their mercenaries in our
country. To my children whom I leave and whom perhaps I will
see no more, I wish that they be told that the future of the Congo
is beautiful and that ... without dignity there is no liberty, without
justice there is no dignity, and without independence there are no
free men. No brutality, mistreatment, or torture has ever forced
me to ask for grace, for I prefer to die with my head high, my faith
steadfast.... History will one day have its say, but it will not be the
history that Brussels, Paris, Washington or the United Nations will
teach, but that which they will teach in the countries emancipated
from colonialism and its puppets. Do not weep for me, my dear
companion. I know that my country, which suffers so much, will
know how to defend its independence and its liberty. Long live the
Congo! Long live Africa![28]

Lumumba was flown to Élisabethville, the capital of Katanga, on
17 January 1961. He was taken by Katangan troops, commanded by
Belgians, and driven to Ville Brouwe. There, Belgian and Katangan
soldiers beat him, while Tshombe decided what to do next. That same
night, Lumumba was bundled into a military vehicle and driven out
into the bush to a place near a large tree. Three firing squads had
been assembled, commanded by a Belgian officer. Another Belgian
had responsibility for the execution site. Lumumba and two colleagues, Maurice Mpolo and Joseph Okito, were lined up against

the tree and shot, one after the other. The bodies were thrown in a shallow grave. Tshombe and two of his ministers were present. A Belgian police officer, Gerard Soerte, exhumed the bodies, hacked them into pieces and dissolved them in acid. When he ran out of chemicals, he burned the remains.[29]

Lumumba: icon of struggle

The biography of Lumumba, writes Ludo de Witte, is the story of the transition 'from nationalist to revolutionary'. This process can be traced through Lumumba's struggle against the secession of South Kasai and Katanga, his attempt to re-establish a Congolese government from nationalist Stanleyville, his refusal in captivity to cede to Mobutu.[30] In his short period as a national political figure he had become known all over the world. In many countries, the murder of Patrice Lumumba was met with protests. In Shanghai, a crowd estimated at half a million staged a mass rally against the crime. In Belgrade, demonstrators shouted 'Lumumba will live for ever'. For his part, President Tito declared that the death of Lumumba was a 'murder, which had no precedent in latter-day history'. A crowd estimated at 30,000 broke into the Belgian embassy and threw furniture on the streets. In Warsaw over 2,000 demonstrators charged the Belgian embassy and the ambassador had to flee for his life. There followed a day-long flow of news of the murder from the Polish press and radio. In Rome, a session of the Italian Chamber of Deputies broke up in shouting and pandemonium and about fifty demonstrators were driven away by a strong cordon of Italian police when they threatened to march on the Belgian embassy. In Damascus, demonstrators swept through the city carrying placards and hailing Lumumba as a glorious martyr and denouncing his murder. Thousands of Syrian students missed classes to join workers parading in the city's streets.[31]

In the Congo itself, the response was more muted. The forces controlling the Congo did everything in their power to keep the news concealed from the people. Nothing was said for three weeks. When Patrice Lumumba's death was formally announced on the Katanga radio, it was accompanied by an elaborate cover story, involving an escape and murder by enraged villagers. No one believed it. The mood was one of shame. There was no burial. The bodies of Lumumba and his colleagues had been destroyed. Hochschild writes: 'Like millions of Congolese before him (and one might add, after him also), he ended up dumped in an unmarked grave.'[32] In Léopoldville, a funeral procession of around one hundred people was allowed. Pauline Opano, Lumumba's wife, marched at the head of the procession. Mourners carried white flags to symbolise their peaceful intentions. Luluabourg saw a general strike, called to protest against the killings.

> But in Stanleyville, where the armed nationalists had begun the apparently unstoppable reconquest of the country, the announcement of the death of Lumumba, Mpolo and Okito produced no immediate visible reactions. On the contrary, a deathly, supernatural calm fell over the city, as if Lumumba's death could not be true, as if Lumumba's personality had already taken on the mythical proportions it would assume in the decades to come.

On 16 February, the town witnessed a great Mass, held to commemorate the life of Lumumba. Some 25,000 people took part, then went home peacefully.[33]

The fact that no one moved to stop Lumumba's murder points to an awkward truth. Despite the universal popularity of Patrice Lumumba among the people of the Congo in summer 1960, his regime was toppled in less than a year. Despite the fact that most Congolese still revere his name, they or their parents did little to stop his murder. The ordinary people of the Congo wanted Lumumba to live. They lacked the know-how, the techniques of popular insurrection that might have saved his life. They believed desperately in Lumumba and everything for which he stood. After his death, however, no politician made any serious attempt to repeat the strategy of 1960.

Mobutu makes his first move

Shortly after the Lumumba–Kasavubu rift in September 1960, Joseph Mobutu, the army chief of staff, had taken power in Léopoldville. He ejected the parliament and the Russian and Czech embassies and, when attempts to reconcile Lumumba and Kasavubu failed, declared for Kasavubu, who in turn acquiesced in Mobutu's coup.[34]

Mobutu was now the ruler of the city, and through those last few months of 1960, as Lumumba struggled to survive, he took over the government. Mobutu handed over power initially to a group of 'general commissioners', a collection of the country's few university graduates, who were supposed to run the country while the politicians took stock of the problems confronting them. With four separate governments in existence – one in the eastern city of Stanleyville, loyal to the ousted Lumumba; one in Katanga under Moïse Tshombe, supported by the Belgians; one in Kasai under Albert Kalonji; and one in Léopoldville under President Kasavubu – partition was a reality. Mobutu had an opportunity now to play a decisive role in his country's future.

It has been suggested that Mobutu was a key figure in the Congolese forces that arranged Lumumba's murder, but his complicity is not certain. On the other hand, it is hard to believe that the head of the army, the man who now held real power, would have been unaware of the many vested interests, inside the country and outside, concerned to eliminate Lumumba once and for all. Certainly, the Western powers had spotted Mobutu early on as someone who would look out for their interests. He had received payments from the CIA while Lumumba's murder was being planned.[35] Whoever actually was responsible, Mobutu always bore the moral responsibility for Lumumba's murder in the eyes of the Lumumbists.

Mobutu now introduced a new constitution and some degree of order, but though supported by the West, failed to establish a viable regime. The provinces did not respond sympathetically to his action, and the resources available to him, communications and retained personnel, were inadequate. The army, moreover, was divided. General Victor Lundula and the forces in Orientale province remained pro-Lumumba, as did many politicians and, so far as could be determined, the Congolese people. By February 1961, it was apparent that the Mobutu–Kasavubu axis had failed, and a new government was appointed under Joseph Ileo.

The Ileo coalition was to last only six months until August, when Cyrille Adoula succeeded him. During this period, the Lumumbists, led by Antoine Gizenga in Stanleyville, and the Katangans, led by Tshombe and Godefroid Munongo in Élisabethville, staged incompatible revolts. Various attempts were made to bring all the factions together, but moves in the direction of Stanleyville usually caused Élisabethville to shy away, and vice versa. The Stanleyville secession had only limited support, however, within the country or on its borders, and Sudanese hostility sealed its fate in Orientale province.

Efforts to build a coalition

On 21 February 1961, the Security Council explicitly authorised the UN to use force in the last resort to prevent a civil war. It did not, however, authorise the use of force against Katanga, or to ensure the removal of the Belgians, or to secure a political solution, although it did call for the expulsion of the mercenaries who had flocked to the Congo in support of Tshombe's coup. This marked a return to better relations between Hammarskjöld, the independent African states and the West, or at any rate the United States, where John F. Kennedy had just assumed the presidency, but it alienated not just Tshombe but also the Kasavubu–Ileo government, which suspected the UN of being in Western pockets and now drew closer to Tshombe.

In July 1961, the Congolese parliament assembled at Lovanium, the university town near Léopoldville, in an attempt to patch together a grand coalition of the rival parties. The coalition was not achieved. This time, Tshombe was the odd man out. There followed military operations against Katanga. By now Katanga was a formidable power, equipped since the beginning of the year with men, supplies and aircraft from Belgium, France, South Africa and Southern Rhodesia (today's Zimbabwe). Over the previous year, Tshombe had also recruited a significant force of some 500 predominantly white mercenaries to fight his cause. On 21 February 1961, the UN Security Council passed a resolution urging that measures be taken for the immediate withdrawal and evacuation from the Congo of all Belgian and other foreign military personnel and political advisers not under the United Nations Command, and mercenaries. Some 273 were repatriated in August 1961, but there were still 237 present in November. On 24 November 1961, a further resolution authorised the use of whatever force was necessary to carry out this decision. Although those countries that had nationals serving as mercenaries in Tshombe's army undertook to get them out, they made little real attempt to fulfil their promises. Some had their passports withdrawn for a time, or endorsed 'not valid for the Congo'. Belgium, whose duplicity and determination to remain closely involved in its former colony was largely responsible for the fighting, professed to have no power to stop its own 'private citizens' becoming mercenaries. A few Belgians had been removed as a result of laborious negotiations, but UN representatives were convinced that Tshombe was playing for time and had no intention of dismissing the Belgian and other mercenaries, or of coming to terms with Léopoldville. These suspicions were confirmed when at the end of August, UN forces seized about 100 foreign mercenaries who had been declared undesirable aliens by the Adoula government. The Belgian consul in Élisabethville dealt with the matter. 'To avoid difficulties' he guaranteed the voluntary departure of these men, and then failed to honour his word. Other mercenaries not in Élisabethville remained untouched.[36]

Hammarskjöld arrived in Léopoldville to find confusion, and hostility towards the UN actions from Britain, France and the United States. He determined to seek out Tshombe, who, aided by the British, had temporarily fled Katanga, and talk to him. He left Rhodesia, the temporary refuge of Tshombe, by air on 17 September. He was killed when the aircraft crashed en route. On 21 December, Tshombe renounced secession and the Katangan assembly endorsed the Kitona agreement two months later. The failure of operations against Katanga revived Gizenga's suspicions, and he returned to his own base in Stanleyville, thereby re-creating the tripartite pattern. Attempts to induce him to return to the capital failed, and he was brought there under arrest in January 1962, put in jail, and expelled from the government.

Through much of 1962, Tshombe and Adoula engaged in a series of fruitless discussions concerning the implementation of the Kitona agreement, which was opposed in Katanga by Munongo and European secessionists. Tshombe seemed unable to decide what to do. The Katangan bid for secession collapsed in January 1963, when he departed for a prolonged stay in Europe. Although Adoula took three Katangans into his cabinet in April 1963, no genuine reconciliation took place. The central government continued to suffer from economic problems and inadequate law and order, and early in 1964 a more serious revolt broke out in Kwilu, under the leadership of Pierre Mulele, who had recently made a trip to China, and also in south Kivu and northern Katanga. Within a few months, the rebels had established their capital in Stanleyville (Kisangani).[37] UN troops were now departing. The last planeload left at the end of June 1964, the fourth anniversary of independence.

Descent into civil war

Congo remained divided, formally and in reality. As the UN forces left, civil war started again. The Adoula government was first reconstituted and then replaced by a new administration, under Tshombe, who returned from Europe as the United Nations departed. He tried to form a broad coalition but Gizenga, whom he had released from prison, formed a new opposition party.[38] A new constitution came into effect on 1 August 1964, establishing presidential government and a federalist structure. The country was renamed the Democratic Republic of the Congo (DRC). Tshombe now began, once again, to make use of foreign mercenaries as well as the army to crush Pierre Mulele's rebels. Tshombe's force was organised in a number of commando groups. Six Commando was composed largely of French-speaking mercenaries, originally commanded by the Belgian colonel Lamouline. Five Commando was led by the British Colonel 'Mad Mike' Hoare. This force was quickly successful and the rebels, who had taken Stanleyville (Kisangani) in August, found themselves threatened with the loss of all their principal strongholds. They had, in the meanwhile, however, taken hostages. In an attempt to mount a rescue operation, and with the permission of the newly elected Labour leader Harold Wilson, Belgian parachute troops were flown in October in American aircraft from the British island of Ascension to Stanleyville, which they recaptured from the rebels. About 200 hostages were killed, in addition to some 20,000 Congolese.[39]

Africans outside the Congo were divided between those who denounced the Belgians, Americans and British as imperialists and those who, stifling their dislike of Tshombe, defended the right of the Congolese government to ask for outside help. The Organisation of African Unity (OAU) was active in condemning the use of mercenaries and encouraging legislation to suppress them. In September 1964, the OAU's Council of Ministers expressed its abhorrence of the practice and appealed to the government of the Democratic

Republic of the Congo to stop the recruitment of mercenaries and to expel those on its territory. Tshombe, who had already refused an invitation from the OAU to its Conference of Heads of State in Cairo, was kept out of the Conference of Non-Aligned States (also in Cairo) in October. He flew to Cairo but was escorted to a hotel and kept there until he decided to return to Léopoldville.

The effect of these events was to galvanise radical African governments against the Tshombe government, with Ben Bella of Algeria and Nasser of Egypt promising to supply the rebel Congolese with arms. In was in this context that Cuba became directly involved. The government of Castro commanded a great deal of respect among liberation struggles, and an equal measure of fear and paranoia among the Western powers. When Algeria, which Cuba had helped by supplying US weapons seized after the failed Bay of Pigs invasion in 1961, asked if Cuba would assist in the Congo, they agreed. The Congo again became a crucial battleground for what many saw as a fight between 'national liberation movements' on the one hand and imperialist nations and their proxy armies on the other.[40]

After only four short years of independence, the Congo was divided and awash with foreign troops. The United States was desperate to defeat what seemed to them to be a left-wing insurgency, part of a Communist threat that they saw spreading across the continent after the successful 'takeover' of Zanzibar. The renewal of the struggle in the Congo, however, also frightened American politicians nervous of being embroiled in the conflict in Vietnam. The Cuban leader Che Guevara summarised the farce of the so-called 'independent' Congo when he addressed the United Nations in December 1964: 'Belgian paratroopers transported by United States aircraft, took off from British bases … Free men throughout the world must prepare to avenge the Congo crime.'[41] Not relying on words alone, Guevara attempted to bring Cuba to intervene in the military campaign.

In Kinshasa, meanwhile, the new rulers of the Congo remained divided. Kasavubu's appointment of Tshombe as prime minister did not herald reconciliation. Given his role in the events of 1960–61, Tshombe could do no more than crystallise the lingering anger of those who had pinned their hopes on Lumumba. In March and April 1965, the Tshombe government organised legislative elections. Tshombe's coalition (Conaco, the National Congolese Convention) won 122 of the 167 seats in the Chamber of Deputies. An opposition bloc (the FDC, the Congolese Democratic Front) soon emerged and a political deadlock developed. Kasavubu dismissed Tshombe. But Kasavubu himself failed to put together a new government, however, and there followed yet another destructive period of paralysis.

Rebellion or revolution?

Through the months after the UN forces had left, it became clear that the Congo was heading into a second period of turmoil. In April 1965, Che Guevara attempted to export rebellion into the country. His allies were the forces of the Simba (Lion) rebellion. The leaders of this second insurrection saw themselves as Lumumba's heirs. Several writers have agreed, portraying Pierre Mulele, leader of the rebels in Kwilu region, in particular as a heroic personality, the man who could have saved the Congo.[42] A leader of the Parti Solidaire Africain, which had its strongest base of support in the west of the Congo, Mulele was indeed a striking figure. 'State employees, teachers, students and the unemployed urban youth', writes, Nzongolo-Natalaja, 'joined peasants in what became a profoundly popular and rural insurrection.'[43]

By January 1964, Mulelist forces held much of Kwilu province. Inspired by Maoist ideology, including its idealisation of peasant life, they were unable to capture the cities of Idiofa and Gungu; nor were they able to spread their insurrection to surrounding regions. Mulele was, however, able to maintain a base in Kwilu until October 1968, despite Mobutu offering rewards of up to $10,000 for his arrest. Drawn back to Kinshasa only by the promise of national reconciliation, he was captured and finally killed. Mulele's insurrection had some success in the west, and was soon joined by a second guerrilla uprising in the east. Once again, the MNC and the PSA provided the bulk of the leaders. On 4 August 1964, the Armée Populaire de Libération took control of Stanleyville, by which time it also held most of the east and much of the south, including North Kantaga, Sankuru and parts of Eastern and Equateur provinces. More successful than the Kwilu *maquis*, the fighters in the east nevertheless suffered from deeper political weaknesses. They encouraged habits of xenophobia and ethnic hatred, they were divided among themselves, they relied on structures of personal charisma and hierarchy. Some of this may have been apparent to careful observers; to Guevara none of the problems seemed insurmountable.

Pierre Mulele, Laurent Kabila and others argued that the anti-Lumumbist forces that held Kinshasa and Élisabethville could easily be overthrown. Invited by the Congolese National Front, Guevara entered the country through Tanzania with a column of 100 men. Guevara hoped to spark a national uprising. The leaders would appear. Concealing themselves from a hostile state, they would work among the people. The peasants would see the justice of their cause, and would join the rebellion in large numbers. Military successes would encourage a politics of rebellion. The only way to defeat the menace of 'Yankee imperialism', according to Guevara, was to open many guerrilla fronts, and to make it impossible for the United States to fight them all, 'Create two, three, many Vietnams' was his idea. The Cuban expedition remained in eastern Congo for seven months. The soldiers stayed near Uvira, Kivu, in front of the Bay of Kigoma. Guevara hoped that a successful uprising in the Congo would be felt all across the continent. Yet reality proved more difficult than the plan. The local troops appeared to the Cuban veterans to be ill prepared, poorly trained and armed. Their leaders were frequently absent.[44]

Much subsequent debate has turned upon the role played by Laurent Kabila. According to former Cuban Army General William Galvin, 'Kabila's organization had a lot of money and military supplies stored in Tanzania. But Kabila and most other leaders of the movement were flying from African capital to capital raising more money and having a good time.' Another Cuban source, Coleman Ferrer, was stationed at the Cuban embassy in Tanzania. He suggests that the main problems were political. Kabila and other leaders offered no message to their people other than one goal, the overthrow of President Tshombe. The rebels were organised along ethnic lines. They were dependent on the personality of local leaders, and they lacked any sense of wider purpose. Thus when Mobutu took power in 1965, he found little difficulty in consolidating his position. 'The same day the radio station announced the overthrow of Tshombe, the majority of the freedom fighters threw their weapons away, because for them the war was finished at that very moment.'[45]

Meanwhile the Cubans were themselves cut off from the local people, not speaking any Congolese languages. Their diet was poor, and they suffered from frequent bouts of illness. The field intelligence they received was scanty, and Cuban troops were repeatedly led into battle against larger numbers of government forces, backed up by Belgian mercenaries. When Guevara came to look back on the mission, he drew out various causes of its failure. One was the low population density of the region, and the limited development of capitalist agriculture. These narrowed the opportunities for the Cubans to introduce reforms. Maybe, Guevara asked himself, they would have done better to start in Katanga or Kasai, among workers rather than peasants?

> What could the Liberation Army offer those farmers? We couldn't talk about an agrarian reform and property, because the land was there, and everybody could see it. We couldn't talk about credits for purchasing equipment, because the farmers got enough to eat from the labour they performed with primitive tools, and the physical conditions of the region weren't appropriate for machinery.[46]

Guevara left in November, promising never to repeat the same mistakes again. The Simba movement continued to hold a base in eastern Congo, which the army could not penetrate. But neither was the movement able to threaten Kinshasa.

Why the army?

What was it about the army that enabled it to take over, after 1965, the running of an entire society? The American academic Crawford Young spent much of the early 1960s in the Congo, and his account of the officers is worth recording.

> The military elite constitutes a distinct group in Congolese society, with a social experience very different from that of the political-administrative elite. Even when posted in camps near large cities, the officers do not belong to the same social circuits as other leaders. They are generally stationed outside their home region and frequently marry women of other ethnic groups. The careful ethnic interrogation of military units meant an ethnically diverse officers' mess. Apoliticism is inculcated as a political ideal.[47]

Two points follow: first, the army was largely immune to the appeal of Lumumba. Second, the army had a strong interest in a single, unitary state. This part alone of Lumumba's legacy they judged to be worth defending.

Behind the initial success of Patrice Lumumba, as we have argued, there stood large numbers of people. There were the *évolués*, rapidly dividing along lines of class, generation and ideology, but open to a radical politics. There was the majority of the people in Stanleyville, and a smaller majority in the other cities. There was not an actual working class, so much as the chance of its formation.[48] Martens argues that one in five of the employed population was engaged in productive work in 1956, or just over 750,000 people out of a Congolese population of 13 million.[49] The largest groups of people in this category were porters, miners, soldiers, farmers and people working in different degrees of forced or indentured labour. Porters could be organised; and the copper miners of Élisabethville had shown their power during the war. The other 10 million people, however, lacked the same social power.[50]

Nzongolo-Ntalaja insists that, as a group, the miners of Katanga remained loyal to Lumumba.[51] The truth seems to have been slightly more complex. Among the veterans of 1941, there was a clear hostility to Tshombe and federalism. Among the newer workers, supporters of millennial cults and those who alternated between work in the mines and as sellers and tradesmen, support for Lumumba was less automatic.[52] Whether or not they supported Lumumba, one effect of the civil war was to cause a sharp decline in the number of employed workers. The Union Minière workforce, for example, fell by 20,000 between 1962 and 1965.[53]

In spring 1960, it had seemed possible that some sort of alliance between workers, peasants and *évolués* could rule, through Lumumba. Yet the *évolués* split, and without their leadership the alliance of classes crumbled. Other radical possibilities were then opened. Stanleyville took on the character briefly of an insurrectionary city-state. The vast crowds who marched to remember Lumumba in other countries of Africa and elsewhere showed that the revolutionaries of the Congo were not alone. In Ghana, President Kwame Nkrumah addressed the entire population by radio: 'Our dear brothers, Patrice Lumumba, Maurice Mpolo and Joseph

Okito are dead.... The colonialists and imperialists have killed them, but what they cannot do is to kill the ideals which we still preach and for which they sacrificed their lives.'[54] If only they could have channelled this collective will of millions, the radicals of the Congo might have escaped their isolation at home.

Every society requires leadership, and in the absence of Lumumba or any successful radical alliance to carry on his work, other forces rose to fill the gap. Prior to independence, the Congolese army, the Force Publique, was arguably the one public organisation that could claim to represent the entire nation. As in so many other newly independent African states, the army represented both an organised unified force and a vehicle for ambitious men often from humble backgrounds to acquire power and influence, and respect, within the wider society as well as within the confines of the military itself. The soldiers were generally well paid, well trained, and, with the obvious exception of the 'insurrection' of July 1960, normally loyal. The army represented a rare chance of advancement. Especially in the period following independence, it was possible to experience rapid promotion. While everywhere else in society, authority was something difficult to comprehend, depending on shifting alliances, money and history, in the army, it seemed, the hierarchies were clear. The Force Publique served different purposes. It existed to protect the country's external borders, and her embryonic divisions of class. It served the interests of the Belgian and then the Congolese rich. No matter how well or badly the Congolese economy performed, the army would always be the first item of expenditure.

The all-conquering warrior

It was from within the ranks of the military that a politician now emerged who was able to control the state. For three decades, between 1965 and 1996, the figure of Joseph-Désiré Mobutu was to dominate the Congolese nation. He would restructure the state more than once, changing its name to Zaïre. He would preside over periods of both 'Westernisation' and 'Africanisation'. Transplanted to the particular conditions of central Africa in the post-independence era, Mobutu was the complete tyrant, possessing as much control over his people as Napoleon or Stalin had before him. Any history of Zaïre in this period must convey something of the character and background of the man who ruled the country for so long.

Joseph-Désiré Mobutu was born in October 1930, in the central town of Lisala on the Congo river. His father, Albéric Gbemani, was a cook for a colonial magistrate in Lisala; his mother, Marie Madeleine Yerno, had previously been married to a village chief but left him and fled on foot to Lisala, where she met and married Mobutu's father. Mobutu's family were Ngbandi, one of the smaller of the country's 200-plus ethnic groups, scattered on either side of the Ubangi, a subsidiary of the Congo river, with one foot in what is today the Central African Republic and another in the Congo. Mobutu managed to mythologise his background and his upbringing. His great uncle had been a diviner in the village of Gbadolite. And he, in one, almost certainly apocryphal, story, killed a leopard with a spear: 'from that day on', said Mobutu, 'I was afraid of nothing'.[55] In the early 1970s, when Zaïreans were obliged to adopt 'authentic' African names, Mobutu adopted his uncle's name Sese Seko Nkuku wa za Banga, meaning 'all-conquering warrior who goes from triumph to triumph'.

Mobutu's father died when he was only 8, but his mother, whom he adored, was able to see him grow up and come to power. Mama Yemo, as she was eventually to be known to the Congolese people, was always a powerful influence. Mobutu learned French from the wife of the Belgian judge for whom his father worked, but was unable to study regularly as his mother moved around the country after his father's death, with her four children, living on the generosity of relatives. Mobutu finally settled with an uncle in the town of Coquilhatville (Mbandaka), an expanding colonial administrative centre. There he attended a mission school and did well academically. In 1949, he absconded from school, stowing away on a boat heading for Léopoldville and living it up for several weeks in 'the big city'. This must have been one of the reasons for his expulsion from the school at the end of the year, when he was sent to the Force Publique for a seven-year apprenticeship in a service still tainted by a reputation for brutality acquired during the Léopold era.[56]

Mobutu joined the Force Publique in 1950 and found both discipline and a surrogate father in the form of Sergeant Joseph Bobozo, a stern but affectionate mentor. Looking back, Mobutu recalled his period with the Force as the happiest period of his life. He read voraciously and was impressed by what he read. Later his favourite authors would include Charles de Gaulle, Winston Churchill and Niccolò Machiavelli, author of *The Prince*. He also studied French and accountancy. He was rapidly promoted, leaving the army in 1956 with the rank of sergeant major, the highest grade open to Congolese. On his return to civilian life, Mobutu got married. His wife, Marie Antoinette, was only 16 but loyal and feisty. She would provide support for many years as he rose to power and struggled to maintain it. He began to work as a journalist, with the support of Pierre Davister, Belgian editor of *L'Avenir*, contributing initially under a pseudonym to a new Congolese magazine *Actualités Africaines*. A visit in 1958 to Brussels to report on the Universal Exhibition led him to stay on for journalistic training, making contact with young Congolese intellectuals and political activists now challenging Belgium's colonial policy in the Congo and elsewhere in Africa. He met and became a friend of Lumumba.

Congolese youths studying in Brussels were at this time systematically approached by the Belgian secret service with an eye to future cooperation. Several of Mobutu's contemporaries say that by the time he had moved from journalism to act as Lumumba's trusted personal aide, deciding who he saw, scheduling his activities and sitting in for him at economic negotiations in Brussels, he was also an informer for Belgian intelligence.[57] Caught writing for the nationalist press in the Belgian Congo, and given the choice of exile or prison, Mobutu chose the former, becoming head of the MNC–Lumumba office in Belgium. This allowed him a perfect cover, if indeed he was working for Belgian intelligence at this time. It was also in this period that Mobutu came to the attention of CIA operative Larry Devlin. They first met in Brussels in early 1960 while Devlin was watching Soviet efforts to court the Congolese delegates to the independence negotiations.[58]

Following Lumumba's election in 1960, Mobutu became army chief of staff, a position of considerable authority and power, second only to the loyal Victor Lundula. In the crucial months of July and August, Mobutu took effective control of the army, displacing Lundula, sending foreign aid to loyal units, controlling promotion to tie individual officers to him. His methods were modern. Mobutu was a twentieth-century plotter; his success was based on money and control of a bureaucratic machine. After President Kasavubu removed Lumumba as prime minister on 5 September, Mobutu staged his first coup on 14 September. With the support of United States officials, Mobutu installed an interim government, which replaced parliament for six months in 1960–61. During the next four years, Mobutu acted as the power behind the throne, supporting but barely tolerating a series of weak civilian government, while the real influence was held in the hands of a 'Binza' Group – Mobutu supporters named after the prosperous district in which they lived. In 1961, according to Adam Hochschild, Mobutu 'received cash payments from the local CIA man and Western military attachés while Lumumba's murder was being planned'.[59] He was rewarded for his loyalty, and 'wearing dark glasses and his general's uniform with gold braid and a sword, he later met President Kennedy at the White House in 1963. Kennedy gave him an airplane for his personal use, and a US Air Force crew to fly it for him.'[60]

Mobutu in power

In 1965, as another clash broke out between prime minister and president, Mobutu staged a second coup. In November, the army, in the person of General Mobutu, stepped in, dismissed the president and established military rule. Once again he received the backing of the United States. This time, Mobutu assumed the presidency himself, rather than hiding behind the scenes. For over thirty years he maintained a highly personalised system of control. After 1965, Mobutu had on his side several advantages. He had the support of the old colonial power, Belgium, and of its regional successor, the United States. He had the guns and the organised force of the Congolese army. His supporters could point to the failures of an entire generation of rivals. Mobutu had the support of most local leaders, whether their power was tribal in origin, political or military. Above all, he had the promise of peace. To call for a second Patrice Lumumba, in 1963 or 1965, was to argue for years of further conflict. Most people would not risk the possibility of further war.

Mobutu established the Popular Movement of the Revolution (MPR). Under Mobutu's one-party state, human rights violations were widespread throughout virtually the entire period of his regime. Mobutu defeated Pierre Mulele's revolt in 1966, and the next year survived an attempt, assisted by mercenaries, to restore Tshombe to power. His political domination was not without opposition within the country. Laurent Kabila, who had led rebellions in the early 1960s, founded the Parti Revolutionnaire Populaire (PRP) in 1967. For years, it carried on intermittent guerrilla activity. There were other armies also, in this area, including the Front de Libération Nationale du Congo (FLNC), which had its roots in the Lunda and Chokwe refugees who fled into Angola after the failed secession attempt by Katanga in the early 1960s.

In the meanwhile, Mobutu consolidated his position at home and abroad. He repaired relations with Belgium, which he visited in 1969, concluding financial and technical agreements, and played host to King Baudouin in Kinshasa. He restored law and order, albeit through repression and control, and embarked on an ambitious programme of national economic development. In 1970 he stood in a sham election for president. He was the only candidate and the voting tickets were green for hope and red for chaos. He was 'elected' on the green ticket with a majority of 99.999 per cent – and became president for a term of seven years. Further US military aid helped Mobutu repel several attempts to overthrow him. Some of his political enemies he ordered tortured and killed; some he co-opted into his ruling circles; others he forced into exile. Mobutu was to impose his mark indelibly on the country he renamed Zaïre.

4

the great dictator

The early years of independence were marked by a complex struggle for power. From the outset, however, one man had figured repeatedly: Joseph-Désiré Mobutu. Always close to the centres of power and influence, he was an *éminence grise* providing support to Patrice Lumumba, even before independence was achieved. When the armed forces rebelled only five days after the independence of the Republic of the Congo was proclaimed on 30 June 1960, it was the replacement of the Belgian chief of staff by Colonel Mobutu that helped assuage their concerns. When President Kasavubu dismissed Prime Minister Lumumba in September 1960 Mobutu staged his first coup, ruling with the assistance of the Collège des Commissaires Généraux (CGC). For a year, the CGC governed the Congo, but failed to establish control in the north-east, where Lumumba's allies had established a rival government in Stanleyville, later Kisangani. Mobutu restored power to Kasavubu in February 1961, and a few days later Patrice Lumumba was murdered. In August a new government was formed, with Cyril Adoula as prime minister. Over the next few years, as the secessionist bid by Tshombe in Katanga eventually collapsed, but new rebellions developed in the Kwilu region, in southern Kivu and in northern Katanga, a divided political leadership struggled to hold the country together.

Following elections in 1965, the army intervened once more, and on 24 November 1965 Mobutu assumed full executive powers and declared himself Head of the 'Second Republic'. He was swift to prioritise the creation of new administrative structures to centralise the authority he had achieved through his position as chief of the army. He became president and sole legislator. Mobutu defeated Mulele's revolt and Mulele himself was lured back from exile with the promise of an amnesty. He was tortured to death, his eyes pulled from their sockets, his genitals ripped off, his limbs amputated one by one as he slowly died. His remains were dumped in the river.[1] The following year, the new president survived an attempt to restore Tshombe. By 1970, Mobutu had successfully eliminated all potential political opposition.

Mobutu's ambitions extended beyond short-term control. The earlier efforts of different regional and tribal leaders to establish their own fiefdoms within a federal Congo had failed to develop sufficient momentum, despite the very real, but temporary, secession of Katanga. More radical populist movements had been crushed and their leaders eliminated. The predicted disintegration of the Congo had not taken place, although something akin to it, a deeply fragmented state, was forged, as the original six provinces of the colonial state proliferated to twenty-one. Mobutu now tried to reduce the centripetal forces of Zaïre's political structure by reducing the number of provinces from twenty-one, first to twelve and then to eight. He further reduced the likelihood of secession by nationalising the assets of the Union Minière, a measure that was part of a larger package of nationalisation. Mobutu promised to hold together a fractious and divided country and create an authentic basis for national development.

The creation of Zaïre

The fact that Mobutu had been partially responsible for many of the earlier divisions and conflicts within the newly independent Congo did not matter; he was now going to secure the future of the nation and the people of Zaïre. This 'project' became known as 'Zaïreanisation', an ideological programme to legitimise the 'Mobutu revolution' and bring the political and economic centre of gravity back home after decades of external rule. For a time Mobutu gathered around him radical supporters for this unifying nationalist project. He drew upon Lumumbist slogans and emphasised the autonomy of the Congo as a 'popular' nationalist project.[2]

During the first two years after Mobutu's 1965 coup, student groups supported his programme of nationalisation and Africanisation; the national student body Union Générale des Étudiants du Congo (UGEC), though cautious, took his radical rhetoric at face value. This relationship is easy to dismiss today, but, as we have seen, Mobutu was speaking from a radical script, condemning tribalism and calling for a new nationalism that would return the Congo to its African roots. The renaming of cities, towns and provinces with 'authentic' African names was a confirmation for many students of Mobutu's sincerity. Mobutu also saw the co-option of the student body, and principally its main representative body the UGEC, as a key element in his control of potentially the most important opposition group in society. The organisational and political coherence of student groups, in the national union and university affiliates, was far greater than most other groups in civil society, a situation that was common in many sub-Saharan African countries after independence.[3] Mobutu was desperate to control the often critical and unruly students, and to convince them of his national project. Taking its lead from the UGEC, the new government even recognised Lumumba as a national hero.

The alliance did not last. The tension between the regime and students was demonstrated on 4 January 1968, when the US vice-president, Hubert H. Humphrey, attempted to lay a bouquet of flowers at the Lumumba memorial in Kinshasa. Students from Lovanium University who had turned up for the occasion pelted Humphrey with eggs and tomatoes. A UGEC communiqué stated that the protest had been called to prevent 'a profanation by the same people who had yesterday done everything [so that] the great fighter for Congo's and Africa's freedom disappear[ed]'.[4] The event caused the regime obvious embarrassment, but also clarified the reality of Mobutu's fake anti-imperialism. A rupture came later in 1968, when the regime arrested UGEC president André N'Kanza-Dulumingu. Student protests in Lubumbashi, Kinshasa and Kisangani led to the banning of the student movement.

The MPR would not tolerate an independent voice of student organisation, so the ruling party created the rival Jeunesse du Mouvement Populaire de la Révolution (JMPR), whose leadership saw their political futures tied to loyalty to the regime. Although N'Kanza-Dulumingu, the leader of UGEC, refused co-option for years, other leaders eventually caved in. The acquiescence of the UGEC did not silence student activism. The late 1960s were marked by violent demonstrations and strikes across the country. In 1969 sixty students from the University of Kinshasa were killed. In what was to become a familiar gesture of solidarity, students in Lubumbashi marched through the city bare-footed and bare-chested in support of their fallen comrades in the capital almost 2,000 miles away. Other universities came out in support, and hundreds of activists and student leaders were expelled.[5]

Students continued to resist the regime throughout the 1970s but, although they had been able to advance some of the first criticisms of the regime, ultimately they remained isolated. Despite the fact that they were well placed in university campuses to organise swift protests, often bypassing the state security apparatus, without the support of wider social forces they were easy to pick off. George Nzongolo-Ntalaja is correct in identifying the importance of the student movement as 'the single most important civil society organisation to challenge the Mobutu regime at the height of its power'.[6] But the capacity of the regime to co-opt the student movement as a whole was a crucial element in its overall ability to stifle criticism and prevent significant opposition throughout the 1970s and even into the 1980s.

Despite some early difficulties with the former colonial power, Belgium, as a result of his apparently 'radical nationalist' stance, it was not long before Mobutu revealed his willingness to restore links. Already in 1969, he had begun to repair relations with the Belgian government, with an official visit that concluded with financial and technical agreements. Later the 'radical nationalist' played host to King Baudouin in Kinshasa, a clear statement that he intended to retain a 'special relationship' with Belgium. At the same time he embarked on an ambitious programme of national economic development, which was to make him and his immediate entourage extraordinarily wealthy but which also promised initially at least to bring economic advancement to his countrymen as well.

In 1970, Mobutu had been 'elected' president for five years with a vote of 10,131,699 with only 157 'against'. In 1971, he changed the name of the country to the Republic of Zaïre, implying an intention to draw on the strengths of the whole country for its development. A process of 'Zaïreanisation' was to be implemented, which would not only replace foreigners with locals in key positions, in the public and private sector, but would provide an inspiration for the creation of a new nation, Zaïre.

The original Constitution of 1960 had given Congolese nationality to 'all those persons at least one of whose parents were members of a tribe or ethnic group established within the territory of the Congo before 18 October 1908'. Twelve years later, in January 1972, in an attempt to clarify continuing questions regarding the definition of Congolese identity, the Banyamulenge, a group in the east of the country, many of whom originated in Rwanda, were given Congolese (Zaïrean) nationality, at the instigation of Barthelemy Bisengimana, Chief of Cabinet to President Mobutu. The status of the Banya-mulenge would re-emerge on several later occasions.[7] Regions were renamed and people were encouraged to abandon their Christian names; it was then also that Mobutu's own name was changed.

There was even a token struggle against corruption and nepotism. On the surface, this was consistent with a programme of nation-building. The reality was more sordid. Crawford Young and Thomas Turner wrote that 'What … transpired was a tumultuous, disorderly, and profoundly demeaning scramble for loot.'[8] In 1973, decrees were passed that ensured the transfer of foreign-owned businesses to Zaïreans. Mixed up with genuine redistribution were other processes, directing resources towards the supreme ruler of a fabulously rich country and his family. In the words of one commentator, 'The pie waiting to be divided up was enormous'.[9]

From boom to bust

For more than fifty years, the production and export of copper had dominated the country's economy, producing huge wealth for the foreign companies that controlled it, and leading to the rise of a new economic mining 'sector'. In 1960, one enterprise alone, the giant Union Minière du Haut Katanga, a Belgian copper-mining company operating in Katanga, generated 60 per cent of Zaïre's entire exports. Copper was a major source of foreign-exchange earnings, together with coffee. In 1965, the 'industrial sector' contributed some 32 per cent of the Congo's GDP, most of it from mining. Mineral deposits, not just of copper, cobalt and diamonds, but also of zinc, gold, cassiterite, manganese, cadmium, germanium, silver, wolframite and coltan, were known to be vast. Copper, cobalt, zinc and germanium were found mainly in the south-eastern Shaba province (formerly Katanga) adjoining the Zambian copper belt; diamonds were located mainly in Kasai province, particularly around the towns of Mbuji-Mayi and Tshikapa, although some mining activity was conducted in Bandundu and Orientale province (formerly Haut-Zaïre) regions. Cassiterite, wolframite, gold and coltan were exploited from the Kivu region in the east. The independent Congo inherited an unparalleled legacy of mineral wealth.

When in 1966, the Mobutu regime announced that all companies operating in Zaïre must move their headquarters to the country, Union Minière initially refused. The regime proceeded to block all exports of copper and any transfers of the company's funds. Soon, however, a compromise was reached. The Congolese state formally took over Union Minière in 1966–67 and renamed it Générale des Carrières et des Mines (Gécamines). One of the central pillars of Belgian colonial rule was nationalised. The new national company did not in fact cut the old colonial owners out of the picture; on the contrary, the new arrangement helped to secure their profits. Thomas Turner was absolutely correct when he wrote, 'The settlement proved lucrative to Union Minière and brought unanticipated costs to Zaïre.'[10] Despite some complications, the involvement of foreign companies in copper production was never fundamentally disrupted.

The years between 1968 and 1974 were a period of significant economic growth for the Congo, powered by the high prices for copper on the international market. In the early 1970s, with copper output hovering at between 400,000 and 470,000 tonnes a year, and production of the far more valuable cobalt at between 10,000 and 18,000 tonnes, Gécamines alone could be counted on to produce annual revenues of between $700 million and $900 million.[11] It was the dominant producer in Zaïre, accounting for more than 90 per cent of the copper output, and all production of cobalt, zinc and coal. It was the mainstay of the economy and accounted for up to 70 per cent of export receipts. During the 1970s, Gécamines became the world's sixth largest mining company. Informed commentators did not think that Mobutu's 'plan USA', to reach the level of economic development of the West by 1980, was wholly far-fetched. On the contrary, as Ingrid Samset writes, 'From 1967 to 1974, the Democratic Republic of the Congo was one of Africa's main economic powers.'[12]

Not all commentators agreed with the image of a sleeping giant about to 'take off'. According to Michael Barratt Brown, by contrast: 'Zaïre was engulfed in civil war, then locked into the grip of the transnational copper companies through the agency of a monster who tyrannised the country, while lining his own pockets, and continued to do so from 1965 [onwards].'[13] Claude Ake suggests that, 'in some extreme cases, such as Zaïre, the assumption of a development project and of a political leadership bent on development is patently absurd. In Zaïre, as also in Togo, Somalia and Sudan, rulership appears to be an exercise in "how to ruin a country".'[14] Certainly these more critical commentators were right to emphasise the role of Mobutu's dictatorship, and his effective encouragement of extreme corruption in undermining the potential of the Congo. Zaïre's fortunes came to hinge on the price of copper.

The 1960s were a period of global economic confidence linked to the capacity of state-led economic growth. This was particularly true in newly independent countries of Africa. Political leaders, far from seeing the involvement of the state as providing the conditions for foreign investment, regarded state intervention as the key element in the country's national development. Mobutu had been following continental trends, politically as well as economically. In Zambia in the late 1960s, Kenneth Kaunda was centralising power and nationalising previously foreign-owned industries. Kaunda took personal control of all major policy decisions in 1968, and the partial nationalisation of twenty-five major companies in 1969. These extensions of state control were regarded as prudent economic projects at the time.[15] The *Economist* wrote about the region as a whole in the late 1960s, saying that 'The shrewdest businessmen in that part of the world have argued for some time that ... a business whose success is underwritten by government participation may be more valuable than 100 per cent of a concern exposed to all the political winds that blow.'[16] There was little international opposition. Colette Braeckman argues that far from opposing the nationalisation of Union Minière, the United States actually favoured it.[17] Mobutu was following orthodoxy when he increased the state's role in the Zaïrean economy in the late 1960s. And for a while, it has to be said, the strategy was successful.

In the light of Mobutu's role in the murder of Patrice Lumumba, given his jailing and torturing of dissidents, and his own extraordinary personal corruption, it is almost impossible to believe that any group of people might actually have supported his regime, for any length of time. Yet a historian looking back at the Congo detects not a society constantly at war with its rulers, but something more complex, an atittude of at times ambivalence, with some surprising evidence of support for parts of Mobutu's programme. That nationalist logic which sees the Congolese moving always collectively, as 'a people', has extreme difficulty in explaining how the dictator was able to remain in power so long. Torture alone cannot keep any tyrant in power for thirty years. It is far more accurate to say that Mobutu had some success, in certain periods, in the absence of any sustained or serious rival, and above all in a climate of economic growth, so that the rhetoric of Zaïreanisation did not always ring completely hollow. A small but revealing example comes from the world of music. One of the most successful songs of 1972 was Tabu Ley Rochereau's 'Nakomitunaka'. It was written in the context of Mobutu's promises of cultural authenticity, at a time when the dictatorship was being heavily criticised by the Roman Catholic Church, in a context of economic growth, at a moment when the Congolese music industry was thriving, and when small producers (in this area and in other fields) could look on the future with a certain modest optimism. For all these reasons, Ley's song takes the side of Mobutu against his critics, who he associates with the legacy of white rule:

I ask myself
My God, I ask myself,
Black skin, where does it come from?
Our ancestor, who was he?
Jesus, Son of God, was a white man.
Adam and Eve were whites.
All the saints were whites.

Why then, oh, my God? ...
Black skin, where does it come from?
The uncles keep us from understanding.
The statues of our ancestors, they refuse them...
My God, why have you made us this way?
Where is the ancestor of we blacks?
Africa has opened its eyes.
Africa will not go back, ah mama.[18]

In so far as there was any tacit support for Mobutu, and from particular classes in Zaïrean society, it drew on two promises: African cultural pride and economic prosperity. But in 1973 industrial production slumped in the advanced economies by a full 10 per cent in one year, while international trade fell in the same year by 13 per cent.[19] The resulting recession had a devastating effect on Africa. Still locked into economic dependency, most African economies relied on the export of one or two primary products. By the mid-1970s, for example, two-thirds of exports from Ghana and Chad were accounted for by coffee and cotton respectively, while Zambia in 1977 depended on copper for half of its GDP. Such dependent economies were hard hit by falling primary commodity prices.[20] Regions and countries already crucially weakened by their integration into the global economy on the basis of one or two single sources of exports were now further debilitated, and even the protective edifice of state capitalism was impotent to resist the violence of these global forces.

For Zaïre, the mid-1970s marked a turning point that signalled the beginning of the rapid decline of copper that had been at the heart of the country's post-independence growth. Now and for the first time GNP stagnated. The economic boom was over. Economic growth declined annually between 1975 and 1978 by 3.5 per cent.[21] The collapse of copper prices was at the centre of this decline. From 1976 copper production began its inexorable tumble from a high of 502,000 tonnes to 50,000 tonnes in 1993, a 90 per cent decline.[22] The slump in world commodity prices coincided with a growing tendency on the part of Mobutu and his cronies to 'bleed off' a significant proportion of Gécamines' earnings. Sozacom, the state-owned subsidiary set up to market minerals abroad, would redirect a share of the foreign exchange earned from the sale of cobalt, zinc and copper on the international markets to numbered presidential accounts held abroad, a practice referred to by the World Bank and IMF as 'uncompensated sales' or 'leakages'. Other devices were also used to siphon off funds into presidential accounts. In 1978, an IMF official discovered that the governor of the central bank had simply ordered Gécamines to deposit all its earnings directly into a presidential account. It has been estimated that $240 million a year was stolen from Gécamines by President Mobutu and others.[23]

The implosion in the late 1970s of the copper-producing giant Gécamines, once the country's economic powerhouse, undermined the economy's hitherto largely positive trajectory. There was now rampant corruption, and the distinction between the public and the private economy was ill defined in many sectors. Mobutu and his family became extraordinarily rich. The programme of 'Zaïreanisation' put substantial new sources of wealth directly into the hands of the new Zaïrean elite. As Riley and Parfitt observed,

> Mobutu's rulership has been secured through his skilful use of patronage, which has entailed the development of an elite that owes its power to his. Virtually all positions of state influence are in Mobutu's gift, and so advancement is dependent on loyalty to the leader, or Guide, as he prefers to be known. Such advancement has been made particularly attractive by Mobutu's utilization of state resources to finance patronage for his political elite. It is accepted that appointment to office carries with it the right to misappropriate any resources associated with that position. Consequently, corruption has run completely out of control in Zaïre.[24]

If the economy was a crucial source of personal wealth for some, it also remained the only security for public borrowing. As in so many other countries, the government had borrowed massively. The increase in oil prices in the early 1970s contributed to a rapid increase in the demand for loans. Across the global South, as the global recession developed and deepened during the mid to late 1970s, these loans turned into major debts. In Zaïre, much of the money borrowed went into military hardware, dubious public projects and luxury expenditure that did little to propel Zaïre closer to its stated objectives and much to swell the national debt.

By 1975 the regime did not even know how much it owed or to whom; it stopped paying any interest on its commercial bank debt, which amounted to around $700–800 million. This prompted the first of a succession of interventions by the World Bank and the UN. The first task was to assess the scale of the debt. By 1976, the total debt was already more than a third of Zaïre's total expenditure and 12 per cent of its GDP. In 1977 the total debt was estimated at over $4 billion. Debt-service payments were now the equivalent of 43 per cent of export earnings and almost half of total state revenue. Despite its enormous wealth in natural resources and potential, the Zaïrean economy was bankrupt. While the ruling elite fed off the ailing economy, for the mass of the people survival became more difficult. At this time life for most Zaïreans ended at 40. Economic and social conditions were to worsen rather than improve during Mobutu's second decade in power.

Mobutu's first decade

Jacques Depelchin sees the first decade of Mobutu's regime as falling into two phases, the first from 1965 to 1973 and the second from 1973 to 1975. In the first period, Mobutu used to his own advantage the so-called 'recourse to authenticity'. His own change of name and title, the change of the name of the country itself, and of towns and streets; and the official proclamation of Lumumba as a national hero – all were part of a proclaimed attempt to forge a new African national identity. There were various efforts also to increase the resources available to the state, making use of 'nationalist' slogans. In 1972 there was an attempt to revive the National Savings Account, which originated during the colonial period; among the measures used for this was compulsory saving by parents for school-age children. There was also a suggestion that the National Pension Account be made a credit institution, not out of concern for the workers' well-being but as a means of again taking advantage of all possible sources of 'revenue'. There were efforts also to improve the taxation system, evidently to appropriate more funds.

The next stage can be seen in the institutional and economic consolidation of the process, which was initiated in the 'second phase', with the Zaïreanisation of the bureaucracy and the progressive 'nationalisation' of sectors of the economy previously in private or corporate Belgian hands into either private Zaïrean ownership or state ownership. This development tended to encourage the development of two different, and conflicting, social formations. At first, the process involved small and medium businesses, mainly in the transport and service sectors, and a transfer from expatriate private ownership to Zaïrean private ownership. One of the major forces behind this process was a concern to gain greater control for the political elite over the resources of the Zaïrean economy, so that the profits generated could all the more easily be appropriated; another was to extend the range of resources under nominal state control, to increase the profits available to be taken.

The process was associated, however, with a bitter struggle between those within the bureaucracy and the government and those in the private sector, for access to the spoils of nationalisation, prompting Mobutu to castigate 'profiteers' as targets for criticism, even as he engineered the transfer of private enterprises into state ownership in his so-called 'radicalisation' of 1975. This involved a more radical programme to transfer into state ownership around 120 large industrial and commercial enterprises. Depelchin suggests that 'outwardly, radicalisation was aimed at the new owners who had proved themselves incompetent as well as against those who had appropriated the business so skilfully that were perceived as a threat to the very group which had opened up this new cornucopia.' The 'radicalisation' of November 1975 was provoked by a realisation that Zaïreanisation had failed.[25]

For various reasons, the 'nationalised' companies tended to perform poorly. It would be wrong, however, to attribute the variable performance of enterprises taken over by Zaïreans from their European predecessors entirely to incompetence, greed and corruption. There was also the fact that, in most cases, the companies taken over were the remnants of the previous companies and often only the shells or rump of those companies bereft of capital, technology and management. Often, moreover, the Belgian owners and entrepreneurs had foreseen the end of the colonial regime and made preparations for the days when they would be limited in the extent to which they could run these enterprises as their own. As Depelchin put it,

> the Belgian joint stock companies had well prepared themselves for such moves by only leaving in the Congo subsidiaries which could not operate without a lifeline to the Belgian financial holding. Thus, when nationalisation finally took place, it did nothing to

them since the Zaïrean subsidiaries had by then been reduced to dead branches of a tree.[26]

The few cases where nationalised businesses did well actually threatened the existing elite, in so far as they constituted the basis for the possible development of an independent private capitalist class, able eventually to reproduce itself without reliance on the state. During the early 1970s, Mobutu's speeches contrasted the Zaïrean people and the 'new 300 Zaïrean families', who were 'in control of the economy'. Mobutu sought to present himself as a guardian of the public interest, against an emerging private capitalist class. In *Salongo*, the government newspaper, he described himself as the one who would prevent the emergence of 'a fistful of fatty and pot-bellied bourgeois next to the misery of the people'. He warned that 'some owners turned bourgeois were behaving like incontestable and uncontested owners of the Zaïreanised businesses allocated to them, to the great contempt of the Zaïrean state which they were unscrupulously spoiling.'[27]

The 'radicalisation' programme, which took significant numbers of larger industrial, commercial and agricultural enterprises under state control in November 1975, was a response to both the inefficiency and the ineffectiveness of many of the 'nationalised' enterprises, but also, as we have seen, to the threat from those Zaïrean entrepreneurs who had made a success of their businesses. A new generation of private entrepreneurs were pushed rapidly into positions of great power. One figure who gained from this process was the musician François Luambo Makiadi, 'Franco', who was in 1975 granted ownership of Mazadis, the largest record-pressing plant in Kinshasa. By dint of his control of this factory, Franco was to play a dominant role in the industry for the next fifteen years, which was the country's best-known export, even before copper. Over the length of his career, Franco released over a hundred albums. Under Mobutu's patronage, he amassed huge wealth.[28] In other sectors, and without Franco's talent or his sense of irony, other new fortunes were also being made.

Between 1975 and 1977, Mobutu's speeches vacillated between two incompatible explanations of his county's malaise. Despite having greatly benefited personally from the siphoning off of public resources, he condemned the 'nouveaux riches' of the private sector.

Although it antagonised the owners of private business, he also felt able to criticise the holders of state power. In allowing both forces to grow in society, and in promoting and then weakening each of them, he sought to maintain his place at the centre of power. In a speech setting out his 'diagnosis of Zaïre's malady', in November 1977, Mobutu's principal target was no longer the 'new bourgeoisie' but rather 'those people who use the state or the party as instruments of personal enrichment.'[29] Those who were castigated most now were cadres in the party. The failure of the great programme for Zaïrean development was seen to be due to 'the psychology and action of a certain Zaïrean bourgeoisie which wants to get rich without working, to consume without producing and to rule without being controlled, in short, to replace the colonisers without "colonising"'.[30] Within a couple of years, many of the nationalised businesses would be handed back to their original owners. As Mobutu struggled to manage the growing internal problems of Zaïre, he was also supporting political initiatives outside the country's borders as part of a political strategy that identified him and his regime as a key regional ally of the West.

Wars in Angola, wars in Shaba

Throughout the 1970s, Zaïre under Mobutu was heralded by most of the powers as a stable ally, but the country was in fact a significant source of regional instability. During the mid-1970s, Zaïre sponsored the Frente Nacional para a Libertação de Angola (FNLA), a rebel movement led by Roberto Holden in Angola and actively involved in the recruitment of mercenaries in the war. According to Wilfred Burchett and Derek Roebuck, 'the FNLA was tribal based, with its influence restricted to the northern areas (of Angola) adjoining Zaïre.'[31] The FLNA was permitted by Mobutu to maintain guerrilla bases and refugee camps along the border in Bas-Zaïre province. For some time, it had its headquarters in Kinshasa, and it was from there that it channelled its supplies, weapons and mercenary fighters.

An agreement had been signed in January 1975 between the Portuguese government and the three Angolan independence movements, the Movimento Popular da Libertação de Angola (MPLA), the FNLA and União Nacional para a Independência Total de Angola (UNITA), which were recognised as 'the only legitimate representatives of the people of Angola'. This Algarve (or Alvor) Agreement, provided for a three-member presidential college in the Angolan capital, Luanda, presided over by each of the three movements in turn. A transitional government of thirteen ministers, formed by three from each of the movements and four nominated by Portugal, would be set up. The transitional period would come to an end on 31 October 1975 with elections to form an all-Angola government, with independence to be declared by 11 November 1975, followed by a phased Portuguese withdrawal, to be completed by February 1976.

The agreement never worked, because it accorded the FNLA and UNITA a status beyond their respective contributions to liberation. By March 1975, as conflict between the two parties intensified, a virtual war had begun. The FNLA, strongly supported at this period by Zaïre, was strongest in the north. Alvaro Holden Roberto, the leader of the movement, came from São Salvador, the capital of the ancient Kongo kingdom, and was reputedly descended from the traditional rulers of the Bakongo. As Burchett and Roebuck suggest, 'if there was any place where tribal loyalties were strong, it was there among Holden Roberto's own Bakongo tribal people'.[32]

In 1976, after the MPLA won the struggle for decolonisation, and despite US and Zaïrean support for the FNLA, there was a degree of reconciliation between Mobutu and President Neto of Angola. The FNLA leadership was relocated to Guinea-Bissau and its armed units moved away from the border. It was also agreed that Angolan refugees in Zaïre would be repatriated and that Angola would return to Zaïre several thousand Katangese soldiers, who had been members of Tshombe's forces at the time of the secession of Katanga. In March 1977, however, some of these, distrusting Mobutu's promises of an amnesty, invaded the Zaïrean province of Shaba from Angola, receiving support from many of the disaffected inhabitants. France supported Mobutu, sending some 1,500 Moroccan troops to stiffen the Zaïrean army. By May 1977, the 'First Shaba War' was over. That same year, Mobutu was 're-elected' for a second seven-year term. But now, towards the end of the 1970s, more systematic opposition to his regime began to emerge. Resistance to the regime was not limited to wars or guerrilla movements. Dissidents were regularly detained for weeks or months, usually without trial. Amnesty International estimated (in 1983) that arrests of dissidents ran to about 100 a year during the five-year period from 1978 to 1983. In May 1978, a year after the First Shaba War, a second revolt took place in the same region. Retribution by the army against those who had failed to support the government after the 1977 invasion and uprising sparked a second war. Several thousand men crossed the Zambian border and entered Shaba, occupying Kolwezi. Well over 100 Europeans were killed. Ostensibly to save further lives, 700 French and 1,700 Belgian paratroops were flown in, to assist the Zaïrean forces in recapturing the town. Having done this, and having evacuated 2,500 Europeans, they were replaced in June by a pan-African peacekeeping force, recruited from Morocco, Senegal, Côte d'Ivoire, Togo and Gabon, which remained for over a year.

This African intervention was coupled with a wider international effort to rescue Zaïre from bankruptcy, into which it had been plunged by the collapse in the price of copper, the closure of rail lines to Angola and Mobutu's malpractices. Despite Mobutu's profligate attitude towards the Zaïrean economy, his failure to meet the conditions set by creditors, and his continuing abuse of human rights in Zaïre, the IMF continued to do business with Zaïre. This unusually tolerant line owed much to Mobutu's strict adherence to American foreign policy objectives in sub-Saharan Africa. He was one of the first African leaders to recognise Israel, he sent forces into Chad to fight against Libyan incursions, and he consistently provided logistic and other forms of support to American proxies in Angola, as we have seen.

Towards structural adjustment: the late 1970s

It was the international collapse in the price of copper, more than anything else, which plunged the country into a crisis from which it never recovered. There were certainly other processes at work; and many accounts of this period place most of the blame on Mobutu's 'Zaïreanisation' project for the subsequent collapse of the economy. Janet MacGaffey's account in 1990 is typical: 'In the mid-seventies, an economically disastrous process of indigenisation sent Zaïre into a spiralling economic crisis.'[33] The weakness of such arguments is that they downplay the effect of the transition from high mineral prices on the international markets to high interest rates, large debts and a slump in mineral prices, all within a decade.

The strategy of development through the promotion of specific export industries based upon existing resources, adopted during the 1960s and early 1970s, which might have provided a short-term basis for growth, if not a sustainable framework for development, was undoubtedly hindered by the corruption of the state by the patronage system of the political elite under Mobutu. Zaïre was not the only African state to take this path. Ake remarks that

> in Ivory Coast, Kenya, Nigeria, Ghana and Zaïre, the principle of promoting specific industries to encourage exports was subverted by parochialism and rent seeking … basically, the political elite tended to see such projects not so much in terms of the compelling need for national development as in terms of accumulation, patronage and power.[34]

At the same time as the state was pushing forward with its policy of borrowing for investment for growth, petrol prices tripled and that of copper collapsed. The situation was made worse by the closure of the Benguela railroad in 1975 due to the Angolan civil war; this shut down a major transport route for mineral exports. There followed a period of political zigzagging. The reaction of the state to this crisis in the mid-1970s was first to further entrench state control of foreign enterprises. In 1975, the decree on 'Radicalisation', celebrated at the time as the 'radicalisation of the revolution' by Mobutu, pushed the policy of Africanisation even deeper. The following year these polices were reversed when the government issued a further decree on 'Retrocession' – presumably the 'retreat of the revolution' – handing back companies to their former foreign owners, while maintaining some 'national partners'. Relations with expatriate business interests improved, as the regime promised to compensate those (mostly Belgian) foreigners who had lost out during 'Zaïreanisation'. The regime even allowed those displaced by the earlier reforms to recover up to 60 per cent of their assets. Belgians were back on board before long.

By 1978, the output of copper was 17 per cent below 1974 levels and imports had dropped 50 per cent in the same period. Manufacturing was now functioning at 40 per cent of capacity and wages were approximately a quarter of their 1970 rate. Foreign debt had risen to $5 billion.[35] The answer, provided by the emerging conventional wisdom of the period, later to be known as the Washington Consensus, and the international financial institutions, was 'structural adjustment'. This process was to prove devastating for the people of Zaïre. The government attempted to manage the crisis in the late 1970s by launching the 'Mobutu Plan', which promoted the 'structural adjustment' of the economy and encouraged the employment of expatriates in a reversal of the policies of the previous decade. This 'new' stance was welcomed by the international institutions and by foreign capital, which still saw Zaïre as a potential powerhouse were 'liberalisation' to be effectively implemented, and by the major imperial powers, which saw Mobutu as a crucial source of stability in the 'heart of Africa', a continent which appeared to be increasingly fragile.

Again, Zaïre was by no means unique in its change of policy. The World Bank and the IMF now advocated liberalisation stridently. As the World Bank declared, 'Africa needs not just less government, [but] government that concentrates its efforts less on direct intervention and more on enabling others to be productive.'[36] Such Washington policies meant the stripping of the state, privatisation and poverty. By 1980, Zaïre's outstanding debt already amounted to 30 per cent of GDP. Faced with this economic deterioration and with no local remedies available, Mobutu became, in 1982, one of the first African leaders to submit his country formally to an IMF-prescribed austerity programme. Initially, the government's apparent enthusiasm to fulfil IMF performance targets was favourably received by the creditors. The early 1980s saw the liberalisation of the Zaïrean economy promoted by successive IMF packages. These processes of liberalisation brought about the reversal of the previous fifteen years of Mobutu's state-led economic planning. The first significant stage of these reforms came in 1981, which saw the selective liberalisation of prices for agricultural products and the legalisation of informal or artisanal mining of diamonds. Artisanal traders could now sell diamonds at legal counters that had opened in Kinshasa. These measures were followed by further price deregulation the following year. One stated aim of the liberalisation measures was to undermine the informal market and the extensive smuggling of minerals across borders, through the establishment of authorised counters. Although initially these measures achieved some success they did little to stem the tide of smuggled goods across borders. A key effect of these early measures was to promote the gradual transformation of the Zaïrean economy away from its earlier reliance on copper production and exports under state control in favour of private and informal diamond mining, trading and smuggling. The IMF and World Bank seemed to regard the growth in the informal economy as a potential engine of free-market development in the developing world.[37]

Inside Zaïre, Mobutu encouraged anarchy by publicly recognising that, 'everything is for sale, everything is bought in our country. And in this traffic, holding any slice of public power constitutes a veritable exchange instrument, convertible into illicit acquisition of money or other goods, or the evasion of all sorts of obligation.'[38] That this view was prevalent is confirmed by Janet MacGaffey's studies, which indicated that more and more people in Zaïre during the 1980s began to produce goods and services without registering or declaring their activities to the authorities. Clandestine links began to be forged with the formal sector; factories and offices found that they could obtain supplies of materials, spare parts, repairs and other services more cheaply from this 'second' economy than from the first. They did so, and kept quiet. Jobs which people held in the formal sector came to be valued not for the direct income they gave but for the access to profitable opportunities for doing informal business.

Smuggling became endemic, in both the countryside and the towns. Zaïre borders nine other states, five of them landlocked, and, because it lies at the very centre of the subcontinent, linking north and south, east and west, it was a centre of smuggling in the region. It also took place at all levels. MacGaffey's studies suggest a distinction between informal trading, the small-scale carrying of rural produce, maize flour, sugar, cooking oil, vegetables and cash crops like coffee, across borders, often between members of the same ethnic groups, on the one hand, and the large-scale smuggling of gold, ivory, diamonds and precious stones, vehicles, fuel oil, spare parts and products of the copper mines, on the other. Small-scale smuggling was particularly common between Zaïre and Zambia during the years when in Zambia maize, sugar and cooking oil were subsidised to maintain the living standards of the urban workers.

A smuggler with a bicycle could earn the equivalent of two-thirds of a monthly minimum wage in one day, even after giving bribes to the border guards.

Large-scale crime required, by contrast, the involvement not only of dishonest customs officials but also of middle-ranking bureaucrats as well as private entrepreneurs. The chains of trading connections reached out from Zaïre north into Sudan and Nigeria, and south into Botswana and South Africa, exporting minerals and cash crops on a large scale, and importing fuel, manufactured goods and luxury items. The scale of smuggling can only be estimated roughly, but operations were clearly massive. Already substantial, smuggling expanded hugely in the late 1970s and 1980s, taking in 30 to 60 per cent of the coffee crop between 1975 and 1979, 90 per cent of the ivory exported in the 1970s, until Zaïre's elephants had all but disappeared, diamonds valued at $59 million in one year, and 90 tonnes of cobalt in 1985, valued at $15 million.

During the 1980s, while the informal economy expanded, the ability to generate wealth through the 'formal economy' diminished. As the flow of aid and in particular commercial loans began to decrease, the cost of imports became more burdensome. The production of copper ore remained at around 500,000 tonnes per year, equivalent to about 6 per cent of world output, and export earnings also remained stagnant throughout the decade. The share of agriculture's roughly 30 per cent contribution to GDP remained more or less the same throughout the 1980s. The country's wide range of climatic and environmental zones, as well as its size, ensured that agriculture remained strong. The main food crops grown were cassava, plantains, maize, groundnuts and rice, grown for the most part by small-scale subsistence farmers. Cash crops included coffee, palm oil and palm kernels, rubber, cotton, sugar, tea and cocoa, many of which were grown on large plantations.

Internal road transport remained poor and there was heavy reliance on river transport and rail. The Benguela railway to the Angolan Atlantic port of Lobito offered the shortest rail route to the sea. Domestic air services were reasonably efficient, with the private carrier Scibe Airlift Cargo operating between the major regional centres and towns. By 1985, Scibe was carrying more passengers than the national carrier Air Zaïre. Telecommunications, by contrast (run by the state concern, the OCPT), were possibly the worst in Africa. In

1980, when Zaïre had an estimated 30,000 telephone lines, the ratio to population was less than one line per 1,000 inhabitants.

In 1980, manufacturing contributed about 14 per cent of GDP, but it has been estimated that throughout the 1980s most manufacturers were operating at only around one-third of installed capacity levels. This was for a combination of reasons, including limited domestic demand, lack of foreign exchange to import badly needed spare parts, management deficiencies and corruption, and problems with regard to reliable power sources. The country's huge water reserves and vast potential for producing hydroelectric power, virtually matchless in Africa, were barely developed at all: the state electricity board (SNEL) estimated installed capacity in 1987 to be 2,486 MW. The most ambitious infrastructure project undertaken in Zaïre, thought to account for a substantial proportion of the foreign debt, was the Inga hydroelectric power project, based near the port of Matadi, at the mouth of the Congo river. This comprised two power stations which, in 1986, produced 3,100 million kWh and a 1,725 km high-voltage power line, extending almost the entire length of the country, from Inga to Kolwezi in the heart of the mining region. Inga produced some of the cheapest power in the world, but the ZOFI industrial free zone established beside the power stations, with the hope of attracting major heavy industry, projects proved largely unsuccessful.

Zaïre, in common with most primary-commodity-producing African states, experienced a steady deterioration in its terms of trade during the 1980s as world market prices for most of its exports failed to keep pace with import price rises. Management was chaotic. Investment, which had risen between 1965 and 1980 from 11 per cent of GDP to 25 per cent, now began to fall. The government's extensive deficit spending of the 1970s generated recurrent deficits on the balance of payments current account as new sources of external funding fell away and service payments on debts incurred in earlier years fell due. Despite defaulting repeatedly on debt repayments, however, the country succeeded in securing regular rescheduling. The International Monetary Fund (IMF) played an important role in 'guiding' the Zaïrean government, even appointing Erwin Blumenthal to monitor and advise the Bank of Zaïre.

The characteristic elements of structural adjustment figured in the IMF's programme of reform for Zaïre. Cuts in public expenditure and a reduction in the role of the state in the economy led, in 1981, as part of the IMF structural adjustment programmes, not only to a reduced ability to manage the economy in the national collective interest but also to the sacking of thousands of civil servants and teachers. For ordinary Zaïreans, the effects were dramatic and led to a severe erosion in living standards. In 1979 prices were estimated to be up to 46 times higher than those of 1969, but by 1986 they were 113 times higher. The National Institute of Statistics (INS) stated that the average family food budget was 3,037 zaire for a month yet the median salary for a civil servant was only 750 zaire. By 1983 the real salary of a civil servant was less than a fifth of the 1975 level. But things were to get worse.

By 1983, the Zaïrean debt stood at around $5 billion, which was roughly equal to President Mobutu's own personal wealth in Swiss bank holdings at the time. An agreement with the IMF and the World Bank resulted in a massive 77.5 per cent devaluation of the zaire (the fifth since the mid-1970s). This package sent the prices of staple foods soaring upwards by something like 200 to 300 per cent. Wages were restrained and thousands of workers in the public sector were fired. Barratt Brown notes that 'in Zaïre, as early as 1983, in the public services, salaries in real terms represented less than one-fifth of the 1975 level.'[39] In 1984, the National Institute of Statistics estimated that an average monthly food budget in Kinshasa for a family of six would be over 3,000 zaire, while the salary for a medium-level civil servant was 750 zaire.

The majority of people were obliged to increase their real incomes in various ways, through moonlighting or by various corrupt practices. Barratt Brown asked,

> how then did families survive? The answer is partly through sharing houses, partly through changing consumption patterns, from fish and meat to cereals, but chiefly through supplementing salaries or wages by informal activities. A 1986 survey of households revealed that managers were spending three times their formal salary, skilled workers only a little less and others over double their formal wages.[40]

The informal economy became crucial, not so much for 'development' as a prerequisite of survival for most Zaïreans. By the mid 1980s only 25 per cent of household income came from wages.[41]

The phrase *Je me debrouille* (I cope) became a near-universal statement for those now living between the formal and informal sectors. Remittances from family members living in Belgium or France
became central to many people's survival. It also meant that many
Zaïreans living abroad could not return, Jean-Paul Kasanga explains
that during this period 'I became the state for my family.'[42] This
situation was reproduced across the Zaïrean diaspora in the 1980s.
Whereas previously Congolese families with children in Europe and
North America insisted that they return home after obtaining their
degrees, now the opposite occurred. Téléphore Tsakala Munikengi
and Willy Bongo-Pasi Mako Sangol observe that they now urged
their 'graduates to find jobs abroad so they can send money home.'[43]
If you were able to get out you did not come back, but you might
send money home.

The IMF requirement most fiercely resisted by Mobutu, despite his
publicly stated antagonism towards those who took advantage of their
positions in the state apparatus and public-sector enterprises to enrich
themselves, was the abolition of corrupt parastatals – from which
many members of the political elite gained their illicit income. The
blatantly unequal sharing of the burdens of austerity roused increasing
discontent among the workers and other groups particularly disadvan-
taged by IMF stabilisation, as evidenced by the strike of workers at
Matadi harbour on the Zaïre river during January 1985. The strikers
brought all commercial traffic to a halt in support of their demands
for a 50 per cent wage rise, which breached the 25 per cent limit
agreed by the government with the Fund. Mobutu was clearly aware
of the popular resentment at the austerity programme, commenting
to one Western minister that Kinshasa was 'a powder keg'. Economic
and social protest would soon be accompanied by political protest
and the growth of an organised political opposition.

Capitalism and class formation under Mobutu

The opportunities available in the first two decades of independence
enabled those who had access to the country's resources to become
wealthy indeed. MacGaffey argued in the 1980s that

> a local capitalist class is in the process of formation in Zaïre,
> to which wealth accumulated in the second economy has been

a contributing factor. Profits from smuggling and other second economy activities have been one source of capital for investment in substantial manufacturing, and in agro-business producing for the local market as well as for export, in commerce, and in real estate. The nascent bourgeoisie enjoys a middle-class life-style, educates its children through university, and passes on wealth to them; it is thus beginning to reproduce itself as a class.[44]

Michael Barratt Brown argued differently that

> the very essence of the Zaïrean secondary economy is that the state is itself working the black economy. Many individual enterprises are disparate, even secretive, linked together only within family or wider kinship ties. There is a distinction to be made here between the more profitable operations based on accumulation of wealth outside the law, upon which MacGaffey places her expectation of a capitalist development, and the smaller-scale trades and services in the second economy. These are everywhere lacking in financial and other resources.[45]

Barratt Brown claimed that 'the trickle down effect from the wealth of a very few rich members of the elite... most of whom are involved in trade and not in production, cannot be any guarantee of capitalist development.'[46] For him

> the crucial question concerning the future of the second economy ... is not so much whether it can be translated into formal development or, in the words of the World Bank, become the 'seed bed of development', to be recognised and cultivated by government, but rather whether it can become a centre for strategic challenge to undemocratic government.[47]

One issue left hanging in this debate was the old question of whether an economic ruling class could be said to exist as a class, even if it had roots chiefly in the state, rather than in private industry. Barrat-Brown is surely wrong to argue that the state would continue to dominate production indefinitely: Mobutu's first twists and turns were signs of a deep historical transition beginning. Yet McGaffey is no more persuasive in portraying state enterprise as something antithetical to capitalism. The history of the Congo, and indeed of many of the other post-independence African states, would seem to have disproved this claim. A class can exist, and a capitalist class at that, taking advantage of the state's dominance of the economy. Put like this, the conflicts between Mobutu and the wealthier private businessmen take on new meaning as a factional struggle within the ranks of one propertied class: between stratergies of state and private hegemony. While in 1975 Mobutu could champion the state, through the pressure of structural adjustment he would soon re-emerge as the darling of privatisation. In this transition, he was hardly unusual.

One problem with too loose a use of qualifying terms such as 'nascent' or 'petty' to describe the bourgeoisie is that they tend to lump together quite distinct layers of people – including the poorest of informal traders, who had far less wealth absolutely even than most employed workers, and the leaders of the largest smuggling gangs, whose wealth was comparable to the innermost members of Mobutu's circle. The effect of economic crisis, from the mid-1970s onwards, was to swell the numbers of the country's poor. They scraped together a living, selling dried fish, handfuls of vegetables or cheap manufactured imports to survive. It would be absurd to regard the urban and rural poor, who had seen their living standards crumble, as somehow having benefited from the new opportunities in the informal economy. Instead, at the end of the 1980s, it was the urban and to a lesser extent the rural poor, together with students and employees of the state (faced with annual cuts in expenditure), who emerged as the principal social forces powering opposition to the regime.

Support abroad, opposition within

Constrained by declining copper exports, increased interest on debts, and pressure from the World Bank and the IMF, Mobutu manoeuvred desperately. For much of the period between 1980 and 1985, the regime agreed to measures of austerity. In 1983, for example, Mobutu persuaded the Paris Club (delegates of the main creditor nations) to ignore $1 billion of debt in return for a commitment to liberalise the economy. Subsequent visits by the minister for finance to the Paris Club to request rescheduling of the official portion of external debt (accruing to Western governments and Japan) became virtually an annual event, and rescheduling agreements were negotiated in each of the years from 1983 to 1986. The creditors did this partly in recognition of the regime's willingness to follow IMF advice. But this was not the major reason for their tolerance. Throughout the late 1970s and early 1980s, there were very strong pressures that facilitated Mobutu's good relations with the IMF, the World Bank and other creditors, above all the regime's support for US foreign policy.

The strain of austerity came to a head in 1986, when Mobutu limited debt-service repayments to 10 per cent of export receipts and raised public-sector wages by up to 150 per cent. This was a clear, albeit temporary, break with the IMF. By 1986, following five years of economic austerity, Zaïre had witnessed few gains. There was little real growth in the economy and no improvement in the balance of payments. Net outflows of foreign exchange exceeded inflows, and the proportion of export earnings devoted to servicing the external debt was more than 25 per cent. The break from orthodoxy was both short-lived and unpunished.

Mobutu was engaged in intensive diplomacy at this time with the Reagan administration, stressing his role in helping the Americans supply arms to UNITA in Angola, and allowing them to make use of the Kamina airbase near the Angolan border. As a long-standing ally of the United States, Zaïre was rewarded increased aid and, as Turner notes, 'pressure on the IMF to treat Zaïre leniently,'[48] prompting one senior IMF official, C. David Finch, to resign in protest. Once again, Mobutu had used Zaïre's strategic value to the USA to win political support and reluctant IMF backing for his corrupt and inefficient regime. In fact, American support continued right up to the end of the 1980s. In 1989 the Bush administration also put pressure on the IMF to accord Mobutu yet another agreement, resulting in further accords in June 1989.

Others also came to Mobutu's rescue. A major obstacle to an agreement with the IMF had been the growing arrears on previous IMF credits. At the end of May 1989, there was an unexpected announcement that the government had liquidated these arrears, reportedly by means of a short-term credit of $120 million from a Belgian commercial bank. This opened the way to the release in June of a second tranche of funding agreed earlier, in 1987. Accommodation with the IMF as the 'lender of last resort' encouraged further loans from other 'donors' and from the Paris Club, the World Bank and the European Community. This was at a time when Zaïre's economic disorganisation had contributed to an expanding debt amounting to $8.8 billion and to consumer price inflation running at well over 100 per cent, and aid from the IMF and Europe was officially conditional on internal reforms, which Mobutu was unwilling to accept. In the face of overwhelming evidence of human rights abuses, economic corruption and mismanagement, and effective bankruptcy, the international community continued to back the regime, financially and politically.

In December 1980 and January 1981, eighteen members of Mobutu's Council were arrested and charged with subversive activities. They had written a 52-page letter condemning the dictatorship and calling for sustained democratic reform. They were eventually released, but in 1982 the core of them, later referred to as 'The Thirteen', were re-arrested for forming an illegal opposition party, which came to be known as the Union pour la Démocratie et le Progrès Social (UDPS). They were sentenced to long prison terms. During 1982, there were more than 200 arrests of political opponents of the Mobutu regime. By the early 1980s students, who had been privileged recipients of state patronage in the 1960s and 1970s, were also suffering from the structural adjustment programmes that bled resources from the public sector. The universities were now regarded officially as bloated and mismanaged institutions. Student opposition to the regime, which had been relatively muted during the previous decade, now began to gather strength again, and many began to look to the new political formations and opposition groups that were emerging abroad.

In October 1982, a year after he had resigned as prime minister while overseas and publicly condemned the Mobutu regime, Nguza Karl-i-Bond spearheaded the formation of a coalition of opposition groups in exile called the Front Congolais pour le Rétablissement de la Démocratie (FCD). The FCD was formally established in January 1983; it included the UDPS, which was to remain the major opposition movement in Zaïre throughout much of the next decade. During 1983, 'The Thirteen' who had been detained in 1982 were released; but six were immediately re-arrested and sent into internal exile. In March 1983, the French section of Amnesty International published a report alleging that 'most of the political prisoners in Zaïre are held without charge or trial and are often tortured'. Soon after, Mobutu offered an amnesty to all political exiles who returned to Zaïre by 30 June. A number of exiles accepted the offer, but a substantial opposition remained active in Belgium.

The most important opposition party was the UDPS. Étienne Tshisekedi, its founder, had been an important political figure from independence onwards. After Mobutu's first effective *coup d'état* on 14 September 1960, he was named as a member of the Collège des Commissaires responsible for justice until February 1961. He was in government during the murder of Lumumba.[49] He took up several high-profile jobs, including Minister of the Interior in the government that was formed after Mobutu's coup in 1965, and was involved in drafting the 1967 constitution that nominally institutionalised a bipartisan state but was eventually used to justify the one-party state. Tshisekedi remained within the ruling party, although maintaining a degree of independence, until the formation of the UDPS.

The emergence of a more organised urban opposition and the new courage showed by former confidants of Mobutu was linked to wider social discontent. As Tshikala Biaya suggests, 'the economic and social crisis resulted in the deepening of popular discontent from 1976. Mobutu reacted with an illusionary democratisation of government institutions in 1977 followed by the reinforcement of the organs of repression of the one-party state.'[50] Braeckman notes that these rebels were far from being revolutionary; 'some of them ... had been members of the Collège des Commissaires that was put in place by Mobutu in 1960 after the fall of Lumumba.'[51] Their criticisms accorded with those that were now surfacing internationally in the Jimmy Carter administration in the United States and in the World Bank: they all criticised the poor management of the country and the waste of resources. When the UDPS was formed on 15 February 1982, it confronted full state repression, and it quickly became the principal political force of the opposition explicitly committed to the democratic struggle.

The path of the UDPS was hard indeed. Imprisoned and beaten, the founders of the party, and Tshisekedi in particular, demonstrated impressive political tenacity, which won them national respect. In the first few years after the formation of the UDPS Tshisekedi was arrested twelve times for his political activities.[52] In 1985, he was almost the only opposition leader to reject the 'accords de Gbadolite', which saw the reincorporation of other parties into the MPR. The other signatories of the 1980 open letter accepted the accords. Isolated, he was declared insane in 1988 and incarcerated in a psychiatric hospital until Mobutu's 'concessions' of April 1990.

During the 1980s, the illegal 'second party' became a magnet to anyone who opposed Mobutu. It was not, in its political programme or leadership, instinctively radical; and it was not made up of activists who necessarily regarded themselves as Lumumbists.[53] Braeckman says, 'Remember that the middle class were hurt by the austerity measures of the IMF imposed on Zaïre. Many thousands of civil servants and sacked teachers joined the ranks of the opposition.'[54] A more positive eyewitness was Muela Nkongolo, a student leader in Lubumbashi in the 1980s. He explains how the leader of the UDPS, Tshisekedi, 'incarnated the opposition to the regime. In the eyes of the great majority he was the man who attracted the interest of the people; intransigent, persevering and convinced in his struggle to dislodge the dictator.' Although Tshisekedi would emerge at the end of the 'transition' as anything but the incarnation of a determined opponent, at the time he was one of the principle symbols or guides that thousands sought to follow and emulate.[55] The opposition came to be symbolised in the intransigent resistance of Tshisekedi and the UDPS.

Despite the continuing dominance of Zaïrean politics by President Mobutu ('elected' for a third time in 1984, with 99.6 per cent of the vote) and continual harassment by the state security forces, the banned opposition movements, including the UDPS, were able to operate in Zaïre, albeit with difficulty, throughout the 1980s. Opposition to Mobutu's regime continued to manifest itself, often in violent form. In November 1984 and again in June 1985, Laurent Kabila was responsible for armed attacks on the town of Moba on the shores of Lake Tanganyika, in Shaba province.

Ministerial reshuffles in February, April and July 1985, and further changes to the structure of the MPR (separating party and government functions), reinforced Mobutu's position. The return from exile of Jean Nguza Karl-i-Bond in July 1985 and the lifting of restrictions on seven members of the banned UDPS, under the terms of another amnesty for political opponents, appeared to provide some evidence of the president's confidence in his position.

Against this impression of an easing of political restrictions, between October 1985 and January 1986, over 100 people, many of whom were supporters of the UDPS, were arrested in Kinshasa and eastern Kasai, in a clampdown on opposition movements. In February 1986, one of the detained leaders of the UDPS was released, but during demonstrations to welcome his release security forces killed at least one UDPS supporter.

In October 1986, Mobutu appointed a minister for citizens' rights, and announced the disbanding of the military state security agency. His political opponent Karl-i-Bond had been appointed ambassador to the USA in July 1986, a post that he held until March 1988. In June 1987, President Mobutu declared a general political amnesty. Several members of the UDPS took advantage of the amnesty. Regional and municipal elections were held in May and June 1987, but annulled because of alleged electoral malpractice. They were rescheduled for March 1988. September saw elections to the National Legislative Council. In October 1987, four other former UDPS leaders were admitted to the central committee of the MPR, and other former opponents of the government were appointed to senior posts in state-owned enterprises. This was the more congenial, 'softer' aspect of Mobutu's policy to draw the force of the opposition

There was another, more brutal side to his strategy. In January 1988 Tshisekedi, who had taken advantage of the amnesty to return from exile, was arrested along with several others associated with the organisation of a UDPS mass rally. Three people were killed when security forces broke up the rally, and there were 200 arrests. A crackdown on the opposition movements saw 600 people detained. Tshisekedi was tried for 'threatening state security', but the trial was suspended to allow him treatment for 'psychological disorder'. He was released in March 1988, but immediately detained again in April along with other UDPS supporters and put under house arrest. He withdrew from political activity and was eventually released from house arrest in September 1988 and allowed to return to Kinshasa. Elections were again postponed until March 1989, for 'budgetary reasons' and to 'ensure that they were conducted democratically'. There was mounting pressure on Mobutu to respond more effectively to the growing opposition.

The country saw rising opposition to Mobutu's regime during 1989 and 1990, with much activity coming from student groups, which clashed violently with the security forces. Munikengi and Bongo-Pasi Mako Sangol describe the collapse of student status at the University of Kinshasa: 'Until the 1990s, students believed that their university diplomas were equivalent to titles of nobility.... By the early 1990s ... degrees still constituted social capital and [a chance, but] if a job opportunity did miraculously present itself, they no longer ensured automatic recruitment.'[56] The political opposition was growing more active, and linking up with other social forces. In March 1989, Tshisekedi was again arrested for alleged involvement in the student disturbances that broke out in Kinshasa and Lubumbashi at the end of February, in which an estimated 37 people were killed. By 1990, the dictator was no longer able to hold back the growing oppostion forces pushing for profound change.

5

the failed 'transition'

On 23 September 1991, the 31st brigade of the Zaïrean Air Forces mutinied. Tired of miserable pay, high inflation and the slow progress of democratic transition, they led a riot across Kinshasa. Baptised the 'people's army', they marched into the city centre, encouraging the city to join in. Soon thousands of men, women and children from the city's poorest neighbourhoods were marching. Shops and warehouses were gutted. Locks were blown off cold-storage units and banks with machine-gun fire. The houses of wealthy businessmen and members of Mobutu's inner circle were targeted. The houses of expatriates were also attacked. The former headquarters of the Mouvement Populaire de la Révolution (MPR) was ransacked, with the rioters scribbling on the ruins of the building 'All's bad that end's bad.' René Devisch described a 'carnival-like ambience'.[1] Looted goods were passed from soldier to civilian.[2] The riot went on for days. For more than four years afterwards, the protest movement blossomed. Students were joined by the masses of the urban poor, workers, informal traders, the unemployed and the army. When Mobutu agreed to accept political changes in April 1990, he had no idea of the extent of the rebellion that he was about to unleash. The dictator looked as though he might be consumed by the popular revolt. Riots, general strikes, religious marches and political meetings punctuated the Congo's second and frustrated revolution.

The changes that were taking place were not exclusive to Zaïre. Reform was now sweeping across many parts of the continent, a second 'wind of change' comparable to the earlier mood of euphoria which had accompanied decolonisation. From 1989, protests broke out across sub-Saharan Africa. In 1991 alone, eighty-six major protests took place in thirty countries. By 1992 many governments were forced to introduce reforms; in 1993 fourteen countries held elections. In a four-year period, from the start of the protests in 1990, thirty-five regimes were swept away by street demonstrations, mass strikes and other forms of protest, and by elections that were often the first held for a generation.[3]

For more than ten years, many Africa states had been forced by the IMF and World Bank to implement 'reforms' and cuts in the public sector, including reductions in health and education budgets, as a condition for new loans. Zaïre experienced these pressures, forcing the government to reduce expenditure on health, education and research.[4] One student described the conditions of life at the University of Lubumbashi, one of the country's largest universities, in 1989:

> We, students and tomorrow's elite of Zaïre, the Youth of the Mouvement Populaire de la Révolution (JMPR), were compelled to go to the toilet in the bush, like animals. We went there every day, in the hot and rainy season. The night like the day ... even the 'largest library in central Africa' was not saved, and was used as a WC. The outside world must know the extent that Mobutu had humiliated us.[5]

Protests broke out across the continent. In Zaïre, Mobutu was forced to respond.

However significant the role of mismanagement and corruption, the deterioration in economic conditions as a result of policies recommended by the international financial institutions and implemented by the government in a context of global recession was ultimately to blame. Despite the country's great mineral riches, by 1988 the Congo was ranked the eighth poorest country in the world. The World Bank reported that it had a per capita income of $160 a year, while real incomes had fallen to just 10 per cent of their pre-independence level.

Between 1973 and 1985, the average income fell by 3.9 per cent a year. The agricultural picture was no better. By the late 1980s Zaïre had gone from being a net food exporter to paying out more than 20 per cent of its foreign exchange on food imports. Twenty-eight years after independence the country was saddled with a $7 billion foreign debt.[6] The road and transport infrastructure had almost completely disintegrated, cutting off agricultural producers from their buyers in the cities. As Zaïre approached the last decade of the millennium, people in the countryside retreated to subsistence existence and in the cities to an informal economy. The rapid decline in nutrition levels and health care was killing a third of children before the age of 5. Yet this was not the experience of everyone. Journalist Blaine Harden reported privilege in high places: 'Mobutu, his family, his European business partners, his CIA friends, and the eighty or so nimble-footed lickspittles who continue to play musical chairs.'[7] This 'exchange of places' that had animated Zaïrean politics since the 1970s now became one feature of the transition. Ever resilient, Mobutu managed to manipulate 'reforms', and to disorientate the leaders of the opposition, who were only too willing to bargain with the great dictator. One observer, Loka Ne Kongo, a minster of higher education in 1992–93, characterised the opposition leadership in the following terms: '[they] suffered failure after failure, in large part because of their own impotence; all of the paths that could have led to the removal of the dictator, by non-violence, had more or less been exhausted.'[8] These failures eventually destroyed the protest movement.

Economic collapse

One of the striking features of the economy in 1990 was the massive scale of the unofficial or informal economy that had now become for many people the principal source of income.[9] The background to the expansion of the informal economy was a profound crisis in the Zaïrean economy that stretched back to the 1970s. As we have seen, mining in Zaïre was crippled by the collapse of world prices and by state-led plunder and corruption. Mining production took a downward turn from 1988 onwards. The future of copper production was evident for all to see. The sharpest fall in production cut right through the period of transition. Between 1987 and 1995 production of copper fell from 499,421 tonnes to a mere 25,000 tonnes.[10] In February 1989, the prime minister, Kengo Wa Dondo, claimed that only Gécamines was still paying any money to the state treasury. The international copper market was increasingly competitive. Other producers, such as Chile, established open-cast, lower-cost mines. In the period 1990–93, production was further hampered by theft of equipment, technical problems and the political situation. Nor was Gécamines immune to corruption and misappropriation. During negotiations for an IMF loan in May–June 1989, it was revealed that $400 million in copper revenues had gone missing. This amounted to some 30 per cent of a year's earnings.[11]

Diamond extraction grew in copper's place. By 1995, this new mining sector accounted for approximately 47 per cent of export earnings. Much came from small-scale operations. After the legalisation of artisanal extraction in 1981, such 'production' expanded rapidly, and within seventeen years had become responsible for 70 per cent of all diamond exports. Even in 1990, copper production by Gécamines was still responsible for more than 50 per cent of national export earnings. Yet, as MacGaffey and Bazenguissa-Ganga have shown, 'By 1994, Gécamines, the copper mining company that had been Zaïre's principal exporter, was barely producing.'[12] The fall in copper production was devastating. Diamond production continued its seemingly relentless upward spiral, expanding further in the 1990s, with the opening up of new diamond beds in the north-east. In 1994 it became the main source of foreign exchange, a process that was inextricably linked to the expansion of the informal economy.[13] Although the artisanal diamond industry had officially replaced the mining of copper by the 1990s as the principal source of foreign exchange, three-quarters of diamonds mined were being smuggled out of the country.[14] Even so, the impact of this new mining sector on the overall economy was limited.

The collapse of Gécamines, however, had a profound effect on the economy of the Congo. Thousands of professionals, doctors, academics, engineers and skilled workers suddenly found themselves without work. Many who had spent years working directly or indirectly for the company in Katanga now migrated to South Africa. By 1992, Zaïreans made up approximately half of the migrant workers in South

Africa, largely because of the relative ease of securing South African visas. Many more travelled to South Africa illegally on the trucks that drove from Lubumbashi loaded with copper and cobalt. Once in South Africa, many Zaïreans became involved in the now ubiquitous circuits of informal trade. In the early 1990s, Congo specialist Colette Braeckman described how flights were 'daily from Zaïre to South Africa carrying diamonds, coffee, gold and cobalt, and have bought back fresh meat to be sold at very high prices in Kinshasa.'[15]

At the centre of all these developments was Gécamines. By the mid-1990s it was a shell of its former self, and faced a haemorrhaging of capital, collapsing infrastructure and corruption. In 1995–96, the country launched a programme of privatisation in certain parts of the mining sector. The decline of copper from the 1970s was symbolic also of the end of a particular economic regime: the collapse of state intervention in the economy with the onset of systematic privatisation – the phenomenon now known as globalisation. The measures introduced by the government in the early 1980s to legalise artisanal production of diamonds were the valedictory gestures of a state that was increasingly powerless to control the circuits of the informal economy. The rise of the diamond industry was not going to bring about an influx of 'foreign direct investment', as promised by the IMF; on the contrary, it was hand-dug in privately owned plots and frequently sold through criminal networks that made use of the pre-existing informal economy.[16] These were not the 'imperfections' of globalisation, as Erik Kennes describes them. The convergence of 'criminal' activity in areas outside the control of 'legal' international and national political actors is rather a defining feature of the new globalised world. Zaïre was one example at the frontier of these developments.[17] The promise of democratisation was thus undermined by economic developments that made the majority weak.[18]

The regime challenged from below

The last days of the 1980s saw further decline in the living standards of much of the population. Minor civil servants and public-sector employees were poorly paid, with an average civil servant earning 20,000 zaire a month (around $25) and a soldier only a third as much. In February 1990, the UDPS organised demonstrations in Kinshasa and three other towns to commemorate the twenty-ninth anniversary of the assassination of Patrice Lumumba. Unrest followed in April, when students staged protests in Kinshasa to demand larger study grants and the removal of Mobutu from power. Mobutu was forced to respond. In what was seen by many observers as an attempt to defuse the growing tension, Mobutu announced proposals for political reforms, including the recognition of opposition parties and the possibility of a transitional government prior to multi-party elections. Many commentators were enthusiastic, with Stephen Riley and Trevor Parfitt arguing that 'even the most uncompromising dictatorships, such as those of Mobutu in Zaïre and Banda in Malawi, are being forced to consider reforms that would previously have been inconceivable.'[19] In an unprecedented initiative, Mobutu decided to survey popular opinion as to a way forward. He invited traditional leaders, associations and individuals to make their views known. Yet, as Claude Ake observed, the process went rapidly out of Mobutu's control.[20] Demands were made for his resignation, and for fair elections.

The failure to announce expected reforms after a cabinet meeting early in April 1990 led to extensive student rioting in Kinshasa. This prompted Mobutu to take more decisive action. On 24 April, he declared Zaïre's Third Republic and indicated that a multi-party system, initially comprising only three parties, including the MPR, would be introduced within a year. During a televised address, Mobutu himself was seen crying. He stopped momentarily and said, 'Understand the emotions.' The long-banned UDPS would be legalised. At the same time, he announced his resignation as chairman of the ruling MPR. Professor Lunda Bululu replaced Kengo Wa Dondo as prime minister. In early May, a new 'transitional government' was formed. Mobutu announced that a commission would draft a new constitution by the end of April 1991 and that presidential elections would be held before December of that year, with legislative elections to follow. He also announced the imminent depoliticisation of the armed forces, the gendarmerie, the civil guard and the security services.[21]

These proposals led to further unrest. At the end of April, the security forces broke up a UDPS rally, reportedly killing two people, giving more strength to the opposition. In April 1990, Étienne Tshisekedi wa Muluma, who led the UDPS, was released from house arrest to the jubilation of his followers. Mobutu revised his plan for democratisation, meanwhile, announcing that the MPR would not, after all, be divided into two, but would compete with the UDPS and a third, unspecified, party for power. There was widespread criticism of this 'to-ing and 'fro-ing' and the attempt to implement so-called 'multi-Mobutism'. In an interview for Belgian television, Tshisekedi referred to Mobutu's 'close friend the Romanian dictator Nicolae Ceausescu', who had been executed months before during a popular uprising. Mobutu had indeed maintained close relations with the Romanian dictator, while Romania remained one of the regime's foreign allies. The close relationship extended to cooperation between the Romanian Communist Party and Zaïre's MPR. Images of the ignoble trial and execution of Ceausescu reached Zaïre, making a strong impression on Mobutu and his enemies. In Kinshasa popular humour contemplated a similar fate for 'Mobutu Sesesescu'.

Students at the University of Kinshasa were the first to initiate the protests. They demonstrated on 5 May, asserting that the reforms announced ten days previously were 'irrevocable'. The demonstration ended violently, after security forces attacked it. The students then issued an appeal for other universities and colleges across the country to rise up in solidarity, 'Do not cross your arms. Follow our example. The dictatorship is finished. We cannot go back. Take on the state. Demonstrate! March!'[22] The call was answered. Students at the University of Lubumbashi responded, demonstrating daily in the city and at the university from 9 May.

On 11 May, the student uprising in Katanga was bought to a violent end. The president deployed a 'squadron of death'. Dozens of students who had led the demonstrations were killed. Without wider protests the students could be isolated. There was strong condemnation of the massacre from humanitarian organisations, and the Belgian government announced the suspension of bilateral aid. After denying the reports, Mobutu authorised a parliamentary inquiry, as a result of which the provincial governor was arrested. Despite a news blackout, it emerged that the massacre had sparked serious clashes between students and government forces in other towns, including Kisangani, Bukavu and Mbanza-Ngungu. The massacre was in many ways pivotal to the early stages of the 'transition'. Though many of the witnesses were students, a number of observers confirm the scale of the killings.[23]

International changes and internal struggle

The students had demonstrated Mobutu's unpopularity. The Lubumbashi massacre marked a turning point in Zaïrean politics. Crucially,
it prompted many of Mobutu's external guarantors to distance themselves. Mobutu, like other dictators supported by the Western powers
during the Cold War as a bulwark against Communism, was now
seen as dispensable. The new international discourse resonated with
the rhetoric of 'good governance' and 'democratisation', as the waves
of protest that broke out across the world, including Africa, and
that had brought down the Communist regimes of Eastern Europe,
redefined international politics. The end of the Cold War signalled
by the collapse of the Eastern bloc and the Soviet Union in 1989–93
profoundly affected Zaïre's relations with the West. By November
1990, the US Congress had withdrawn military and economic aid
from Zaïre, basing their decision as much on corruption as on the
abuse of human rights, but referring directly to the events at the
University in Lubumbashi. The regime's strategic importance was
beginning to wane. Mobutu was forced to hire Washington public
relations firms to lobby on his behalf.

Belgium and France had funded the regime, traded military equipment for influence and spoken on behalf of Mobutu in international
discussions. The French government of Valéry Giscard d'Estaing
had in 1975 negotiated prospecting rights for copper in return for
a moratorium on debts. Belgium was, of course, even more heavily
implicated in the regime's survival.[24] Yet both governments now
came to oppose Mobutu, with the executive in the US moving more
slowly in the same direction.[25]

The massacre in Lubumbashi also prompted a wave of civil unrest
during the second part of the year by civil servants, teachers, medical
staff and nurses, as well as workers and the urban poor. State employees went on strike from July to October, demanding increases of up
to 500 per cent for the lowest paid; the protests ended when 100 per
cent pay rises were promised. Hyperinflation reduced the value of even
quite dramatic pay increases and prices of staple foods rose by the day.
These conditions provoked anger and outrage as well as desperation.
The strikes were not only economic; they reflected the moral economy
of the Zaïrean crowd. One of the favourite slogans was 'Mobutu,
thief!' There were food riots in Kinshasa and Lubumbashi.

In June 1990, as part of the process of reform, the legislature passed amendments to the constitution. These ended presidential control over foreign policy. The establishment of independent trade unions was also authorized. In early October, Mobutu announced that a full multi-party political system would be established, and in November the enabling legislation was adopted. It was now possible to register a political party. The announcement of a timetable for the restoration of multi-party politics led to the proliferation of parties. Prominent among these was the Union des Fédéralistes et Républicians Indépendants (UFERI), led by Jean Nguza Karl-i-Bond, another previously intimate member of Mobutu's inner circle, prime minister under Mobutu and minister of foreign affairs.[26] In 1977, Mobutu had broken with him, accusing him of having supported the regime's opponents in Katanga. In 1978 Mobutu pardoned him and months later he became minister of foreign affairs. By 1981 he had fallen out again with his boss. From then on, he led a campaign from exile against the regime. In 1982 he wrote *Mobutu ou l'incarnation du mal Zaïrois,* describing the torture and hardships he had experienced when he was imprisoned. For a brief period he was the figurehead of the opposition to the regime abroad.

When, following an amnesty in 1985, Karl-i-Bond had returned to Zaïre and to Mobutu's fold, he alienated those who had previously supported his anti-Mobutu crusade. His return to Mobutu's circle was well rewarded when in 1986 he became the ambassador to Washington. Karl-i-Bond continued to astonish former sympathisers when in 1989 he met with President Botha in South Africa and subsequently argued that the Organisation of African Unity should revisit the strategy of isolating apartheid South Africa. Following Mobutu's speech in April 1990, however, he now proclaimed his desire to stand against Mobutu in elections scheduled for 1991.

In November 1990 an anti-government rally in Kinshasa, organized by the UDPS, was violently repressed; in the following months, anti-government demonstrations took place in Kinshasa and Matadi. The USA announced in the same month that it was to terminate all military and economic aid to Zaïre. By the end of 1990, Zaïre's external debt had exceeded $10 billion, with outstanding long-term debt of $8.85 billion. There now seemed little chance that these sums would ever be repaid.[27]

By July 1991, the new coalition of opposition groups established by the UDPS, including the Parti Democrate Social Chrétien (PDSC), the Union des Federalistes et Républicains Indépendants (UFERI) and the Union Sacrée de l'Opposition Radicale (USOR), had expanded to include 130 political parties. As in so many countries undergoing cautious reforms, the floodgates proved hard to shut. In February 1991, hundreds of thousands of workers, civil servants and public service employees held a three-day general strike to demand the resignation of the government. Later in the same month, 20,000 people attended an anti-government rally in Kinshasa, organized by the UDPS. In March 1991, a new and enlarged 'transitional' government included representatives of several minor parties. Yet co-option proved only partially successful. In April 1991, Mobutu announced that a National Conference would convene at the end of the month to draft a new constitution, but the main opposition parties refused to participate unless Mobutu relinquished power. Widespread anti-government demonstrations followed, and in mid-April forty-two people were reported killed and many injured when security forces opened fire on demonstrators in the town of Mbujimayi in central Zaïre. Mubutu then suspended the national conference.

In July, in an attempt to incorporate the more powerful elements of the opposition, Mobutu offered the post of prime minister to Étienne Tshisekedi. Tshisekedi refused. But the real story is more complex. In fact, secret negotiations had been going on between the two men for some time. When national television and radio declared in July that Mobutu planned to appoint Tshisekedi as prime minster, thousands of his supporter were shocked, but they were not passive. If the state media was reporting events correctly then this was in contradiction to everything that Tshisekedi had said for years. Nzongola-Ntalaja explains what happened next: 'The politicised masses of Kinshasa ... immediately after the announcement ... descended on Tshisekedi's residence in Limete to force him to back down. For the masses, their "saviour" should not cohabit with the "devil".' Although he bowed to popular pressure, Tshisekedi made it clear that he had been prepared to accept the post. While attempting to protect his democratic credentials, he damaged his reputation among his followers, perhaps irreparably.[28]

The opposition had previously been opposed to a national conference but now changed tactics. The National Conference was reconvened on 31 July 1991 to discuss constitutional and administrative matters. Some 2,850 delegates participated, including 900 from the opposition. By late September, the Conference, from which representatives of the powerful Catholic Church had withdrawn, had become overshadowed by a worsening crisis beyond its confines. Violent clashes had taken place between opposition supporters and the security forces. While the demonstrations represented growing popular frustration with the national conference, it was also the case that massive inflation had aggravated hardship, so that political concerns were fuelled by the flames of anger and despair at the worsening of economic conditions.[29]

In late September troops led thousands of people onto the streets of the capital, sacking the warehouse at Njili International Airport and taking over the city. But it was not simply a question of mindless 'looting', as much of the literature maintains; clashes instead expressed anger at the slow pace of democratic change. From 1989, when the inflation rate was 56 per cent, it had climbed by 1990 to 233 per cent, and an extraordinary 3,642 per cent by 1991. Another force driving people onto the streets was the collapse of pyramid investment schemes. One such scheme was run by Bindo Bolembo and promised effortless rewards in return for a small initial investment. When Bolembo declared himself bankrupt in May 1991, large numbers were made destitute.[30]

By late September protests had developed into widespread looting. The people of Zaïre were not prepared to wait until the political crisis had resolved itself. The military were heavily involved, but the civilian population also participated on a significant scale. Large numbers were reported killed or injured. French and Belgian troops were sent, ostensibly to evacuate foreigners, and suppressed the rioting. There was much suspicion in Kinshasa regarding Mobutu's role in the rioting. It was noted that the troops did not attempt to execute a coup, even though those at the airport could easily have taken over Njili's control tower and the troops at Kokolo were less than 500 metres away from the main state radio and television transmitters. Mobutu, for his part, did not attempt to intervene to quell the disturbances until he called for a curfew on

26 September. To many, all this indicated that Mobutu was playing his old games.[31]

Tshisekedi was appointed First State Commissioner by Mobutu on 2 October 1991, albeit with MPR loyalists in defence, foreign affairs and planning. The last was no sinecure as the economy was in free fall. Inflation had increased in the wake of the riots to some 10,000 per cent and salaried workers in the public sector were openly contemptuous of pay offers in the region of 100–200 per cent. Nor did the government have much prospect of raising money, since Gécamines had ceased payments to the state treasury in early 1991. Just twelve days later, Mobutu dismissed Tshisekedi, installing 'a government of crisis'.[32] It soon became clear that the new government lacked the confidence of the Zaïrean people. A demonstration of 15,000 people in Kinshasa accompanied Tshisekedi's departure. There were also demonstrations in Lubumbashi. Tshisekedi now called on the army to revolt. According to Ludo Martens, the opposition

> should have called for a popular insurrection against Mobutu and the MPR, against the Presidential Guard and the total overturning of the dictatorship … Such an appeal even if it had not been immediately understood, would have made a start. The impotence of the National Conference would have proved the accuracy of such an approach.[33]

While Martens might exaggerate the potential that existed to turn these disparate riots into a nascent 'revolutionary struggle', it is clear that the opposition always regarded mass mobilisations only as a means to an end, as a method to pressurise the dictatorship to share power. The factions continued to evolve through autumn and winter 1991–92.

The march of hope

During January and February 1992, tension increased again as different sections of the opposition made their views felt. In January, troops briefly seized the national radio station, urging the removal of the government and the resumption of the National Conference. Violence intensified as USOR and Christian churches attempted to mobilise demonstrations against the suspension of the Conference and moves against certain sections of the opposition. A number of strikes broke out in February as civil servants and public-sector workers generally demanded better wages and living conditions and the resumption of the national conference. One eyewitness, Nzongola-Ntalaja, writes, 'As in the past, ordinary people stepped in to change the situation.'[34]

On 16 February, the Catholic Church organised a 'march of Christians' in the capital. Reports describe a 'million people' in the street. In 110 parishes there were committees that mobilised for the protests, where radical voices could be heard.[35] The demonstration took place demanding the restitution of the national conference. The army was reinforced by elements from Angola's rebel army UNITA. Even today the memory of that mobilisation of a million people, a demonstration on a scale never before seen in the country's history, remains with those who were present. However, the significance of the march and its bloody repression requires careful analysis. The organisation of the demonstration, marking perhaps the high point in the popular struggles during the 'transition', gives us an opportunity to examine the dynamics and organisation of the protests. An important collection of eyewitness accounts from the demonstration, *Marche d'éspoir*, published two years after the protests, provides a unique insight into the nature of the popular struggles that were sweeping Zaïre.

The Catholic Church occupied a highly ambiguous space. Church and parish groups were at the centre of the protests. They organised neighbourhoods, and brought together local militants from a range of political parties. These groups discussed how to stage local protests, and coordinated their action with other parish groups. Radical intellectuals, invited to address parishioners by local groups, would advocate the overthrown of the regime, the same groups called lobbies and protests. They instructed newcomers on how to protect themselves against tear gas, by carrying water and scarves to cover the face, and how to behave when under attack by the police.[36]

Church groups began to organise themselves in the 1980s. In 1989 *Le Groupe Amos* in Kinshasa was formed. Its founder was a priest, José Mpundu, who together with the group was going to play a decisive role in the politicisation of thousands of Kinois. One of their first meetings, in August 1989, was described by the group:

'The Parish of the Resurrection, of which José Mpundu is the curé, organised a mini-session of two mornings, Tuesday and Wednesday 22–23 August, dedicated to non-violent evangelism. Thirty people participated.' In December, the same group, still without an official structure and organisation, arranged further meetings, this time more political but still connected to the question of the Church and political change:

> During a second meeting, held on 4 December 1989 at Saint Joseph, we had the opportunity to listen to the experiences of the struggle for justice in other parts of the world. Sister Pétronille shared with us what she had seen and lived through in Latin America, and the lessons that she had drawn from this experience.... We gained another image of the church: a church which is united with humanity in its struggle ... and one that raises the consciousness of the people. Sister Marie told us about her experiences in Cameroon and the Commission for Justice and Peace, which was composed of laymen and the religious community. This commission denounced injustices and sought to construct a new, just order in society. The two accounts stimulated us and made us question.

On 8 January 1990, members of the group held their inaugural meeting. They set up a coordination committee. They agreed to elect members responsible for spreading information across the region. Similar church-based organisations were taking place in many areas, often drawing their specific motivation from 'the wind of perestroika which shook Eastern Europe'.[37] Gustave Lobunda, a young priest from Kisangani, went on hunger strike in 1992 in protest at the closure of the conference. He describes how his actions were animated by a combination of ideas, including the example of the life of Jesus as well as other sources:

> My hunger strike was also inspired by Gandhi and Martin Luther King, for whom I have always had a profound admiration. I have seen the film of Gandhi at least nine times ... I had time to get to know him in the book *This night, freedom*. And learnt about Martin Luther King through articles and by his biography written by Stephen B. Oates. Gandhi and King have helped me to understand the value of human freedom, which is a gift from God ... this consciousness of freedom is so strong that I cannot continue to live under a dictatorship.

The demonstration on 16 February was organised by the Comité Laic de Co-ordination, made up of members of the National Conference and local militants who had the ability to mobilise their neighbourhoods. José Mpundu from *Le Groupe Amos* attended a meeting of the Comité in February, when the idea of a demonstration was first discussed. Parish activists spread the word in their neighbourhoods:

> People of God, this call comes to you from men and women from all levels of society: researchers, teachers, employees, trade unionists, members of NGOs, businessmen, students.... Everyone who is called by their Christian faith and animated by a profound sense of justice ... who sees every day the suffering endured by the people of God.
>
> People of Zaïre, this country is a gift from God. It belongs to us all.
>
> The political, economic and moral crisis that has shaken Zaïre for three decades demands a response.
>
> Our country, potentially one of the richest on the planet, finds itself paradoxically, among the poorest of the world ...
>
> In this situation the regime has thrust us into intolerance, ethnic hatred and state terror.
>
> Today, like yesterday, Zaïreans are constantly victims of a society expressly organised for one aim, to assure the profits and the power of a minority, through denying the rights of the overwhelming majority ...
>
> Respond to the last man to the call that our churches have made: the Conférence Nationale Souveraine is irreversible.
>
> The *Marche d'éspoir* will take place on 16 February 1992. This day of the Lord, the people of the capital will descend into all of the streets of Kinshasa to demand the return of the Conférence Nationale Souveraine.
>
> Rise up Christians, free the people of God.[38]

The Comité were lay delegates in the National Conference. The only way they could call an effective demonstration was by appeal to the parishes where local militants were organised. They called for people to support the *Marche d'éspoir* on the authority of the churches of Zaïre. The National Conference needed the 'people of God' to force the regime to back down, but they could not organise these people independently of the structures that had been set up over the last two years. José Mpundu describes the day of the demonstration: 'On the day itself we only had one Mass at 6 a.m.... I must confess that I was a little scared. Scared that there wouldn't be a large enough turnout. But when I saw the number of people at the assembly point my fear disappeared.' He estimated that some 200 members of his parish and neighbouring parishes had gathered. Shortly after they had set off they encountered an obstacle, 'the army blocking the route... we sat down together according to our plans... the soldier then tried to disperse us, by kicking us... We left the avenue and reassembled in a parallel street where there were no soldiers.'[39]

Demonstrators marched holding crosses, Bibles and images of the Virgin Mary. The crowds sang hymns and prayed. One eyewitness explains what happened when the police started to fire:

> we were scared by the firing and were advanced slowly towards the soldiers. Priest, nuns ... Christians were on their knees praying and brandishing branches, Bibles ... as the soldiers fired into the air. The crowd were singing. Thirty minutes later the soldiers had exhausted their ammunition and we continued singing religious songs, and we had crossed the first military barrier.[40]

Another eyewitness writes,

> despite the fact I couldn't walk easily as a result of being hit by the police, a young man saw I was having problems walking and supported me though the march. There were lots of similar gestures. Even our behaviour towards the soldiers – we tried to make them understand the reasons for the march.

Expecting the police to use tear gas,

> We had prepared ourselves: we had handkerchiefs and water, and we put these wet cloths against our eyes. The soldiers had nothing. I saw how mothers and fathers were helping the soldiers, wetting their faces. I saw how soldiers who had nothing to drink were given water. The soldiers were asking themselves 'What has happened to us?' They could not understand.... It was in this way that the march took place. Nothing was stolen from small shops among the route, nothing! Everyone had the door of their house open to help the demonstrators: people were leaving and entering and nothing was stolen. Really this was a march of non-violence.[41]

Other marches took place in Kitwit, Kananga, Mbujimayi, Kisangani, Goma and Bukavu. The level of state repression varied. In Goma and Bukuva there was little disruption. In Kisangani and Mbujimayi, however, the demonstrations were brutally suppressed. Lobunda, who was on hunger strike at the time, describes the Catholics of Kisangani responding to the call from Kinshasa, but only at a day's notice. Young Christian militants from Mangobo, a poor neighbourhood in the city, wrote and signed a leaflet, and distributed it to all the parishes in Kisangani on Saturday morning. 'The result: despite the small amount of preparation all the parishes of the city marched, even if the numbers from parish to parish varied.'[42]

Activists convened meetings to discuss the march, exchange stories, establish who had been killed and plan for the next mobilisation. A female activist describes how

> two days later we had a meeting with the *Comité* to evaluate the march from across the city. We attempted to get those who had been imprisoned out, and organised visits to the hospital.... And as the government had not ceded to our demand to reopen the National Conference, we wanted to organise a further march the following Sunday.[43]

Anyone who has been involved in a demonstration will be familiar with such 'evaluation', and the planning for the next action.

Some commentators question the motives of demonstrators. De Villers and Tshonda write of the 'imaginary world' of the Christian marchers. They observe that 'people chanted psalms and demonstrated with Bible in hand. They were motivated by the hope of a new Christian reign.... This Catholic crowd had the deliberation, calm and peacefulness of ... a procession. Its strength was belief rather than politics.'[44] It is wrong to oppose belief and politics in this context. The aim of the demonstrators was not a 'new Christian reign', but much more practically the reopening of the National Conference. The demonstration was motivated by the ideas of non-violence inspired by a range of political movements. In 1992, Catholic churches were synonymous with protest, encouraging communities to become involved in the changes sweeping the country. There was a widespread belief in the involvement of the church in liberation. Inevitably the movements were contradictory and the tactics questionable, but people were drawing on their own experiences in which religion played a real part.[45] Nzongola-Ntalaja understands the importance of the demonstration for the National Conference:

In Kinshasa, the paramilitary forces opened fire, killing over thirty people. To the martyrs of independence who fell on Sunday 4 January 1959 were now added the 'martyrs of democracy'. Their sacrifice would compel the dictator to give in to internal and external pressure by reopening the conference.[46]

The National Conference reopened on 6 April.

Resuming the 'transition'

The demonstration and its suppression revealed again the cowardice of the opposition. On 17 February, hours after the massacre, the old-time oppositionist Antoine Gizenga intervened in the political debate. Gizenga had been dismissed as vice-prime minster along with Lumumba in 1960 but became one of the principal rebel leaders in the 1960s. In 1992 he addressed a letter to the dictator:

> Just returned from twenty six years of exile, I take the liberty to write in my capacity as one of the fathers of independence, and former vice-Prime Minster under Lumumba ... [On] the 24 April 1990 you proved your courage in announcing ... the end of the one party state ... it only remains for you to announce ... your resignation ... at the same time I will take up again the affairs of state and guarantee you and your family security.

Gizenga seemed to assume his own return to power on a mandate he had received as far back as June 1960. Gizenga took the precaution of copying the letter to the US, French and Belgian ambassadors.[47] Not surprisingly, there was little response.

It still seemed that Mobutu would hang on to power, at any cost. As Parfitt and Riley remarked in mid-1992, 'at the time of writing... Mobutu continues to cling on to power in his bankrupt and chaotic country, clearly oblivious to the suffering of his people.'[48] This, despite the fact that a leaked cable in which the Belgian ambassador was reported to have said 'it is impossible to continue with Mobutu'.[49] In the southern town of Mbujimayi, which had a history of opposition to the Mobutu regime dating back to the 1970s, later in the year, security forces opened fire on UDPS supporters protesting at earlier arrests and at looting by soldiers; over forty people were reportedly killed. On another occasion, dozens were injured and a woman reportedly killed when security forces took violent action to prevent a UDPS demonstration in Kinshasa. The deterioration inside the country brought negotiations with the IMF to a halt. Zaïre in return suspended payments on much of its international debt. Increasingly isolated, Mobutu agreed to reconvene the National Conference. This in turn declared itself 'sovereign', with power to take binding legislative and executive decisions. Mobutu was permitted to remain head of state. The main role of the conference was to define a new constitution, to be put to a referendum, and to establish a timetable for legislative and presidential elections. The political situation within the country was now extremely confused. At a formal level, it was not clear who ruled. Mobutu was still president and maintained control of the army and security forces and much of the state apparatus; but there was no effective government, the National Conference remained in session, and the various opposition movements were in disarray.[50]

In June it was announced that a transitional government would take office in July. In August 1992, Tshisekedi was elected interim prime minster. According to Nzongola-Ntalaja,

> From 5 pm on Friday to 5 am on Saturday 15 August, the Congolese people witnessed the freest and most transparent elections ever held in the country's history. Nearly 71 per cent of the delegates voted for Tshisekedi, as against 27 per cent for Kanza [the pro-Mobutu candidate]. Few in Kinshasa slept that night. At dawn, hungry and exhausted honourable members of the CNS were met by enthusiastic crowds of citizens, who thanked them for having respected the popular will in choosing Tshisekedi. Like Kinshasa, the whole country erupted in joyful dance from dawn to sunset on 15 August 1992.[51]

In September, the National Conference adopted a multi-party constitution, only for Mobutu to reject it. In October, attacks on opposition leaders became increasingly frequent in Kinshasa, while Katanga was alight with what seemed like ethnic violence. In November, the National Conference adopted a draft constitution providing for the establishment of a Federal Republic of the Congo, the introduction of a bicameral legislature and the election of a non-executive president with largely ceremonial functions. Executive power was to be held by the prime minster.

Mobutu opposed the draft document. He attempted, unsuccessfully, early in December to declare the Tshisekedi government dissolved. The national conference dissolved itself and was succeeded by a 453-member Haut Conseil de la République (HCR) with the Catholic Archbishop of Kisangani, Laurent Monsengwo Pasinya, as its president. As the supreme interim executive and legislative authority, the HCR was empowered to amend and adopt the new constitution and to organise legislative and presidential elections. In response to this effective seizure of his powers, Mobutu ordered the suspension of the HCR and the government, and decreed that civil servants should replace ministers in the supervision of government ministries, a demand they refused. Attempts by the Presidential Guard to obstruct the convening of the HCR ended following the organisation of a public demonstration in Kinshasa in protest at the actions of the armed forces. The HCR received the support of Belgium, France and the USA in its declaration of Tshisekedi as head of the government. By the end of the year there was a major political crisis in Zaïre.[52]

Had the National Conference been successful? Most commentators see it as a failure: Mobutu was still in power and there was no timetable or framework for a genuine transition. Yet George Nzongola-Ntalaja responds that there were in fact many positive dimensions to the work of the National Conference. He notes the work of the twenty-three commissions that produced well-documented reports exploring the country's history and present-day social problems. The proceedings of the Conference were broadcast live to the nation. In addition, 'ordinary people had the opportunity to influence the proceedings through letters, public forums and ... this had the effect of strengthening Congolese civil society.'[53] Political debate was, indeed, widespread. An organisation of young people calling themselves 'politicians of the street'

> organised in each municipality in Kinshasa and with a central organ for the city as a whole ... debated current issues, took decisions and sought ways of implementing them. Major actions involved publicly denouncing opposition politicians who were seen as faltering in their resolve for democratic change, and organising rallies and demonstrations in support of the various demands of the democracy movement.

Although many of these groups were vocal supporters of Tshisekedi, they were not controlled by the UDPS and were free to criticise whomever they wanted.[54] These street politicians drew on traditions of free discussion. For years people would refer to 'street radio' (*radio trottoir*), to describe such informal channels for communicating news.[55]

In January 1993, the HCR issued its first ultimatum to Mobutu, stating that he would be removed unless he reversed his decision to dissolve the transitional government, and then declaring him guilty of high treason. Throughout January there were demonstrations and strikes by those opposed to Mobutu. Troops opened fire on more than one occasion and several demonstrators were reported killed. A brief general strike and campaign of civil disobedience, organised by the USOR, resulted in five fatalities and numerous injuries. The Presidential Guard was called out to quell riots by disaffected troops, protesting an attempt by the president to pay them with discredited banknotes, indicating serious divisions within the army and security forces. Order was eventually restored, but only after the deaths of some 65 people, including the French ambassador, and the intervention of French and Belgian troops. Once again, these stepped back from deposing Mobutu.[56]

In December 1993, at a rally in Kolwezi attended by Nguza Karl-i-Bond, the governor of Shaba province declared the autonomy of the province, reverting once again to the name of Katanga. In January 1994, Mobutu issued an ultimatum to all parties, in an attempt to end the impasse, which led to an agreement to form a government of 'national reconciliation'. Encouraged by an unexpected level of support, Mobutu dissolved the HCR and the National Assembly and dismissed the government of his own appointed prime minister, Faustin Birindwa. He announced a contest between Tshisekedi and Mulumba Lukoji for the premiership, to be decided by a legislature to be known as the Haut Conseil de la République–Parlement de Transition (HCR–PT). This new parliament was convened on 23 January under the presidency of Archbishop Monsengwo. The HCR–PT immediately rejected Mobutu's procedure for the selection of a new prime minister and eventually, in June 1994, ratified the candidature of seven opposition representatives (but not Tshisekedi) for the premiership. Elections for the position of prime minister were held, and Leon Kengo wa Dondo was elected, with IMF support – an election bitterly criticised by the UDPS. During June, Tshisekedi was briefly detained, only to be released following violent protests by his supporters in Kinshasa. By July, a new government was in position, with a couple of portfolios held open for candidates from the UDPS. But elements of the radical opposition, including the UDPS, called for demonstrations in Kinshasa. In February 1994, the World Bank closed its office in Kinshasa, and in June Zaïre was suspended from the IMF. Since the civil disturbances of 1991, private investment had virtually ceased. The collapse of the mining industry meant that the foundation of the wealth that had sustained the political process was gone. Mining output fell in 1994. A modest improvement followed in 1995 and 1996, with output rising to 34,000 tonnes and 42,425 tonnes of copper respectively. But the second half of the decade saw decline in the sector, with production stuck at around 30,000 tonnes. In 1997, production declined to 4,041 tons. Gécamines now barely existed.[57]

Frustrated transition

There were several moments between 1990 and 1994 when Mobutu could have been removed. But the main opposition party the UDPS and its leader Tshisekedi failed to provide any lead. De Villers and Tshonda argue that 'Tshisekedi's preoccupation with the premiership caused the opposition to lose sight of its real political objectives. Moreover, his confusing strategy disorientated supporters. "Moses the saviour" was transformed into the "Sphinx" without a clear political stance.'[58] Other observers express similar frustration. Martens despairs of the failure of the opposition to move when the optimism of the masses was at its height, in the aftermath of Mobutu's speech on 24 April 1990. The effect of delay was eventually to demobilise and discourage the popular movement, the only force that could have swept Mobutu aside.[59]

By 1994 politics had reverted to a pattern of ethnic mobilisations, akin to the crisis of the 1960s. Even the leaders of the major proponent of the 'transition', the UDPS, looked increasingly to their ethnic fiefdoms among the Luba of Kasai. By 1996 the opposition had exhausted the energy that had animated the first years of the transition. The experience of Nzongola-Ntalaja in 1996 is revealing. He had arrived back in Zaïre in April 1992 after years out of the country. His commitment to the transition was determined and principled. Yet at the end of 1996 he resigned from his official role on the Commission Nationale des Elections (CNE). He writes that eleven months away from the long expected birth of the Third Republic it was evident that the ... institutions responsible for managing the transition would fail... one by one, each of the major components of the institutional framework of the transition ... failed to help effect the democratic transition in the Congo ... the democracy movement had lost confidence.

This was the result, Nzongola-Ntalaja tells us, of the 'undermining of the democratisation process by the political class'.[60]

The opposition had not only failed to dislodge the dictator, it seemed increasingly unwilling to do so. As late as November 1996, Tshisekedi repeated the mantra, 'The transition recognises two political families; that of President Mobutu and that of the opposition, of which I am the leader. These two leaders today, that is two families, will be welded together.'[61] The struggle shifted to resistance in the countryside, particularly in the east of the country. But it also meant a return to a more 'basic' form of politics, involving local and ethnic allegiances rather than political ideology or class politics.

How, then, can we understand the processes that were taking place during the transition? In many ways they bore remarkable similarity to the democratic struggles that had swept away old regimes elsewhere across the continent. Even where these 'transitions' had been successful, the new governments were easily persuaded to adopt an agenda of neoliberal privatisation. Those implementing these reforms were, in effect, members of a limited political class, who, in the words of two critics, have done 'little more than ... stabilise property-threatening situations by a momentary re-circulation of elites'.[62] Martens argues that what was needed was a different type of organisation, one that would have helped lead and coordinate the popular, grassroots forces that were emerging between 1990 and 1994. There was certainly an embryonic alternative in the parish committees, neighbourhood groups and among trade union militants that could have found more consistent leadership with an organisation that refused to compromise with the regime. Martens outlines what such an organisation might have been able to do, 'A revolutionary organisation could have expressed these needs: the immediate departure of Mobutu and all the dinosaurs; prosecution of all Mobutists responsible for repression and corruption; [and] the end to the foreign domination of the Congo.'[63] Yet, while we can share some of Martens's frustration at the lack of a serious organisational force, there were many factors militating against the creation of such a phenomenon. One of the central weaknesses was lack of an organised left with a tradition of coherent, rank-and-file politics. The generation of political leaders, militants, trade-union activists and intellectuals, precisely those who could have formed such an organisation, were left without their ideological moorings following the disintegration of the Soviet Union and its bloc. One of the reasons why the opposition kept deferring to the National Conference was that it needed something to fill this ideological vacuum. There was no other serious political force in the cities and towns that offered a viable alternative.

Some commentators argue that the entire political class, government and opposition alike, were simply determined to secure the largest share of state power and patronage for themselves and aimed not at a change of regime but just of government. Such a view suggests that the people of Zaïre, who expressed their fundamental opposition to Mobutu's regime throughout the period of 'transition', were effectively betrayed by the political leadership of all parties. Such was the opinion of Loka Ne Kongo, who wrote in 1995:

> Hunger, illness, ever-present death, social and physical insecurity have devastated our population. The successive failure of the opposition, the betrayals of our leaders, discourage and disarm… the population is hungry. One fears that tomorrow they will not listen anymore to the opposition.

Six months after writing these words, Ne Kongo called for a programme of 'civil disobedience' that would include a popular refusal to cooperate with the state on any level. He was clear that 'this supposes that the opposition organises itself to install across the country a parallel administration, police force and justice system.'[64]

Martens's retrospective call for a revolutionary struggle to emerge from social forces left unnamed is consistent with the familiar narrative of Congolese resistance that sees only lost opportunities and conjectures as to what might have been. Nzongola-Ntalaja marvels at the popular expressions of protest and democracy during the transition, but sees their role as reinforcing the work of the National Conference. Nowhere was there a politics that put the organisation of the street, community and workplace at the centre of change.

In April 1996, after many months of struggle between the president and the opposition, it was announced that presidential and legislative elections would be held in May 1997. But during May and June 1996, the scale of fighting in eastern Zaïre increased. In August, President Mobutu went abroad 'for several months' for medical attention. During September and October, a major rebellion took shape in the east, and at the end of October a state of emergency was declared in north Kivu. The rebels extended their control over the region, however, and captured Goma. The fighting and breakdown of law and order in the east generated a massive humanitarian crisis which, combined with the rebellion, threatened the integrity of the Zaïrean state. In this context, the struggle between the president and the legal opposition became secondary. It was in eastern Zaïre, engulfed in violence, that new forces emerged.

6

speculators and thieves

In May 1997 the forces of Laurent Kabila took Kinshasa and announced the liberation of what now was called the Democratic
Republic of Congo. Two and a half years later, on Christmas Day
1999, the Bishop of Bukavu, Emmanuel Kataliko, described Kabila's
revolt in the most critical terms. His honesty proved fatal.

Foreign powers, with the collaboration of some of our Congolese
brothers, organise wars with the resources of our country. These
resources, which should be used for our development, for the
education of our children, to cure our illnesses, in short so that
we can have a more decent human life, serve only to kill us. What
is more, our country and our people have become the object of
exploitation. All that has value is pillaged and taken to foreign
countries or simply destroyed. Our taxes, which should be invested
in the community, are embezzled.... All this money, which comes
from our labour and saved in the bank, is directly taken by a small
elite that come from we don't know where.... This exploitation is
supported by a regime of terror, which ... means that some of our
compatriots don't hesitate to sell their brothers for a dollar or ten
or twenty.[1]

Several days later Kataliko was deported to Butembo in the north
of Kivu by the rebel authority controlling the region. Fleeing to seek
asylum in Rome, he survived only a few days before dying of a heart

attack. His description of the Congo was brave and honest. The war that unfolded after 1998 testifies also to its considerable truth. Laurent-Désiré Kabila's rise was mercurial. The aftermath of the Rwandan genocide was a crucial element. So, too, was the nature of American and French influence in the region. Yet the conflict cannot be understood simply as the product of Western intrigue. To write in that way is to ignore the central role of African nations, or more accurately, African regimes, intervening for their own reasons. Analysis therefore requires a rejection of that part of Kataliko's analysis which portrayed the war simply as a manipulation by Western powers. We argue rather that the war brought together a shifting constellation of forces: African nations, Western powers and a complicated array of multinational companies, artisanal commerce and criminal networks.[2] Such analysis does not in any way exonerate the West. The Congo exists not in an obscure and primitive place in 'darkest Africa' but in a modern and globalised world. Commentators frequently emphasise the 'complexity' of the war; but under the constantly shifting alliances of the various rebel groups there was one overriding and predictable motivation: control of the country's vast mineral wealth.

Understanding the east

The war of the late 1990s was the product of a crisis in the Eastern Congo and in post-genocide Rwanda. The eastern provinces, north and south Kivu, were the engines of war. These provinces had long been the source of conflict, including groups that had for generations been regarded by the Congolese state as 'non-indigenous minorities'. The war that spread across the Congo, but was waged most violently in the east, had it origins thus in what Mahmood Mamdani has described as 'the internal crisis of citizenship, and the external impact of a traumatised post-genocide Rwanda.'[3] The fault lines in the east, writes Mamdani, date back to the colonial imposition of ethnic-based customary law. Mamdani's is the most sophisticated explanation of the crisis: it is rooted in an understanding of an earlier period. Authority in the Belgian Congo, Mamdani argues, came in three tiers. The first was the chief of the locality, the second the *chef de groupement*, and the last the Mwami of the *collectivité*. Each 'indigenous' ethnic group was allocated its own Native Authority. Although non-indigenous 'refugees' or 'immigrants' were allowed a 'first-level' chief, their chiefs remained answerable to the governing authority of other established Native Authorities. Membership of a Native Authority was absolutely crucial, as rights to land use were granted only on this basis. Being 'non-indigenous' meant that a people had no 'customary' access to land.[4]

This division between indigenous and non-indigenous peoples was, even on its own terms, artificial. Both in Rwanda and in the eastern Congo, Belgian rule served to displace entire peoples. Belgian companies were awarded millions of hectares of land, and they in turn allocated land to white settlers.[5] The effect was to pull in black labour. As we have already seen, mines in Katanga had imported workers from as far afield as modern-day Zambia, Rwanda and Uganda. Repeatedly, the Belgian authorities in Kivu also encouraged immigration from Rwanda. Mamdani gives examples:

> A decree of 19 July 1926 authorised Rwandans to seek employment freely outside their country and legally opened the country to labor recruiters from outside. Three types of recruiters came to Rwanda: Union Minière, the mining conglomerate; CNKI, the plantation oligopoly; and individual settlers.[6]

The process of independence in the Congo in 1960, Mamdani argues, saw only a partial deracialisation of the colonial state. In the cities, white power passed into black hands. In the countryside, much less changed. There were no whites to displace. The system of Native Authorities remained entirely unreformed. Ethnic divisions were entrenched. Not every ethnic group had its own Native Authority. Relative 'newcomers' were put at a disadvantage. These divisions crippled the three principal Kinyarwanda-speaking immigrants in the two Kivus, the Banyamulenge, the Banyamasisi and the Banyaruchuru. By not having their own Native Authority they were ethnic outsiders, continuously scrambling for recognition by the state.

The immediate post-independence period witnessed a 'Kinyarwanda War' in north Kivu. It was a rebellion of various minorities against local authorities. At the Roundtable Conference that preceded independence, the issue of citizenship for the Kinyarwanda minorities was discussed but decision postponed. Over the three decades this minority was alienated from local authorities, and sought representation instead with higher or national authorities. These developments upset the local 'indigenous' majority, which worried that national representation would be wielded to acquire power locally. The issue of citizenship buffeted the independent state repeatedly; it forced Mobutu in 1972 to introduce a Citizenship Decree that extended citizenship to those who had come to Kivu from Rwanda in 1959. Another 1981 Citizenship Law reversed this rule, insisting that only those who could establish a connection to the area dating back as far back as 1885 could hold citizenship.

The period of transition in the 1990s again cast rights for the Kinyarwanda minorities into flux. Instability was further aggravated by attacks made by the Rwandan Patriotic Front, a rebel army made up mostly of Tutsi immigrants from Uganda, into Rwanda. These conflicts inspired considerable numbers of young Tutsis living in Kivu to cross into Uganda and join the RPF. Mobutu responded by instigating a Mission d'Identification de Zairois au Kivu in October 1990 to establish who among the Kinyarwanda-speakers were from the Congo. This decision in turn further thickened the flow of Tutsis moving into Uganda. By the time the Sovereign National Conference met in 1991, the fault lines in Kivu had hardened. Elsewhere in the country, the holding of this new convention represented a moment of hope, as we have seen.[7] In Kivu, the constitution threatened a 'non-indigenous' minority growing through the influx of refugees.[8]

Refugees, the UN and Rwanda

The genocide in Rwanda in 1994 further destabilised the region. The war in Rwanda was part of a global process that has undermined the state. While ethnic divisions played a central role in Rwanda's recent history, having been constructed and maintained by Belgian colonialism, it was more recent forces that gave rise to the genocide, including privatisation, structural adjustment and the relative decline of primary production in the world economy.[9] The destructive spiral of events in Rwanda was triggered by the collapse of the International Coffee Agreement in 1989, instigated by the US administration acting in the interests of US coffee importers. The period also saw an equally devastating collapse in tin prices that left the country with almost no resources. As a consequence the Rwandan economy plunged into crisis. In its midst, the regime turned to ethnic militias. Between 1990 and 1994, the Rwandan president Juvenal Habyarimana used funds that had been made available to him through structural adjustment loans to purchase $83 million of arms. The most infamous symbol of the killings, the machetes, were manufactured by British firms.[10]

In June 1994, the killings in Rwanda subsided, following the victory of the rebel RPF. As this army spread across the country, another catastrophe began to unfold. Millions of mainly Hutu refugees fled across borders to neighbouring states. In the camps that spread across eastern and southern Zaïre, Hutu extremists and the Interahamwe, the organisers of the genocide in Rwanda, regrouped their dispersed forces in the hope of a renewed attack on the Rwandan regime. Camps sprang up in Goma and Mulunga in north Kivu, and Bukavu and Uvira in south Kivu. They contained an estimated 30,000 fighters from Habyarimana's vanquished army.[11] The presence of up to a million Hutu refugees across central Africa created impossible tensions. As the attention of the world shifted to the squalid camps in Zaïre, the remnants of the scattered Hutu army began to regroup. Using north Kivu as their power base, they took control of both the camps in the region and the surrounding areas. Gangs of Hutu militiamen treated the local Banyamulenge viciously.

The camps that became centres of training and organisation for the ex-soldiers of the Forces Armées Rwandaises (FAR) and the Interahamwe were funded and supported by the United Nations High Commission for Refugees (UNHCR). This was a grave mistake that assisted in the export of the Rwandan genocide to the already fraught Kivu provinces. In the United Nations' defence, Kurt Mills insists that the UNHCR operated courageously in difficult circumstances, let down as they were by the international community's refusal to send in a military presence: 'given the extreme circumstances, it is hard to rate the UNHCR as a failure in eastern Zaïre.'[12] But the UNHCR cannot be exonerated so easily. The funds that were made available to the camps perpetuated the cycle of killings. The UNHCR even collaborated with Mobutu to mobilise a Zaïrean Camp Security Contingent (ZCSC), theoretically to undermine the grip of the armed militias in the camps. These troops, finally deployed in February 1995 were nicknamed 'Ogata's troops', after the High Commissioner for Refugees, Sadako Ogata. Even Mills is forced to admit the results were disastrous, with the forces providing 'resources to the militants and rather than wanting to undermine their position, worked to strengthen it.'[13] One Bukavu-based priest described other consequences of the United Nations' work:

> One talks of all the humanitarian organisations that came here but one doesn't talk ...[about] how they ruined our economy through its dollarisation, its rents going up, local Zairois finding life increasingly beyond their reach. In short, amazing resources were deployed in an unreachable endeavour, one which did not correspond to our vision.[14]

When the refugee camps were broken up by the RPF in late 1996, perhaps as many as 300,000 Hutu refugees fled deep into the Congo.[15] While some of these refugees had participated in the genocide, many had not. Thousands died in the long march across the region, and in the impromptu camps set up to shelter them.[16]

The export of the Rwandan crisis also saw an outflow of Congolese Tutsis to Rwanda, as they faced increasing attacks by Hutu extremists. These Tutsis were then armed by the RPF. In the Congo, meanwhile, the Interahamwe, often in league with Mobutu's army, terrorised the region. The consequences were catastrophic. Local Native Authorities responded, logically, by creating their own militias. It was out of these processes that the first rebellion against Mobutu launched in the east emerged. The AFDL, Alliance des Forces Démocratiques pour la Libération du Congo, was formed, initially as an umbrella organisation for Congolese Tutsis. Rwanda was the principal force behind these developments. This 'front' group became the organisation that fought the first rebellion. Its success necessitated rescuing a rebel leader, Laurent Kabila, from relative oblivion. One commentator on the war, Timothy Longman, describes how Rwanda believed that the rebellion was 'its own initiative and the ouster of Mobutu as something that the Congolese alone could not have accomplished'.[17] Rwanda was not the only sponsor of the AFDL. The Alliance was a motley group of disparate interests, reflecting the recent history of the region.

We agree with Mamdani when he writes that 'the crisis in eastern Congo cannot be understood unless we see it as the result of a confluence of ... social crisis of post-genocide Rwanda and the citizen-ship crisis in the entire region.'[18] However, Mamdani's analysis falls down when he discusses the reasons Rwanda became involved in the Congo. He sees the genocide turning Rwanda into a diasporic state, where the state was driven by an 'overwhelming sense of moral responsibility for the very survival of all remaining Tutsi, globally'.[19] The motivation for their involvement in the war, Mamdani argues, was to protect the community of Tutsis living in the Congo. As we will see below, the real reasons were far more sordid and tied to a desire, supported in part by the United States, to continue the plunder of the country.

The first rebellion

The new Rwandan government before long started to supply arms to groups of Banyamulenge fighters. Some had trained with the Rwandan RPF and many even fought with them. Soon these arms were supplemented by Rwandan soldiers. After the coup in Burundi in 1996, Major Pierre Buyoya also became embroiled in the conflict, adding his own troops. By September, the Banyamulenge 'offensive' had reached such a level that the deputy governor of South Kivu ordered the immediate expulsion of all Banyamulenge, or they would be hunted down as rebels.[20] The rebels had already metamorphosed into a formidable army. Their offensive was widened to take on the Zaïrean state. The situation demonstrates how easily ethnic identity was manipulated at a time of war. During the Rwandan intervention, the term 'Banyamulenge' was transformed into a politicised category, defining all Tutsis in eastern Congo. Myths grew up to explain that, that although many had not lived in the Congo previously, there had been a 'Banyamulenge' migration from Rwanda to the Congo centuries earlier: now they were simply coming home.

Rwandan troops gave impetus to the anti-Mobutu rebels in the east. There was no shortage of Zaïreans motivated by a desire to rid the country of Mobutu's allies.[21] Mobutu could no longer rely even on France or Belgium to intervene. The wave of democratic struggles that had gripped Africa since the late 1980s had not left Zaïre untouched. On the contrary, the country had been rocked by demonstrations and revolts that forced the regime to convene a sovereign national assembly. Zaïre, like many other new 'democracies' or polities 'in transition' in Africa, could not be treated in the same way as before, not only for geopolitical reasons but also because of the changes brought about by the struggles of the African people.[22]

If the old colonial powers were no longer willing to intervene, one power, America, was. Indeed, its strategy towards the Rwandan intervention shaped the processes that were to unfold in the Congo for years. The RPF-led Rwanda was not peripheral to their plans but central to the new alliance that the Clinton government sought to carve out in the region. The plan expressed clearly by the White House at the time was to use the Rwandan army as an instrument of American interests. One American analyst explained how Rwanda could be as important to the USA in Africa as Israel has been in the Middle East.[23] By September 1996, the United Nations arms embargo on Rwanda was lifted, as a result of American pressure. Even before the invasion in 1996, a large number of US intelligence operatives converged on Zaïre. Wayne Madsen describes US embassy staff in Rwanda travelling to eastern Zaïre to initiate intelligence work with members of the AFDL. Madsen explains that US strategy in the region rested on two connected policies: military aid and trade. US Special Operations Command (SOC) and the Defense Intelligence Agency (DIA) carried out these programmes. As the rebels advanced on Kinshasa in 1996 and 1997, a US embassy official with the rebels in Goma expressed American thinking at the time: 'What I am here to do is to acknowledge them as a very significant military and political power on the scene, and, of course, to represent American interests'.[24]

American troops and spies poured into Rwanda. At the end of 1996 the deputy assistant secretary of defence for African Affairs, Vincent Kern, justified American military assistance on the grounds that the RPF were being trained under a programme called Enhanced International Military Education and Training (E-IMET). Frequently America used private military training firms and logistics, which had the advantage of being immune from the Freedom of Information Act. The increasing use of 'private military contractors', a contemporary euphemism for mercenaries, was a prominent feature of American involvement. By late 1996 *Le Monde* cited French intelligence sources that indicated that as many as sixty American mercenary advisers participated in the RPF massacre of thousands of Hutus around Goma.[25]

In a testimony before the Congressional Subcommittee on International Operations and Human Rights Committee on International Relations (May 2001), Madsen went further. He argued that the AFDL-CZ advanced effortlessly on Kinshasa because of American military assistance. The technical assistance provided by America was accompanied by US Special Forces who followed the AFDL advance. Again the French press confirms these arguments. *Valeurs Actuelles* reported that a French DC-8 Sarigue electronic intelligence aircraft flew over eastern Zaïre shortly after the notorious Oso river massacres. The aircraft reported US military involvement in the region.[26] Supporters of the American government were unapologetic. Élizabeth Rubin argued in *Harper's Magazine* that

> when an African political crisis does erupt into international attention, as in Zaïre (now the Democratic Republic of the Congo, DRC) and Rwanda this past fall, it is treated by the powers-that-be in the UN Security Council as a purely humanitarian crisis, often with disastrous results. Although the idea of killing to end killing confounds the genteel sensibility, the fact remains that wars need to be won, one way or another.[27]

Within a few months of the arms embargo being lifted in 1996 it was announced that a new group of countries, including Eritrea, Ethiopia and Uganda, were to receive millions of dollars in military aid from the US government. This alliance displayed an American nervousness about Sudan and an anxiety not to make the kind of intervention that had led to the catastrophe in Somalia in 1993. It was much easier for Clinton to use Rwandan forces than it was to risk US casualties.

The motives of Rwandan politicians may initially have been to limit the military threat posed by refugee camps and rebel movements and to establish a buffer zone in eastern Zaïre. But once they saw that there was no reaction from Mobutu's army, their ambitions rose, as did their allies' hopes. The AFDL, led by Laurent Kabila, seemed to sweep all before it as it advanced on Mobutu's seat of power in Kinshasa. Kabila's movement, backed by Ugandan and Rwanda, had marched more than 2,000 kilometres across the country. However, there was what might seem a bizarre twist to Kabila's route to power.

Although he could be seen on international television networks throughout 1996–97 lambasting imperialist powers, his Alliance was a travelling trade fair. While Mobutu might have had only token legality as president in 1996, mining companies wasted no time to meet with the rebel leader. De Beers and American Mineral Fields signed contracts with Kabila that were worth an estimated $3 billion a year. Days before Kabila's victory, *The Times* reported that:

> Mining multinationals have signed billion-dollar deals for mineral rights with Laurent Kabila, Zaïre's rebel leader, to get ahead in what is being billed as the 'second scramble' for Africa. Executives with the companies said that they are happy to do business with rebels, who control all of Zaïre's mineral resources other than its off-shore oilfields, because they do not ask for bribes ... The unusual alliance [brings together] big business and revolutionaries, many of whom were Chinese-trained Maoists and Marxists in their youth.

While the American government played an active role in the crisis, we should not exaggerate the significance of the American businesses that actively courted the new regime. Smaller companies hoped to sell on concessions granted by Kabila to larger companies, who were not directly involved at this stage. The risks were enormous and the chance was low of turning concessions into profitable mines. Frequently the noise from these speculators drowned out reality. Kennes describes the main effects:

> For speculative purpose, rhetoric often prevails over reality.... In Africa, the pressure of globalisation in the mining sector contributed to the final breakdown of the formerly existing model of integration of mining interest into the nation state structure. This model was one of a long term engagement of major companies with the government of the country where a de facto monopoly was granted to the company.[28]

By the 1990s, the state was unable to provide guarantees to foreign companies. The state's collapse had come about as a result of the pressures of global restructuring that broke down national capital across the world. While Mobutu continued to make promises to foreign capital, he was quite unable to honour them. Laurent Kabila was dragged, probably willingly, into the new reality.

Kennes is correct when he asserts that American Mineral Fields' interests were mainly speculative. By 1998, the boom was largely over, and the ambitious projects of mineral extraction had come to nothing. American Mineral Fields may have been listed on the Vancouver and Toronto stock exchanges, but it lacked sufficient capital to develop mines on its own. The logic of its own situation required it to over-advertise its role. Braeckman writes, 'what counts for the "juniors" is to play an "avant garde" role, [to] find the deposits in high risk zones where more important companies would not dare to go and then secure a contract that can be developed by more experienced companies.' The money that was given to Kabila's Alliance was made available under these conditions, and the 'juniors' expected their speculation to be followed by the involvement of more 'senior', bigger capital.[29]

American interests

Long historical processes of change were at work. By 1990, the United States was willing to revise its thinking towards the continent. Mobutu had already started to lose some of his importance. Throughout the decade, American firms had begun to desert the country, so that by the mid-1990s there were few companies planning any new investment. The largest American investor in Zaïre in 1995 was Chevron International, but revenue from oil production was insignificant compared to the wealth garnered by the same trade in Nigeria and Angola.[30] Many countries were suffering from the reorientation of US interests. Africa's net share of world production and world trade fell in the wake of divestment. Zaïre was hardly alone.

There was a degree of confusion in the United States, which was reflected in a 1995 US Department of Defense document claiming that the United States had 'very little traditional strategic interest in Africa'.[31] Yet, as we have seen, the USA was involved in providing extensive military support to the Rwandan military from 1995. Literally hundreds of Rwandan soldiers and officers were enrolled in American training programmes in 1995 and 1996.[32] The American administration was clear in supporting Rwanda in the east of the Congo.[33] Over 1996 the USA stepped up its military assistance to Rwanda as the government helped establish the AFDL and prepared for the assault on Mobutu.[34] Behind the involvement was a shifting set of regional interests. A central element was the importance of 'containing' Sudan. The regime was targeted for its support of Islamic militancy, and a new set of regional allies, a 'new African bloc', was sought to undermine the government in Khartoum. These regional powers included Eritrea, Ethiopia and Uganda. In late 1995, for example, President Clinton allowed several million dollars military assistance to this 'new bloc', the largest amount of military aid to these states since the end of the cold war.[35] Support for Rwanda was consistent with these strategic priorities.

The strength and survival of the RPF was regarded as central to the stability of Uganda. Equally the rebellion against Mobutu was consistent with Uganda's interests as it promised to dismantle rebel groups amassed against the country in Zaïre. Both Uganda and Ethiopia were also regarded as models of successful implementation of IMF programmes, and could be held up as representative of 'good governance': paradigm cases of the so-called 'African renaissance'.[36] In candid language, assistant secretary of state for African affairs to George Bush senior Herman Cohen stated: 'our last connection with [Mobutu] was mainly to use [Zaïre's] airfields to help the anti-Communist rebels in Angola, but that ended in 1991 ... [Zaïre] has not been providing much to the United States in recent years.'[37] In the early 1990s the USA withdrew support for Angola's largest rebel movement UNITA. A failure by UNITA to achieve military hegemony coincided with the discovery of oil reserves in the early 1990s. The American government swapped sides soon after. The Angolan regime's subsequent conversion from Marxism to the free market was seen in Washington as conformation of the regime's good will.[38] Angola, too, was hostile to Mobutu, precisely because of his previous role in backing the UNITA rebels.[39]

Uganda also benefited from the shifting interests of American power in the region. In the 1990s the country was regarded as a useful ally on the border with Sudan. In 2001 Uganda received $81 million in 'development assistance and food aid' from the USA; in 2003 the total amounted to approximately $70 million. The Bush government awarded Uganda in 2002 favoured trading status under the African Growth and Opportunity Act (AGOA). The Department of State's annual *Country Reports on Human Rights Practices* for

2002 withdrew criticism of Ugandan soldiers in the DRC, perhaps as a reflection of the country's deepening alliance with the USA.[40] Influenced by alliances with Uganda, Ethiopia, Eritrea and Rwanda, the US administration was prepared to let Mobutu, its ally of thirty years, fall to a rebel army headed by the former Maoist Laurent Kabila and supported by an Angolan regime that it had formerly seen as the very embodiment of the Communist threat.[41]

Kabila

Who was Kabila? Initially he was one of the young Lumumbist cadres disaffected after the debacle of 1960–61. His name first comes up as the secretary general of social affairs of the Comité National de Libération (CNL), an organisation created in 1963 in Brazzaville by exiled rebels. In the various splits that ravaged that organisation, Kabila allied himself to the left and to Gaston Soumaliot, who in 1964 had become the military leader of a so-called 'provisional government' helping to lead the rebellion in north Katanga. Kabila was vice-president of the CNL, with responsibility for foreign affairs. After the capture of Albertville he escaped to Burundi. The best source on Laurent Kabila in the early days is Che Guevara, who met him in Kivu in 1965. Guevara was in direct contact with Kabila during his abortive period in the Congo and notes that he was 'always on missions to Dar-es-Salaam or Nairobi' and there was even a rumoured, although uncorroborated, visit to China. Kabila was, according to Guevara, always promising to come to the camp, and when he finally arrived months later, with cases of whisky, he managed to rally the Congolese troops, who chanted his name 'Kabila ya, Kabila eh', but quickly left again for Tanzania to resume his disputes with other rebels. In a letter to Fidel Castro after he had left the Congo, Guevara made his opinion clear: 'I know enough of Kabila to have no illusions about him.'[42] Kabila later travelled extensively through the Eastern bloc.[43]

Laurent Kabila went on to form the Parti de la Révolution Populaire (PRP) in 1967 and, accompanied by a small group of sixteen men armed with three revolvers, he crossed Lake Tanganyika to establish a 'liberated zone' in the territory of Fizi-Baraka. Kabila's forces were able to hold a larger area until the 1980s. The 'red zone' was tightly controlled by the structures of the PRP, with elaborate political organisations that included youth groups and a revolutionary women's organisation. The economy was entirely collectivised, with no salaries or money, but cheques and a bank account for members of the collective. According to Justin M'Molelwa, 'We produced ourselves everything that we needed… we were very organised, in cells, in zones, in communes. In our base at Hewa Bora we had created schools, health centres and administrative structures that bought us all together.'[44] The young historian Cosma Wilungula, who was given unparalleled access, is more critical.[45] Wilungula observed that the inspiration for the zone was a Maoist socialism with a decidedly contradictory character. The zone survived through trade in gold and ivory with Zaïrean troops and functionaries living across the border in the 'white zone', and although officially no one was allowed to grow rich from this trade, by the early 1980s the benefits had accrued almost exclusively to Kabila and his loyalists. A cult of personality built up around Kabila, celebrated as 'the light' and 'the creator'.

By 1984 three-quarters of the zone had fallen into the hands of Mobutu's state.[46] The liberalisation of the production and extraction of gold, found in abundance in the region, made 'desertions' more likely, as Kabila's supporters sought to profit during the mid-1980s from the 'micro-exploitation' of gold extraction. The wider liberalisation of the Zaïrean economy contributed to the collapse of Kabila's liberated zone. By 1987, Kabila was already out of the picture, leaving a rump of eighty rebels sandwiched between Lake Tanganyika and the Zaïrean army. Kabila's next movements are hard to trace as he moved between the south of Sudan and profited from trade in ivory and gold. Kabila was critical of the transition of the 1990s, arguing that it would merely prolong the life of Mobutu's regime. He wrote an open letter in 1992, offering his services to 'his fellow Congolese'. In the letter, no mention was made of the revolutionary struggle and his demands went no further than those being raised across the country by other parties.[47] As late as the mid-1990s, Kabila still had no army, no leadership and no intention of resuming any sort of struggle. He was nothing. Then he became something. The Rwandan alliance was key.

Kabila in power

In May 1997 Kabila's force, the AFDL, triumphantly took Kinshasa. This 'liberation' was hailed as the chance to free the people of Zaïre from thirty-five years of Western-backed dictatorship. Although in the first months, thousands regarded Kabila as a real alternative to the Mobutu regime, many became sceptical of his Alliance. In power the new government sought to balance popular demands and foreign interests. The country was awash with multinational deals and joint ventures in the first six months of 1997. Foreign companies promised to advance the capital necessary to ensure success. Consolidated Eurocan Ventures, from the international firm Lundin, proposed the exploitation of copper and cobalt from Tenke Fungurume in Katanga, a reserve with the highest-quality copper in the world. The Canadian company Barrick Gold Corporation, the second largest company involved in gold extraction after Anglo-American, was interested in the deposits of gold in Kilo Moto. Another Canadian company, Banro Resources, acquired Sominki (Société minière du Kivu), whose deposits were rich in gold and colombo-tantalite (coltan). As for American Mineral Fields, its representatives signed three agreements totalling nearly a billion dollars for the extraction of copper and cobalt in Kolwezi, cobalt in Kipushi, and the construction of a fac- tory for the treatment of zinc in Kipushi. 'In Kisangani, Braeckman writes, 'AMF already had acquired an office to buy diamonds, and in Lubumbashi, the company demonstrated their generosity to the rebels, who benefited by an "advance" of 50 million dollars ... to finance the war still being fought and to secure a date for trans- actions in the future.'[48] Despite the hopes of the foreign companies, the mines were incapable of resuming production to the quality or at the rates anticipated. Mobutu's decline had ravaged all industry. The production of copper and cobalt, which had reached 500,000 and 17,000 tonnes respectively at the end of the 1980s, stood at just 37,000 and 3,800 tonnes by 1997.[49]

Kabila sought initially to maintain a populist nationalism, and among other gestures he printed Lumumba's effigy on the new banknotes. Yet his plans for expanded production did not meet with the approval of the World Bank and the IMF, whose pressure he continued to resist during 1998. It became clear to the govern- ment that the same foreign companies that had previously financed

Kabila's war now desired for Rwanda and Uganda to install another leader, more open to their interests.[50] Under considerable pressure, Kabila's regime took on an increasingly high-handed character. The government promised democratic multi-party elections within two years, while at the same time jailing the former dissidents upon which any rival parties would be based. Kabila's army, which had been supported by the Banyamulenge, now turned against them. The regime failed to grant them the indigenous status that they had long desired. Kabila fell back on his 'clansmen' from Katanga. Guillaume Ngefa, president of the Congolese African Association for Human Rights (ASADHO), explained the process: 'As he [Kabila] has descended into corruption and nepotism, he has left himself with only the tribal card to play.'[51]

Kabila was faced with a choice: face down his detractors or turn against his former backers. He opted for the latter. In an extraordinary reversal he turned against the Rwandan troops. The consequences of this decision were apocalyptic. In order to fight the Rwandans, the government was forced to make alliances with Hutu militias in the east and look for other sources of support. Negotiations with Silver Shadow, an Israeli private company, to provide a special protection unit for Kabila himself were only terminated when the Israeli government intervened to stop the deal.[52]

On 27 July 1998 Kabila made the decision to expel his closest allies, the Rwandan army. This led inevitably to a second war. The members of Kabila's previous Alliance, including Rwanda, Uganda and the Congolese Banyamulenge, now supported a new invasion by an anti-Kabila militia, the Congolese Rally for Democracy (RCD). Some outside commentators have seen in Kabila's manoeuvring the germ of some better politics. Ludo Martens, for example, puts a romantic gloss on the response to this threat:

> In the Congo in the past you rarely saw an army encircle a city without the people panicking and shutting themselves up in their houses. But in three weeks Kabila had realised a veritable miracle. With their bare hands in all the neighbourhoods, in all the streets the youth have raised themselves to attack and kill the rebel intruders.[53]

Behind Martens's 'popular resistance' was a far nastier reality. On the eve of Laurent Kabila's 'miraculous' uprising, the leader addressed the population: 'Everyone must be ready to confront the enemy. In each village people must arm themselves, even with traditional arms, bows and arrows. The aim is to erase the enemy, otherwise we will become slaves to these little Tutsis.'[54] Massacres of civilians quickly followed.

Intervention and the second war: the case of Zimbabwe

Kabila drew on pragmatic associations, against the new alliance of Rwanda and Uganda. He reinforced his positive relationship with the ruling party in Angola, the Movimento Popular de Libertaçaõ de Angola (MPLA). He also cooperated with the MPLA in an intervention in the Republic of Congo in mid-October 1997, an action that resulted in the overthrow of the democratically elected government of Pascal Lissouba and the return to power of the former 'Marxist' ruler, General Denis Sassou-Nguessou. Lissouba had defeated Sassou-Nguessou in a presidential election in August 1992. Kabila's support for Sassou-Nguesso's 'Cobra' militia forces was by way of thanks for the MPLA's support for Kabila in his struggle against Mobutu.

Angola, Zimbabwe and Namibia supplied the troops that protected Kabila's government. We can use the case of Zimbabwe to illustrate some of the problems faced by this new alliance. The country's president Robert Mugabe was eager to prove his credentials as a leader of the regional organisation SADC. Mugabe had loaned Kabila several million dollars for his previous war; this direct intervention was also intended to ensure that all debts would be repaid. Days before the final push on Kinshasa, Zimbabwe Defence Industries (ZDI) sealed a $53 million deal for the supply of food, uniforms and weaponry to Kabila's army.[55] Mugabe's support for the government of the DRC has been rewarded by the gift of vast areas of land. Generals were granted contracts on mines and in logging companies. One company, run by leading members of Zimbabwe's ruling party ZANU–PF, was granted what *Global Witness* calls 'the world's largest logging concession'. It gained rights to exploit 33 million hectares of forests, an area ten times the size of Switzerland.[56]

Regional networks engaged in diamond smuggling and trade with military officials from ZANU–PF but, at the same time, the informality of these networks mitigated against a large-scale exploitation of resources by the Zimbabwean army. A later United Nations report on resource exploitation in the conflict found little evidence of significant increases in trade between Zimbabwe and the Congo. As during the previous war, when Rwanda and Uganda had backed Kabila, allies were attracted by the promise of huge profits, only to discover later that the productive infrastructure was missing. Gains turned out to be modest. The Zimbabwean state had to cajole an unwilling private sector to back its war.[57] Other factors contributed to the decision to intervene. Mugabe's party, ZANU–PF, had introduced an Economic and Structural Adjustment Programme in 1991 that had a devastating effect on the country's economy. The decline in the Zimbabwe economy, evident the year after the implementation of the ESAP, was signalled by a huge 11 per cent fall in per capita GDP.[58] The liberalisation of the economy led to an increase in inflation and decline in exports, generating an increase in interest in the possibilities of closer relations with the DRC. John Mangudya of ZimTrade in 2000 expressed the harsh conditions in the country following adjustment and the various motivations for war among private and state capitalists:

> Within Zimbabwe the small and medium guys were being squeezed out. Thus they are being forced to look outwards. Big (private) Zimbabwe companies, in contrast, think that the margins are low, that there is too much risk. Big (state-owned) companies like the Agriculture and Rural Development Authority (ARDA) are game because of political motivations.[59]

In place of Zimbabwean businesses it was members of the Zimbabwean Defence Force who made use of their monopoly of networks in the DRC to set up commercial outfits. As the war spread, so did these networks and the possibilities for the Zimbabwean military. Their strategic position in the regions under their command, concentrated on trunk roads, airports and border crossings, ensured that they could maximise their influence on informal and local trading networks. De facto tariffs on Congolese diamond exporters enabled the army to recoup some of its costs.

Lubumbashi was a commercial centre for Zimbabwean soldiers and Congolese middlemen. Long-standing expatriates in the DRC, often of Greek, Belgian, Indian, Lebanese or Pakistani origin, imported food and consumer goods. Behind them in turn were business interests in diamond, gold and currency trading. These 'middlemen' guaranteed access into otherwise unreachable parts of the DRC. They had access to entrepreneurs in Kinshasa, Mbuji Mayi, and with local and national officials. The exploitation of commercial interests by Zimbabwe was not only limited to small-scale entrepreneurs riding on the back of the military. Some large-scale interests were involved. The most notorious were invariably those connected to the ZANU–PF regime. The transport millionaire Billy Ractenbach, with a record of supporting Mugabe's government, became the chief executive of the DRC mining group Gécamines. He secured a near-monopoly for his company Ridgepointe Overseas Developments Ltd, transporting supplies to the DRC. Ractenbach's business was inextricably connected to members of the ZANU elite. He also had a working relationship with Emmerson Mnangagwa, Zimbabwe's minister for justice, legal and parliamentary affairs, who controlled the military occupation of the DRC.

Some important 'black' businesses also took part. The general manager of the Zimbabwe Minerals Development Corporation (ZMDC), Isiah Puzengwe, was a shareholder of Operation Sovereign Legitimacy (Osleg), which, though privately owned, was regarded as the commercial unit of the Zimbabwe Defence Force (ZDF). Other shareholders included the permanent secretary of the Ministry of Defence, the commander of the ZDF, General Vitalis Zvinavashe, and the acting general manager of the Minerals Marketing Corporation of Zimbabwe. Some Zimbabwean parastatals also had interests in the DRC, ranging from the Forestry Commission to Air Zimbabwe. While such companies asserted their independence from the state, in practice they often accepted government pressure to take advantage of Zimbabwe's war. The ability of smaller businesses and military officials to exploit informal commercial opportunities often eluded larger parastatals. In late 2001 one observer could note that most ventures involving Zimbabwean parastatals were still modest; 'Clearly this type of investment is long-term, but there are enormous hurdles to overcome before such joint ventures become a reality on the ground.'[60]

Ractenbach's role in heading Gécamines also exposes another myth of the war. It was assumed that Zimbabwe's principal motivation in the war would be the exploitation of mining operations. Yet where these existed, they often proved unprofitable. The commercial units of ZDF and the Congolese Armed Forces (FAC), and the joint ventures that they formed, yielded little of substance. Even the elaborate project that included Osleg, Comiex and Oryx Zimcom faced a questionable future. The contrast between the promises of enrichment and the reality for investors was extraordinary. The Zimbabwean government contributed to a get-rich fever in the Congo that was hard to justify for those without close connections to ZANU–PF. Small investors risked their savings on business ventures that often collapsed. When the home-affairs minister, Dumiso Dadengwa, urged his constituents to 'make a killing' in the Congo, seventy-eight women travelled to the Zambia/DRC border with a lorry carrying their pooled resources, only to see their goods stolen and their savings lost.

By 2000, Zimbabweans had secured the right to exploit two of the country's principal diamond areas, Tshibwe and Senga Senga, as exclusive owners for twenty-five years. The timing could not have been better. As international pressure isolated the ZANU–PF regime, Mugabe's allies could export DRC diamonds through South Africa, thereby securing a steady flow of foreign exchange into Harare. Zimbabwe was never alone, either in their intervention to help Kabila or in the exploitation of minerals. Namibia and Angola also insisted that its intervention be rewarded with vital diamond concessions. At the same time that Zimbabwe was granted the two richest reserves of diamonds in the country, Namibia received a concession in Tshikapa, and Angola sought similar concessions close to its border with the DRC.[61]

Uganda, Rwanda and the role of the military

Turning now to the alliance against Kabila, the involvement of Uganda and Rwanda shows many similarities to the practices of the Zimbabwe state. Again the military, the Ugandan People's Defence Forces (UPDF), played the central role in the plunder of resources.[62] The direct involvement of foreign African troops in the Congo in recent years has indeed led one commentator to describe them as a 'self-perpetuating class of rent-seekers, prospering at the expense of productive civilians whose security and well-being will be correspondingly reduced.'[63] A confluence of military and economic interests lay at the heart of Uganda's role in the war. Uganda had sponsored, with Rwanda, the first rebellion against Mobutu. In the second rebellion it was an important backer of the Rwandan proxy army, the Rassemblement Congolais pour la Démocratie (RCD).

Uganda, again like Rwanda, justified its involvement in the war against Kabila on the grounds of his failure to provide security to Uganda's western borders, and its desire to prevent a further genocide against the Banyamulenge. If this was the case, asked one academic observer, Gerald Prunier, in 1999, then why were the UPDF deployed more than 1,000 kilometres from the Uganda border?[64] Ugandan export figures revealed the reasons for the country's military occupation of the Congo very neatly. In 1997 gold was the country's second largest export earner, an extraordinary fact for a country that has hardly any domestic sources of the metal.[65]

Two distinct periods of plunder can be identified. The first year of occupation saw naked theft. According to a 2001 UN Security Council report, the UPDF stole timber, minerals and livestock from early 1998 onwards. The report named the military commander General James Kazini as the principal holder of timber from Amex-bois in August 1998, and then from La Forestière the following December.[66] It was during a second period from early 1999 onwards that the UPDF became more directly involved in extracting wealth from the Congo. Again military commanders played a leading role. Ugandan businessmen entered into partnership with a Thai company to form DARA–Forest. With the active engagement of the military the new company started to cut and sell timber for export.[67] Unwilling to develop the gold mines under their control in the mineral-rich Orientale province, Ugandan businesses made extensive use of artisanal labour in mines normally operating on an industrial scale. This was despite warnings by members of the state Office of the Gold Mines of Kilo-Moto (OKIMO) that artisanal techniques were dangerous in industrial mines. Impatience led the Ugandan army to use 'reckless mining practices that would destroy Gorumbwa mine, the most important in the region'.[68]

In regions occupied by the Rwandan army, local communities were also forced into mining. One commentator explains how in Walikale people were 'driven into regroupment camps where they were required to mine coltan.'[69] One report noted that in 2000 coltan was earning Rwanda $20 million per month.[70] Between 1999 and 2000, the re-export of Congolese coltan through Rwanda covered all the costs of Rwanda's intervention in the war.[71] In 2001, UN investigators established that the Rwandan army had exported about 100 tonnes of coltan each month the previous year, through two companies, Rwanda Metals and Eagle Wings Resources.

Western politicians knowingly encouraged Rwanda and Uganda in the looting of resources from the Congo. For example, throughout the period of greatest plunder in the late 1990s, which has been extensively documented, the British government was the main international donor to Rwanda and Uganda. While 'concern' was voiced about 'activities' in the DRC, funding was not made conditional on military withdrawal. As a Human Rights Watch report in 2003 explained, 'the British government has continued to support Uganda and Rwanda politically and financially. British authorities abstained from any open criticism of either Uganda and Rwanda.'[72] It was not just the British government. A recent International Monetary Fund report explained, 'Uganda's microeconomic performance has been good ... real GDP growth is expected to remain at around 6 per cent in 2004/5. The economic expansion has been led by strong output increases ... and by strong growth in exports.' In particular the country was praised for its 'export-led growth'.[73]

The Ugandan and Rwandan governments have been kept afloat for some time by aid money. In Uganda between 2000 and 2001 donor funds accounted for 55 per cent of the country's budget, totalling $582.2 million. Uganda has also received debt relief totalling more than $2 billion, most recently as one of the countries earmarked for debt relief by the G8 in July 2005. To qualify for this relief Uganda has to promise further privatisation of utilities, including its water supply, agricultural services and commercial bank. The reforms that wreaked havoc on Uganda's poor have served as a catalyst to military intervention beyond the country's borders.[74]

John Clark argues that the Ugandan army in the DRC was 'engaged in criminal activity that [did] not benefit the Ugandan state'.[75] This is too simple. As Uganda was being lavished in donor monies between 2000 and 2003, it overspent its defence budget by 30 per cent.[76] World Bank rules stipulate that no more than 2 per cent of a country's GDP can be spent on the military. Thus, even with an occasional loss, the plundering of the Congo has proved 'fundamentally self-sustaining'.[77] The Rwandan and Ugandan armies have expanded without subjecting the rest of the state to pressure.

Minerals and multinationals

The UN panel of experts report in 2002 identified eighty-five countries operating in the DRC, but the nature of their involvement changed dramatically over the course of the war.[78] In the first war of 1996–97 the mining companies played an important, speculative role in the conflict. In the ensuing chaos and war of 1998 and onwards, the companies were an essential element. That does not mean that they managed to implement a coherent policy. Neither does it mean that the Congolese mineral economy was consistently better developed in 2003 than it had been five years earlier. At the time of the second war, American Mineral Fields purchased diamond concessions in the Cuango Valley along the Congolese–Angolan border from a firm of Belgian speculators. This was a familiar pattern; entrepreneurs would acquire concessions and then sell them on at increased prices to bigger players. The deal was celebrated by the company in a press release: 'The joint venture asset is a 3,700 square kilometre mining lease in the Cuango Valley, and a 36,000 square kilometre prospecting lease which borders the mining lease in the north.'[79]

Madsen notes how Western mining companies benefited from the de facto partition of the country into separate zones of political control. First, the mineral exploiters from Rwanda and Uganda concentrated on pillaging gold and diamonds from eastern Congo. They increasingly turned their attention to coltan. Rwanda and Uganda conducted the great part of the mineral exploitation in the Congo. Western companies then bought the minerals exported by these countries, presenting a cover for their involvement in the war. The cover, however, was blown by UN reports on the illegal export of minerals. While the World Bank funded and praised Rwanda and Uganda, and the UK's then international development secretary Clare Short went so far as to describe the Rwandan leader Paul Kagame as a 'darling', their economic success was being built on the exploitation of Congolese minerals sold to Western companies.

The report of the UN Panel of Experts on the Illegal Exploitation of Natural Resources and Other Forms of Wealth of Congo was devastating in its conclusions. The UN published four studies detailing the exploitation of natural resources in the Congo, and all showed how the exploitation of minerals was funding rebel groups and feeding into global networks of international business.[80] The report argues that foreign companies 'were ready to do business regardless of elements of unlawfulness ... Companies trading minerals which the Panel considered to be the engine of the conflict in the Congo, have prepared the field for illegal mining activities in the country.'[81] States with few natural resources of their own started to export large quantities of coltan, cobalt and gold. Rwanda's balance of payments increased from $26 million in 1997 to $51.5 million in 1999. Claims that the World Bank was unaware of the sources of Uganda's new wealth received short shrift from the UN: 'Notes exchanged between World Bank staff clearly show that the Bank was informed about a significant increase in gold and diamond exports from a country that produces very little of these minerals, or exports quantities of gold that it could not produce'.[82] During this period the Rwandan Revenue Authority lists thirty-five of the largest companies to profit from the mineral trade, of which twelve were based in Belgium and five each in Germany and the Netherlands. Coltan in all the cases was the largest export. The benefits for Rwanda were clear. The re-exportation of minerals from the DRC provided more than 7 per cent of the country's foreign earnings in 1999 and 2000. Over the same years, revenue from the re-export of coltan covered the entire cost of fighting the war and arming the rebels. The value of diamonds exported from Uganda, meanwhile, rose from $0.2m in 1997 to $3.8 m three years later.[83]

By 1999, Uganda and Rwanda had parted company and were fighting each other in the north and east of the Congo. That left the region divided by rebel groups, funded by a new alliance of neighbouring countries. The Rassemblement Congolais pour la Démocratie (RCD–Goma), led by Adolphe Onosumba, was funded and supported by the Rwandans and controlled the whole of eastern Congo, northern Katanga and parts of central Congo. There was also the RCD–Bunia (known as RCD–ML) based in Bunia and led for a while by a professor, Ernest Wamba da Wamba, who was supported by the Ugandans and installed in far north-eastern Congo. Even terms such as 'supported' or 'sponsored' can fail to express the full extent of the direct involvement of neighbouring states. Both Rwanda and Uganda recruited, trained and armed soldiers to fight in various rebel groups. At all times these developments were noted and the information available to international donors and others.

The third major rebel group that emerged in the first two years of the war was the Mouvement de Libération Congolais (MLC), led by the cellphone entrepreneur Jean Pierre Bemba. These were not rebel leaders forged organically out of guerrilla struggle. Bemba was promoted in early 2001 to rebel leader for his business connections and organisational skills. Clark explains his leadership of the MLC: 'Uganda selected him to head the umbrella organisation.'[84] Such groups clashed as they fought for control and access to minerals. This fighting took place in the second period of plunder, which saw a systematic attempt to organise the 'extraction' of minerals. The first major fight was between the Rwanda- and Uganda-backed armies in Kisangani in the middle of 1999. The fighting was generated by attempts to share the diamond trade through Kisangani. After a year of fighting, the militias agreed to sign a peace accord in Lusaka. The agreement did not hold, but led to further conflict.[85] Rwanda still maintained that its intervention was motivated by a desire to rid eastern Congo of Hutu extremists. The progress of the war should be sufficient evidence against these claims. In 2002, one Interahamwe fighter expressed Rwanda's motivation well:

> During the last years of the war we have not fought the RPF a lot. We think that they are tired of the war like us. Anyway, they are not in the Congo to hunt us, as they pretend. I have seen them exploit the gold and coltan mines and we see how they attack the population. It is for these reason that they are here.[86]

Ituri, gold and multinational companies

No region symbolises the plunder in the Congo in the last five years as graphically as Ituri. The province is even a creation of war, having reached an independent existence only in 1999. Situated on the Ugandan border, Ituri is rich in gold, coltan and timber. Conflicts to control the province have claimed an estimated 60,000 lives since

1999, according to the UN. Although the war has sometimes assumed an ethnic colour, involving conflicts between Hema and Lendu,[87] it has always centred on the control of resources. To speak of the ethnic nature of the conflict is also to conceal the role of Uganda. According to Human Rights Watch, 'Uganda intervened in local administration by establishing a new province, Kibali–Ituri, in 1999, by naming its first governor, and by playing a major role in changing four of the six governors since then. Three governors were removed directly by Ugandans with their army providing the force in two of these cases.'[88] Sometimes the Ugandans did not even bother to disguise their intervention; in 2001, for example, a colonel in the Ugandan army, Edison Muzoora, acted as de facto governor for five months.

The UPDF deployed soldiers to fight with the Hema militas against the Lendu, and in 1999 and 2000 there were reports of Ugandan soldiers killing Lendu civilians. Hema militias have also been known to employ UPDF soldiers to defend their property. The Ugandan initiative to reconcile rebel groups in the region in 2001 stemmed from an attempt to reorganise the plunder conducted by groups under their patronage. However, the merger of different rebel groups into the FLC under the leadership of Jean-Pierre Bemba collapsed as they disputed the division of power.[89] Rwanda has also been involved in the shifting alliances characteristic of the politics of the region. As local groups in control of the region fell out with their Ugandan backers, Rwanda was on hand to trade arms and support for influence. One report describes how in 2003 Kigali was 'delivering arms, ammunition, and even Rwandan soldiers' to the region.[90]

The new province carved out by Uganda has sucked in several international corporations. The gold-mining company AngloGold Ashanti, a subsidiary of the mining giant Anglo American, was connected to one of the province's rebel groups, the Front Nationaliste Intégrationiste (FNI), which assisted the company's access to gold reserves situated around the town of Mongbwalu in the north-east. The company would provide monetary and logistical support to the FNI, describing this support as 'unavoidable'.[91] Although the company initially won mining rights to a gold concession in 1996, it was not until 2003 that it could start serious exploration of the mining opportunities. This exploration had been paralysed by the war and only once the transitional government had been installed in Kinshasa could the area be regarded as accessible. AngloGold Ashanti's Charles Carter explains his company's role, 'While this is obviously a tough environment right now, we are looking forward to the opportunity to fully explore the properties we have in the Congo, believing that we now have access to potentially exciting growth prospects in Central Africa.'[92]

Another company, Metalor Technologies, based in Switzerland, has been identified as purchasing gold from Uganda. It is estimated that in 2003 $60 million worth of Congolese gold was exported through Uganda, much of it bought by Metalor.[93] As a result of an extensive investigation by Human Right Watch the company was forced to suspend gold purchases from Uganda in 2005. However, millions of dollars' worth of gold are still exported from the country. The gold is sold through Uganda, conveniently hiding its origins, on the global gold markets in Europe and America. This 'blood-gold' is sold with Ugandan certification.

The province has also been cursed by the discovery of oil. After the South African peace agreement in 2002, the central government in Kinshasa attempted to reclaim control over the province's resources. The government signed oil exploration licences with the Canadian–British Heritage Oil Company for the Congolese side of the Semliki valley. The discovery of oil in the valley ensured further bloody competition in the area. Oil was found after exploratory drilling on the Ugandan side of the border, with the company claiming that the area had the potential to be a world-class oil basin. In March 2003 it promised to commence exploration on the Congolese side of the border. The company was mindful of the region's political turbulence, and made contacts with local chiefs in Ituri in 2002. One of these, Chief Kahwe of Mandro, who was fighting to take control of the region's capital Bunia from a rebel group the Union des Patriots Congolais (UPC), explained in February 2003: 'I have been contacted by the Canadian Oil people who came to see me. I told them they could only start work in Ituri once I had taken Bunia from the UPC.'[94]

The violent competition for the region's resources requires some illustration. In late 2002 there was an attempt to seize control of the gold-rich town of Mongbwalu by the UPC, a group that claims the 'Congo for the Congolese', and that has been backed by the

Rwandans. This violence was directly connected to the involvement of the multinational companies mentioned above. Even before the town was taken by UPC forces, the rebel commander had invited the general director of OKIMO, the state organisation in charge of mining in the region, to discuss how mining could best be organised once the UPC was in charge. The boss of OKIMO, Étienne Kiza Ingani, was quick to congratulate the UPC on its expected victory, and advocated a 'mixed Executive Council to take stock of the terrain'.[95] One witness describes how they took control of Pluto, a village on the outskirts of Mongbwalu:

> As I was running I saw people being hit by bullets. Women and children were falling. Some people did not run and hid in their houses... I heard afterwards that these people were slaughtered. The assailants continued to kill people for five days in Pluto.

Another witness explains what happened in Mongbwalu:

> A group of more than ten with spears, guns and machetes killed two men in Cite Suni, in the centre of Mongbwalu. I saw them pull the two men from their house and kill them. They took Kasore, a Lendu man in his thirties, from his family and attacked him with knives and hammers. They killed him and his son (aged about twenty) with knives. They cut his son's throat and tore open his chest. They cut the tendons on his heels, smashed his head and took out his intestines. The father was slaughtered and burnt.[96]

Hundreds of others were killed in a similar way; human rights groups have estimated that 800 were killed as a result of the attacks in late 2002 and early 2003.[97] After these attacks, however, the new UPC authorities were faced with a problem: having killed civilians in large numbers, they found most of the experienced 'diggers' were precisely the Lendu *non-originaires* that they had slaughtered or chased out over the past few days. So, faced with a serious labour shortage, the UPC sent messengers into the forests to persuade the population to return. Suddenly the UPC was forced to backpedal from the war it was waging against 'outsiders'; the commander now explained in a town meeting that 'the UPC was for everyone' and it was safe to return. Naturally, most of the former population refused. The UPC forced those who remained in the town to work in the mine. One witness described the experience underground:

There were three shifts: those who worked in the morning, those who worked in the afternoon, and those who worked at night. They were not paid. It was hard labour. They had to dig under big stones without machines. They had only hand-tools like pick-axes. They were given bananas and beans to eat and they were beaten. Some tried to run away by pretending to go to the toilet.... The Ugandans were also there to ensure security.[98]

Forced labour is well documented in the region.[99] Another witness described how the FNI, which had forced the UPC out of Mongbwalu later in 2003 with the support of Ugandan troops, collected 'taxes' and organised forced labour, known locally as *salongo*. This was 'community labour' that was used by the FNI in a host of activities, including a range of 'municipal' projects to fix roads, collect firewood for the military and clean military camps. This *salongo* could be as much as two days per week. One administrator implementing *salongo* admitted in 2004 to the necessity of intimidating 'people to come, otherwise they would not'.[100] Throughout this period, during which ethnic militias fought for control of Mongbwalu, AngloGold Ashanti was involved in discussions with the rebels about access to the mines. Ituri is not the only region that has brought together multinationals and armed groups. In Katanga an Australian mining group, Anvil Mining Group, has been implicated in acts of barbarity carried out by the FARDC, the government forces.[101]

The contradictions in the control and exploitation of minerals can be seen clearly. The mobilising power of the ethnic militias and rebels armies is through an appeal to ethnic loyalty and, frequently, the rejection of those who are regarded as *non-originaires*. Yet exploitation of the mineral reserves often requires experienced labour. This may not correspond with the ethnic politics of the militias. Ethnicity is an imperfect tool for securing control of the region's resources. For the rebels the control of gold reserves is inextricably linked to the division of political power in Kinshasa. So the FNI is able to use the gold under its control and the presence of AngloGold Ashanti to increase its leverage in negotiations with the government in the capital. The peace process can be seen, therefore, as an ongoing process to redistribute power to military networks with the best access to and control of minerals. Even the UN was forced belatedly to accept that competition for the control of gold mining was a major element in the continuing conflict.[102]

Negotiations

Despite repeated attempts to negotiate a settlement, the country remained divided. President Chiluba of Zambia chaired a series of summits under the Southern African Development Community that reached an agreement for ceasefire (the Lusaka agreement) in late 1999. By the winter of 2000 little progress had been made towards peace. The death of Kabila in January 2001, assassinated by his bodyguard, and his replacement by his eldest son Joseph, was reported outside the country as heralding a new period of positive change. The new Kabila committed himself to the Lusaka agreement. The Inter-Congolese Dialogue that he announced was meant to initiate national reconciliations and compromise, promising elections, a new constitution and power sharing. To support the peace process the UN deployed a 90-strong military liaison mission in 1999, and was authorised to deploy a further observer mission in February 2000. The size of the contingent was widely ridiculed as being hopelessly inadequate. The following year the UN agreed to monitor the implementation of the Lusaka agreement; its force, MONUC, the Mission des Nations Unies en République Démocratique du Congo, comprised just over 500 observers and nearly 9,000 military personnel.

By 2003 foreign forces had mostly left the country and the ceasefire held, but despite this progress fighting continued in the east. On 30 May 2003, after massacres in Bunia, the UN Security Council agreed the deployment of an Interim Emergency Multinational Force. the force was finally launched as a EU European and Security and Defence Policy (ESDP) on 12 June. Operation Artemis, as it is known, is in fact a largely French-led initiative. A deal signed at the end of 2003 in South Africa between the Kinshasa government, rebel groups and the political opposition agreed to the formation of a Transitional National Government (TNG). The agreement was finally signed and agreed formally by all parties in Sun City, South Africa, on 2 April 2003, with the TNG coming into being on 30 June of the same year.

The 'peace' signalled by the transitional government triggered two important processes. The first saw the return of some multinational companies to regions that they had previously only watched from a distance. There were attempts to reintroduce gold mining and to start oil exploration, particularly in the north-east of the country.

Yet much of the worse violence took place after these deals were signed. The companies dealt brazenly with rebel groups, indifferent to the history of violence on which the agreements were based. The second process tied to the 2003 peace deal was just as predictable. Rebel commanders, responsible for the killing and slaughter in the war, were incorporated into the Congolese army, the FARDC.[103] In reality, the army has become a fractious amalgamation of rebel groups, responsible for much of the continued violence. In December 2004, for example, FARDC soldiers killed approximately 100 civilians, and raped dozens of women and children during fighting in north Kivu with Rwandan-backed RCD–Goma forces. Despite Rwanda's trumpeted withdrawal of troops in 2002, much of the region remains under its influence, with Rwandan troops still sited in the east and continuing their support for RCD–Goma. When Rwanda is not directly intervening, it is threatening to do so. As a consequence, since late 2004 more than 200,000 people have fled villages and towns, seeking sanctuary in the forests of north and south Kivu.[104]

Since 2003, fighting has continued. Some of the worst has been between the Congolese army and renegade soldiers previously backed by Rwanda, and demobilised as part of the peace plan. The Ituri district in the north-east of the Congo has also witnessed ongoing conflict. Further evidence of the region's continued chaos can be found in north and south Kivu. Here remnants of the Interahamwe and ex-FAR members are still active in the Forces Démocratique de Libération de Rwanda (FDLR). At the time of writing, this army is still reputed to be several thousand strong. In September 2005, its soldiers were still refusing to return to Rwanda in opposition to the predominantly Tutsi Rwandan regime. In May 2005, although a new constitution was adopted by the National Assembly and agreed by former rebel groups, national elections were postponed until early 2006.

Conflict has hardened ethnic identities. One report of a rape committed by Banyamulenge soldiers in 2004 illustrates the legacy of war. After raping his victim the soldier explained that 'until you accept the Banyamulenge as Congolese, there will be no calm in Bukavu ... We leave you that message.'[105] In Ituri rebel groups have targeted *non-originaires*. One witness describes an attack on the gold-mining town Mabanga that targeted these 'outsiders':

[A]ll those who spoke Swahili and were non-originaires should leave straight away... If they saw you and you were light skinned they would kill you shouting 'jajabo' [term for Lingala speakers not from the region]. They were slashing people with their machetes on their arms and heads.[106]

None of the region's communities has been left untouched, and most have sought to defend themselves against the permanent presence of occupying armies and rebel groups. They have done this by arming and defending themselves. Meanwhile the UN mission, MONUC, has proved impotent in disarming the armed groups, which are still the main power in much of the country. The strong 'yes' vote in the referendum for a new constitution in December 2005 showed the desire of the Congolese people for democratic change and an end to conflict, yet the elections promised for 2006 offer little hope of profound change.

One authority, Georges Nzongola-Ntalaja, is scathing about the negotiations that have led to the supposed 'transition' to democratisation. They proceed, he argues, on the false premiss that the fighting in the Congo was a civil war, fought by national groups that all possess some degree of legitimacy. This is, as we have seen, a lie. The result of seeing the conflict as a civil war has justified the inaction on the part of the United Nations Security Council and given comfort to these regional powers that have occupied the Congo. The peace process has reflected this attitude. The reality of the war as a foreign invasion is not recognised. On the contrary the rebel groups are regarded as *interlocuteurs valables* who deserve a place around the negotiating table. Nzongola concludes that peace talks seem to 'legitimise the de facto partition of the country by inviting the signatories themselves, the states involved ... to disarm the rebel'. Though the current negotiated peace, with its scheduled elections, might not result in the immediate partition of the country, it 'ensures both control of some of its richest and strategic regions by trusted allies and undisturbed access to mineral and other resources by transnational corporations'. [107]

The IMF, criminality and the partition of the Congo

It is fashionable to speak of 'failed states' in Africa. The so-called 'complex political emergency' in the Great Lakes in the late 1990s was widely regarded as symptomatic of the 'criminalisation' of the state in Africa. Congo was a prime case, but it was not alone and the category seemed to fit a number of states in Africa at the end of the 1990s. Jean-François Bayart argues that,

> the process of criminalisation ... has become the dominant trait of the sub-continent in which the state has literally imploded under the combined effects of economic crisis, neo-liberal programs of structural adjustment and the loss of legitimacy of political institutions.[108]

Theorists of the failed state emphasise the internal failings and understate the extent of Western influence in the failures they lament. Yet, as we have seen, the involvement of international business in the Congo has sustained the war and the other regional African governments involved in the conflict. The collapse of the DRC can only be explained by the combined effects of economic crisis, neoliberal programmes of structural adjustment, and the consequent loss of state power.

The UN Panel of Experts on the Illegal Exploitation of Natural Resources and Other Forms of Wealth of Congo detail the exploitation of resources in the Congo, and show how the minerals were used to fund rebel groups and nourish global networks of international business. The reports conclude that foreign companies 'were ready to do business regardless of elements of unlawfulness.... Companies trading minerals which the Panel considered to be the engine of the conflict in the Congo, have prepared the field for illegal mining activities in the country.'[109]

War stems not simply from the desire of neighbouring countries to control the Congo's minerals. It is tied to the global restructuring of capitalism. The collapse of Mobutu was significant because it represented, after years of painful adjustment and crisis, the replacement not only of one regime by another, but the triumph of a model of private capitalist development: the annihilation of the nation-state. Mobutu had presided over an earlier system of state control, a malign state capitalism, epitomised by his short-lived project of Zaïreanisation, which proved eventually impossible to sustain in an era that combined the global collapse of commodity prices and the geopolitical earthquake of 1989. It is tempting to argue that Kabila was always doomed to failure as a would-be nationalist leader in a country that had already been transformed. What is certain is that these processes unravelled such national integrity that the country had achieved, preparing it for war.

The gradual collapse of the Congolese state from the mid-1970s onwards facilitated a huge growth in the hand-dug extraction of industrial diamonds and coltan by small-scale private enterprise, often directly linked to outside interests. Increasingly, interest in coltan grew as its potential was recognised. By the late 1990s, coltan was celebrated as a wonder metal. US multinational companies were among those most interested in coltan, and in securing easy access to it. The special alloys needed for the construction of the International Space Station, for example, require massive quantities of cobalt and coltan; and there are many other uses. The rebels made deals tied to the privatisation of state mining companies in 1997, even before the fall of Mobutu. The involvement of American multinational mining companies allowed the introduction of the most advanced technology. Coltan was at the centre of these developments. Diamonds played a similar role. Under pressure from international donors, Mobutu had liberalised the diamond sector in the 1980s, legalising artisanal production in 1981, and before long diamonds provided the country with its principal source of foreign exchange and accounted for 70 per cent of the world's supply. The country's reliance on diamonds proved a mixed blessing, as the economy was badly affected by the decline in global prices for industrial diamonds throughout the 1980s and early 1990s, deepening the country's already terrible economic crisis. Liberalisation, which contributed to the take-off of the diamond sector in the early 1980s, continued through the late 1980s and early 1990s; by 1994 the process of liberalisation was almost complete. The World Bank insisted on the privatisation of the mining sector, leaving the door open for transnational private capital to buy up Congolese concessions. It also contributed to the bloodiest chapter in the country's recent history.[110]

Coltan and diamonds dug by hand were the perfect minerals of war. They played a pivotal role. By the end of the 1990s, the DRC was the fourth largest producer of diamonds in the world; that same year, diamonds were flowing out through neighbouring countries involved in the war at an astonishing rate. During the first few months of that year, artisanal diamonds generated for the state in

Kinshasa only $18.7 million, compared to $328.7 million the previous year. Artisanal diamond production was estimated in 2004 to pull in approximately 700,000 miners, with the diamonds sold to more than 100,000 middlemen. Officially these diamonds should be sold to the country's twelve *comptoirs*, which are then responsible for their export. Recent attempts to regulate diamond production to accord with the regulatory framework set out by the Kimberley process have largely failed to formalise the industry. Only a small fraction of an estimated 500,000 artisanal miners in Kasai Orientale, for example, are licensed. Despite these recent attempts at regulation, Global Witness notes that in Kisangani, a major centre of diamond trading, 'goods are still smuggled out to neighbouring country'.[111]

In January 2000, the market price of coltan fluctuated between $60 and $80 per kilo; by December, the price had rocketed to $380 per kilo. Of course, the prices that coltan reached on the 'open market' contrasted massively with the pittance that the diggers themselves received; most were paid between $10 and $20 per kilo, still enough to provide them with ample incentive to continue production. The high prices did not last; the bubble burst on 5 December 2000. As Colette Braeckman writes: 'when American corporations had established sufficient supplies ... the United States suddenly decided to put their strategic stocks on the market.'[112] The market price of coltan slumped to $3 per kilo. The Congo remains hopelessly buffeted by the violent oscillation in prices of raw materials on the absurdly named 'free market'.

The new Congo, informalised and artisanal, is fundamentally unlike its previous incarnations. In a world dominated by private capital after 1989 it is possible to imagine the country permanently partitioned. As usual the US neoconservative right has led the way. Walter Kansteiner entertained this notion in 1996, when he called for a division of the Great Lakes. It 'would probably necessitate redrawing the international boundaries and would require massive voluntary relocation efforts.' Four years later he was beating the same drum, stating that the 'break up of the Congo is more likely now than it has been in 20 or 30 years.'[113] Today his cynicism is merely reflective of reality. The partition of the DRC is already in effect, and the new territory is again awash with rebels, mercenaries and Western capital.

conclusion

The recent war in the Congo is poorly understood in the West. Our media treat this war in central Africa as somehow different from the many conflicts that have occurred recently in other parts of the world. Instead, it is explained as something inevitable, evidence of recurrent African 'backwardness'. As the *Economist* asked, at the start of the millennium, 'Does Africa have some inherent character flaw that keeps it backward and incapable of development?'[1] The NGO left too has tended to adopt an apocalyptic perspective and to despair at Africa's 'tragedy', seeing only failure across the region and willing the 'liberation' of the continent by external forces.[2]

Another well-known recent account is *In the Footsteps of Mr Kurtz* by *Financial Times* journalist Michela Wrong. *Footsteps* portrays Lumumba and Mobutu as equals, fighting for political power, apparently following the pattern of the 'great parables of mankind: the loving brothers, the best of friends who end up trying to destroy each other... the story of ... Cain and Abel'.[3] Wrong cites uncritically from an extensive interview conducted with CIA operative Larry Devlin, who was implicated in the murder of Lumumba. Devlin becomes her emblematic white hero, described in the text as a 'floating above the pavement with the uncertain grace of a fifteenth-century schooner setting out on its first journey to the new world ... an old-fashioned gentleman who opened car doors for a lady.' Africa for Wrong is an impenetrable place, where the 'African heat' has lead to the 'dull political acquiescence of its people'. She portrays Kinshasa, the stage to so many great popular revolts, as 'a city where everyone seemed to complain about how awful things were but no one seemed ready to try changing the status quo'.[4] The Congolese are an unfortunate and frustrating bunch, unable to liberate themselves and destined to be spectators to the machinations of the political elite.

While this kind of analysis might flatter a certain European audience, it does nothing to explain the recent history of the country. The Congo becomes for the European, a paradigm of Africa, its 'darkness' even greater than the rest of the continent. More than a hundred years later it is still the subject of European pondering. The European imagination of the nineteenth and early twentieth centuries saw the Congo as mysterious place populated by savages but needing to be civilised; today it is a catastrophe whose depths cannot really be fathomed, caused, somehow, by the inexplicable 'acquiescence' of its people in killing.

It is against these absurd arguments that this book has argued that there were no mysteries to the war, or the recent history of the Congo. It was a human catastrophe linked to globalisation, profit and Western manipulation. The war was not simply an African affair, a regional war fought on Congolese territory. Behind the countries and the rebel groups involved in fighting it were Western companies and interests which played a crucial role in setting these forces into motion. The war, so often characterised as primitive, barbaric and inexplicable, was inherently regional and global. The war was international – taking in six African states, with some supporting the regime in Kinshasa (Angola), others (Uganda, Rwanda) attempting to unseat it, and numerous groups, both Congolese and from neighbouring countries, in shifting alliances with the new government and the neighbouring states. More than 200,000 soldiers fought on several fronts, in forest, jungle and on remote plains, in what has been termed Africa's first World War.

The number of those who died in the war was staggering, not even matched in Africa by the cumulative slaughter in the Sudanese civil war over the last fifty years. The International Rescue Committee estimated that, from the beginning of the second rebellion in 1998 to the end of April 2004, the war resulted in approximately 3.8 million deaths. The killing was greater than in any conflict since the Vietnam War.[5] Behind the dead stood the profits of regional powers and multi-nationals. The current phase of plunder was often initiated by relatively small groups of speculators, who crisscrossed the Congo as Kabila's army approached the capital in 1997. There is no better example of this group than American Mineral Fields. Though listed on various stock exchanges they were in reality little more than 'adventurers' who lacked sufficient capital to invest in the concessions that were sold to them by Kabila. They were what the Congo expert Colette Braeckman has described as 'juniors', the advance guard who sought the investment and interest of bigger players.

These 'juniors' are the contemporary versions of Henry Morton Stanley, the nineteenth-century speculator par excellence. His books describing his exploration of central Africa were largely accounts of the riches that could be found in the region. Stanley detailed the precious woods, ivory and minerals found in the Congo. The river that he originally sought to map was presented as the passage that European powers could use to access the resources he had catalogued. Originally his efforts were directed towards the British. After they rejected his advances he turned to King Léopold II, who snapped up one of the last regions of the continent as yet unoccupied by other European gunboats. Faithful to his new paymaster Stanley was charged with setting up trading stations, and dealing with local chiefs who would ensure Léopold's access to the wealth that Stanley had promised. Under the guise of free trade, Léopold doled out concessions, keeping a majority share for himself.

Though the independent state had been used to pillage the country's resources, it was also, and throughout the 1960s and 1970s, regarded as the one force that could develop the Congo. Mobutu was a fashionable and complex symbol, not only of corruption and Cold War politics, but also of the interventionist state, which would in Mobutu's 'Plan USA' raise the standard of living of the Congolese to match that of the USA. By the 1990s, however, the state was unable to provide any guarantees to its foreign backers, let alone its own population. The state's collapse had come about as a result of the pressures of global restructuring that broke state capitalist regimes across the world. While Mobutu continued to make promises to foreign capital, he was unable to honour them. The effect of these transformations was felt powerfully in copper mining, as Kennes has written: 'the pressure of globalisation in the mining sector contributed to the final breakdown of the formerly existing model of integration of mining interest into the nation state structure.'[6]

There is nothing primitive or backward about the Congo, nor is the current period of plunder, which has seen commentators rage against the 'criminality' of foreign companies and multinationals, symptomatic of any 'deviant' capitalism. This is not the 'dark side' of globalisation, as Kennes has written. The convergence of 'criminal' activity in areas outside the control of 'legal' international and national political actors is rather an integral and even defining feature of the new globalised world. Zaïre is one example at the frontier of the processes of privatisation that politicians in the West dub glibly 'reform' or 'progress'.[7] The Congo can be seen most accurately as prefigurative of an essential element of late capitalism, shorn of any of the normal pretence of modernisation and development.

Such arguments are missing from too much of the literature. The problem, we are told, is that the Congo has not had the right development or investment. One study asks how 'criminal activity' can be 'linked up with 'legitimate' economic activities'.[8] Even in the most devastating reports tracing the involvement of Western multinationals in the slaughter, there are appeals for corporate responsibility:

> Congo is at a critical phase in its transition to the rule of law
> and needs investment by business corporations to help generate
> revenues.… Such business involvement needs to support economic
> and political development.… In an environment of continued
> conflict … multinationals need to ensure that their activities do not
> in any way support directly or indirectly armed groups responsible
> for human rights abuses.[9]

This is a strange formulation, indeed. It is these 'business corporations' who have frequently provided the chief *raison d'être* for the armed groups. The war and 'criminality' in the Congo are examples of real existing capitalism itself, transformed by the erosion of national states and by the growth of private capital and also contributing actively to that process.

The conflation of 'criminality' and capitalism is characteristic of a new period of global development that has seen the dismantling of the statist model of economic stability. In the West, state capitalism was seen to be expressed in Keynesianism; in the developing world, during the same post-war period, the modernisation perspective posited the development of poor countries if they followed the statist policies pursued by the West. Today the picture is completely different. The World Bank and IMF preside over enfeebled governments who no longer seek 'large scale institutional and social change' other than privatisation and the reduction of the role of the state to an 'administration to secure debt repayments'.[10]

The global backdrop to the war in the Congo has seen the rapacious growth of private and speculative capital, focused increasingly on short-term profits to which the stability (let alone socialisation) of society is largely peripheral. But this is not simply a return to earlier forms of capitalism. A Belgian colonial officer in the early part of the twentieth century might have looked down the Congo river from his quarters in Léopoldville and envisaged some development and modernisation, couched, of course, in the rhetoric of enlightenment and civilisation.

Today, the speculator and multinational surveys the Congo without any such considerations. Increasingly the country faces the direct rule of private capital, mediated only by local militias and more powerful neighbours. The indignation of commentators at the destruction of mining facilities in the war by the very forces involved in their exploitation is misplaced. It is fanciful to imagine that multinationals properly regulated and controlled can at last bring about the development and investment that will fully develop the Congo. The pattern of Western intervention and capitalist development in the Congo tells us that this will never happen under present conditions.

Yet this has only been half our story. We have also shown that the recent history of the Congo has been set alight by the resistance of the Congolese themselves. Their struggles have so often gone down to defeat, most recently in the 'transition' led by a cowardly political opposition. Still, the opposition was constantly forced on, scrutinised and compelled to push further than they wanted to go by a protest movement that dissected their every move and lamented each compromise. During the independence struggle of autumn 1959 and spring 1960, it was popular resistance that led to the country's first elections and moulded politicians of the stature of Lumumba. During the years 1990–94 the people again took to the streets, almost breaking Mobutu's reign. Civil servants, university students, trade unionists informal traders and other groups were not acquiescent, but fought bravely for a different, democratic Congo in which people would be free of hunger and free to vote. It is to these forces, and to their resistance, that the Congo must again turn.

notes

introduction

1. B. Coghlan et al., *Mortality in the Democratic Republic of Congo: Results from a Nationwide Survey* (New York: Burnet Institute and the International Rescue Committee, 2004).

one

1. B. Davidson, *Africa in History* (London: Paladin, 1974), p. 23.
2. D.L. Schoenbrun, *Gender and Social Identity in the Great Lakes Region to the 15th Century* (New York: Heinemann, 1998), pp. 15–23.
3. S.H. Nelson, *Colonialism in the Congo Basin 1880–1940* (Athens OH: Ohio University Centre for International Studies, 1994), p. 19.
4. D.L. Schoenbrun, *A Green Place, a Good Place: Agrarian Change, Gender and Social Identity in the Great Lakes Region to the Fifteenth Century* (Portsmouth NH: Heinemann, 1998), pp. 15–23.
5. Ibid., pp. 2, 33, 35, 47, 57, 69, 72, 80, 170, 245.
6. Herodotus, *The Histories* (London: Penguin, 1996), p. 229.
7. J. Mark, *The King of the World in the Land of the Pygmies* (Lincoln: University of Nebraska Press, 1995), pp. 41–2.
8. *The Travels of Marco Polo* (London: Wordsworth Classics, 1997).
9. P. Forbath, *The River Congo: The Discovery, Exploration and Exploitation of the World's Most Dramatic River* (London: Secker & Warburg, 1978), pp. 19, 29, 32, 36, 38, 40, 48, 52, 71–6, 81.
10. J. Vansina, 'Equatorial Africa and Angola: Migrations and the Emergence of the First States', in D.T. Niane (ed.), *General History of Africa,*

Volume IV: *Africa from the Twelfth to the Sixteenth Century* (Paris: UNESCO, 1984), pp. 551–77, 575.

11. E. Axelson, *Congo to Cape: Early Portuguese Explorers* (London: Faber, 1973), p. 95.

12. For a fictionalised account of his rule, see E.M. Bkolo, *Afonso I: Le Roi Chrétien de l'ancien Congo* (Paris: ABC, 1945).

13. A. Hochschild, *King Leopold's Ghost: A Story of Greed, Terror and Heroism in Colonial Africa* (London: Pan Books, 1998), p. 13.

14. D. Richardson, 'Shipboard Revolts, African Authority, and the Atlantic Slave Trade', *William and Mary Quarterly* 58, no. 1 (2001).

15. 'The strange adventures of Andrew Battell of Leigh in Essex, sent by the Portugals prisoner to Angola who lived there, and in the adjoyning Regions, neere eighteene years', in S. Purchas, *Hakluytus Posthumus or Purchas His Pilgrimes: Contayning a History of the World in Sea Voyages and Lande Travells by Englishmen and others*; Volume VI (Glasgow: James MacLehose & Sons: 1905), pp. 367–430, 384.

16. R. W. Harris, *River of Wealth, River of Sorrow: The Central Zaïre Basin in the Era of the Slave and Ivory Trade 1500–1891* (New Haven: Yale University Press, 1981), p. 44.

17. H.M. Stanley, *The Congo and the Founding of Its Free State: A Story of Work and Exploration*, 2 vols (London: Sampson Low, Marston, Searle & Rivington, 1885), vol. I, p. 13; K. Thornton, *The Kingdom of Kongo: Civil War and Transition, 1641–1718* (Madison: University of Wisconsin Press, 1983), p. 84.

18. T. Mukenge, *Culture and Customs of the Congo* (Westport CT: Greenwood Press, 2002), p. 13.

19. D. Birmingham, 'Central Africa from Cameroon to the Zambezi', in R. Gray (ed.), *The Cambridge History of Africa*, Volume IV: *From 1600 to 1790* (Cambridge: Cambridge University Press, 1975), pp. 325–83.

20. *Travels of an Arab Merchant in Soudan* (London: Chapman & Hall, 1854).

21. H. Brode, *Tippu Tip: The Story of His Career in Zanzibar and Central Africa* (Zanzibar: Gallery, 2000).

22. W.H.G. Kingston, *Great African Travellers* (New York and London: Routledge, 1871), pp. 8–9.

23. D. and C. Livingstone, *Narrative of an Expedition to the Zambesi and its Tributaries; and of the Discovery of the Lakes Shirwa and Nyassa 1858–1864* (London: John Murray, 1865), p. 6.

24. Ibid., pp. 596–8.

25. J. Marchal, *L'État Libre du Congo: Paradis Perdu: L'Histoire du Congo*, vol. 1 (Borgloons: Editions Paula Bellings, 1996), p. 11.

26. A particularly bloodthirsty account of 'pursuing the Arabs' appears in the work of one of Livingstone's contemporaries, L. Moncrieth-Fotheringham, *Adventures in Nyasaland: A Two Year Struggle with Arab Slave-dealers in Central Africa* (London: Fleet Street, 1891), pp. 64, 127, 206.

27. M. Wrong, *In the Footsteps of Mr Kurtz: Living on the Brink of Disaster in the Congo* (London: Fourth Estate, 2000), p. 213.

28. Stanley, *The Congo and the Founding*, vol. I, p. 148.

29. *Daily Telegraph*, 12 November 1877.

30. Stanley, *The Congo and the Founding*, vol. I, p. 393.
31. Wrong, *In the Footsteps of Mr Kurtz*, p. 33.
32. Stanley, *The Congo and the Founding*, vol. II, pp. 354.
33. Ibid., p. 356.
34. In 1892, Stanley would stand for the British parliament as a Unionist (a Conservative). His candidature received tacit support from the Liberal Party, but was fiercely denounced by socialists, including Belfort Bax. See the following from *Justice:* 'Manifest Destiny', 11 January 1890; 'A Swashbuckler's Success', 19 January 1890; 'Stanley's Present to God', 1 March 1890; 'How They Spread Civilisation', 23 May 1890; 'Stanley Goes Under' and 'Stanley Must Be Kept Under', both 9 July 1892.
35. M. Twain, *King Léopold's Soliloquy: A Defence of His Congo Rule* (Boston MA: P.R. Warren, 1905), p. 23.
36. Marchal, *L'État Libre du Congo*, p. 45.
37. Stanley, *The Congo and the Founding*, vol. II, p. viii; Marchal, *L'État Libre du Congo*, p. 33.
38. Hochschild, *King Leopold's Ghost*, p. 72.
39. C. Miéville, *Between Equal Rights: A Marxist Theory of International Law* (Leiden: Brill, 2005), pp. 254–6.
40. Ewans, *European Atrocity, African Catastrophe: Léopold II, the Congo Free State and its Aftermath* (London: Routledge, 2002), p. 254.
41. P. Singleton-Gates and M. Girodias, *The Black Diaries: An Account of Roger Casement's Life and Times with a Collection of His Diaries and Public Writings* (Paris: Olympia Press, 1959), p. 72.
42. B. Berkeley, *The Graves Are Not Yet Full: Race, Tribe and Power in the Heart of Africa* (New York: Basic Books, 2001), p. 115.
43. N. Ascherson, *The King Incorporated: Léopold the Second and the Congo* (London: Granta, 1999), p. 11.
44. Nelson, *Colonialism in the Congo Basin,* p. 42.
45. Ewans, *European Atrocity, African Catastrophe*, p. 175.
46. J. Stenghers and J. Vansina, 'King Léopold's Congo', in J.D. Fage and R. Oliver (eds), *The Cambridge History of Africa*, Volume 6: *From 1870 to 1905* (Cambridge: Cambridge University Press, 1985), pp. 313–58.
47. W.J. Samarin, *The Black Man's Burden: African Colonial Labour on the Congo and Ubangi Rivers 1880–1900* (Boulder CO: Westview Press, 1989), p. 231.
48. Twain, *King Léopold's Soliloquy*, p. 23.
49. K. Marx, *The Poverty of Philosophy* (Moscow; Progress Publishers, 1975), p. 102.
50. A. Conan Doyle, *The Crime of the Congo* (London: Hutchinson, 1909), p. 29.
51. D. Seddon, 'Popular Protest and Class Struggle in Africa: An Historical Overview', in L. Zeilig (ed.), *Class Struggle and Resistance in Africa* (Bristol: New Clarion Press, 2002), pp. 24–45, 27.
52. Cited in Davidson, *Africa in History*, p. 278.
53. V.I. Lenin, *Imperialism: The Highest Stage of Capitalism* (New York: International Publishers, 1939).

54. E. Hobsbawm, *The Age of Empire, 1875–1914* (London: Weidenfeld & Nicolson, 1987), p. 66
55. C. Kimber, 'Blood Money', *Socialist Review*, December 2003.
56. 'Murder for Money: Congo, First Genocide of the Twentieth Century', in B. Russell, *Freedom and Organization 1814–1914* (London: George Allen & Unwin, 1934).
57. Forbath, *The River Congo*, p. 105.
58. Hochschild, *King Leopold's Ghost*, p. 233.
59. *La Belgique Coloniale*, 14 August 1898.
60. Conan Doyle, *The Crime of the Congo*, pp. 9–10.
61. *Encylopédie du Congo Belge*, Volume I (Brussels: Éditions Bieleveld, 1950), p. 39.
62. G. Nzongola-Ntalaja, *The Congo from Léopold to Kabila: A People's History* (London: Zed Books, 2002), pp. 42–6.
63. Stenghers and Vansina, 'King Léopold's Congo', pp. 333–4.
64. R.L. Wannyn, *Les Proverbes anciencs du Bas-Congo* (Brussels: Éditions du vieux Planquesaule, 1983), pp. 17, 22.
65. Nelson, *Colonialism in the Congo Basin*, pp. 25, 29, 38, 91.
66. Hochschild, *King Leopold's Ghost*, pp. 131–3.
67. J. Hope Franklin, *George Washington Williams: A Biography* (Chicago: University of Chicago Press, 1985); Hochschild, *King Leopold's Ghost*, p. 102.
68. Quoted in S. Lindquist, *'Exterminate All the Brutes'* (London: Granta, 1997), p. 20.
69. R. Segal, *African Profiles* (Harmondsworth: Penguin, 1962), p. 180.
70. J. Polasky, *The Democratic Socialism of Émile Vandervelde: Between Reform and Revolution* (Oxford: Berg, 1995), p. 59.
71. Nzongola-Ntalaja, *The Congo*, pp. 31–2.
72. E.D. Morel, *The British Case in French Congo: The Story of a Great Injustice, Its Causes and its Lessons* (London: Heinemann, 1903), p. 56.
73. Ewans, *European Atrocity*, p. 231.
74. M.H. Kingsley, *Travels in West Africa: Congo Français, Corisco and Cameroons* (London: Macmillan, 1897), pp. 479, 487.
75. Polasky, *The Democratic Socialism of Émile Vandervelde*.
76. E.D. Morel, *History of the Congo Reform Movement* (Oxford: Clarendon Press, 1968).
77. J. Marchal, *E.D. Morel Contre Léopold: L'Histoire du Congo 1900–1910*, vol. 1 (Paris: L'Harmattan, 1996), pp. 12–14, 16, 20.
78. Morel, *The British Case*, p. 177.
79. G. Gudenkauf, *Belgian Congo: Postal History of the Lado Enclave 1897–1910* (Newbury: Philip Cockrill, 1986), p. 52.
80. Singleton-Gates and Girodias, *The Black Diaries*, p. 200.
81. After 1918, Morel considered himself a socialist, yet even now his politics were complex and were shaped by a latent racism, which came to the fore at the time of the French occupation of the Rhineland. Morel's response, *The Black Horror on the Rhine*, accused the French of employing 50,000 African troops, 'savages', to rape German women. The pamphlet went through many editions. Its success with European

readers has been compared to another contemporary falsehood, *The Protocols of the Elders of Zion*. See R. Reinders, 'E.D. Morel and the "Black Horror on the Rhine"', *International Review of Social History* 13 (1968), pp. 4–28.

82. B. Inglis, *Roger Casement* (London: Hodder & Stoughton, 1973); Singleton-Gates and Girodias, *The Black Diaries*, pp. 39, 64–8, 72, 74, 87–96, 104, 120, 138, 140, 183, 190, 194–9.
83. Conan Doyle, *The Crime of the Congo*, pp. 6, 27, 155.
84. J. Conrad, *Heart of Darkness* (Harmondsworth: Penguin, 1973); Hochschild, *King Leopold's Ghost*, p. 145; Lindquist, *'Exterminate All the Brutes'*, p. 74.
85. Conrad, *Heart of Darkness*.
86. B. Parry, *Congo and Imperialism: Ideological Boundaries and Visionary Frontiers* (London: Macmillan, 1983), p. 27; R.E. Lee, *Conrad's Colonialism* (Paris: Mouton, 1969), pp. 40–48.
87. Conrad, *Heart of Darkness*, p. 98.
88. 'An Image of Africa: Racism in Conrad's Heart of Darkness', in C. Achebe, *Hopes and Impediments: Selected Essays* (New York: Doubleday, 1989), pp. 1–20.
89. Polasky, *The Democratic Socialism of Émile Vandervelde*, pp. 10–11, 16, 53, 57–9, 61–2, 67–9, 71.
90. Ewans, *European Atrocity, African Catastrophe*, p. 217.

two

1. É. Vandervelde, *La Belgique et le Congo, le passé, le présent, l'avenir* (Paris: FélixAlcan, 1911); also É. Vandervelde, *Les Derniers jours de l'état du Congo* (Paris: Mons, 1909).
2. M.E. Thomas, 'Anglo-Belgian Military Relations and the Congo Question, 1911–1913', *Journal of Modern History* 25, no. 2 (1953), pp. 157–65.
3. The best single source for this period is R. Lemarchand, 'Selective Bibliographical Survey for the Study of Politics in the Former Belgian Congo', *American Political Science Review*, 54, no. 4 (1960), pp. 715–28.
4. J. Gérard-Libois, 'The New Class and Rebellion in the Congo', *Socialist Register 1966*, ed. R. Miliband and J. Saville (London: Merlin Press, 1966) pp. 267–80, 267.
5. M.D. Markovitz, *Cross and Sword: The Political Role of Christian Missions in the Belgian Congo 1908–1960* (Stanford CA: Hoover Institution Press, 1973), p. 104.
6. C. Perrys, *Black Mineworkers in Central Africa: Industrial Strategies and the Evolution of an African Proletariat in the Copperbelt 1911–1941* (London: Heinemann, 1979), pp. 9–10.
7. D. dia Mwembu, *Histoire des Conditions de Vie des Travailleurs de l'Union Minière du Haut-Katanga/Gécamines 1910–1999* (Lubumbashi: Presses Universitaires de Lubumbashi, 2001), p. 16.
8. A. Yav, *The 'Vocabulary of Élisabethville'* ed. and trans. Johannes Fabian with Kalundi Mango (Amsterdam: John Benjamins, 1990), pp. 75–7.

9. Dia Mwembu, *Histoire des Conditions*, pp. 26–33.
10. Perrys, *Black Mineworkers*, p. 58.
11. D.N. Gibbs, *The Political Economy of Third World Intervention: Mines, Money and US Policy in the Congo Crisis* (Chicago: University of Chicago Press, 1991), p. 51.
12. B. de Melder, *De kampen von Kongo* (Antwerp: Kritak, 1996), p. 77.
13. Perrys, *Black Mineworkers*, pp. 77–8.
14. R.W. Harris, *River of Wealth, River of Sorrow: The Central Zaïre Basin in the Era of the Slave and Ivory Trade 1500–1891* (New Haven CT: Yale University Press, 1981), p. 41; M. Ewans, *European Atrocity, African Catastrophe: Léopold II, the Congo Free State and Its Aftermath* (London: Routledge, 2002), pp. 238–42.
15. Perrys, *Black Mineworkers*, p. 99.
16. D. Northrup, *Beyond the Bend in the Rover: African Labour in Eastern Zaïre 1865–1940* (Athens OH: University of Ohio Press, 1990), p. 206.
17. G. Nzongolo-Ntalaja, *Revolution and Counter-revolution in Africa: Essays in Contemporary Politics* (London: Zed Press, 1987), p. 98.
18. Dia Mwembu, *Histoire des Conditions*, p. 43.
19. Yav, *The 'Vocabulary of Élisabethville'*, p. 77.
20. J. Fabian, *Language and Colonial Power: The Appropriation of Swahili in the Former Belgian Congo 1880–1938* (Berkeley: University of California Press, 1986), p. 101.
21. Ewans, *European Atrocity, African Catastrope*, p. 218.
22. Markovitz, *Cross and Sword*, p. 22, 26, 115.
23. H. Vinck, 'The missionaries' influence on Mongo national consciousness and political activism 1925–1965', www.aeqatoria.be/influenceEnglish.html.
24. Young, *Politics in the Congo*, p. 15.
25. A. Gide, *Travels in the Congo* (Harmondsworth: Penguin, 1986), p. 12.
26. M. Farr, *Tintin: The Complete Companion* (London: John Murray, 2001), pp. 21–7.
27. Markovitz, *Cross and Sword*, p. 19.
28. Young, *Politics in the Congo*, pp. 11, 93–4.
29. Ewans, *European Atrocity, African Catastrope*, pp. 238–42.
30. M.-B. Dembour, *Recalling the Belgian Congo: Conversations and Introspection* (Oxford: Berghahn Books, 2000), p. 48.
31. Ibid., p. 58–9.
32. E. Bustin, *Lunda under Belgian Rule: The Politics of Ethnicity* (Cambridge MA: Harvard University Press, 1974), p. 160; I. Cunnison, *The Luapula Peoples of Northern Rhodesia: Custom and History in Tribal Politics* (Manchester: Manchester University Press, 1959); H. Van Roy, *Les Byaambvu du Moyen-Kwango: Histoire du royaume Luwa-Yaka* (Berlin: Reimer, 1988); E.-L. Adriaens, *Recherches sur l'alimentation des populations au Kwaango* (Brussels: Ministère des Colonies, 1951); J.-L. Vellut, 'Notes sur le Lunda et la Frontière Luso-Africaine (1700–1900)', *Études d'Histoire Africaine* 3 (1972), pp. 61–166.
33. P. De Boeck, 'Post-colonialism, Power and Identity: Local and Global

Perspectives from Zaïre' in R. Werbner and T. Ranger (eds), *Post-colonial Identities in Africa* (London: Zed Books, 1996); O. Likaka, 'Rural Protest: The Mbole against Belgian Rule, 1897–1959,' *International Journal of African Historical Studies* 27, no. 3 (1994), pp. 589–617.

34. M. Douglas, *The Lele of the Kasai* (London: International African Institute, 1963), p. 261.

35. J. Banaji, 'The Crisis of British Anthropology', *New Left Review* 64 (1970), pp. 71–85; J. Copans and D. Seddon, 'Marxism and Anthropology: A Preliminary Survey', in D. Seddon (ed.), *Relations of Production: Marxist Approaches to Economic Anthropology* (London: Frank Cass, 1978), pp. 1–46.

36. O. Lisaka, 'Rural Protest: the Mbole against Belgian Rule 1897–1959', *International Journal of African Historical Studies* 27, no. 3 (1994), pp. 589–618, 607.

37. Ewans, *European Atrocity, African Catastrope*, p. 240.

38. Yav, *The 'Vocabulary of Élisabethville'*, pp. 79–81.

39. For previous millenarian prophecy in the region, associated with the Jehovah's Witnesses, see H.-J. Greschat, *Kitwala: Ursprung, Ausbrieitung uind Religion der Watch-Tower Bewegung in Zentralafrika* (Marburg: N.G. Elwert Verlag, 1967).

40. Yav, *The 'Vocabulary of Élisabethville'*, p. 87.

41. E. Andersson, *Messianic Popular Movements in the Lower Congo* (Uppsala: Almquist & Wiksells, 1958), pp. 50–52, 61, 63–8, 269.

42. P. Manicom, *Out of Africa: Kimbanguism* (London: Christian Education Movement, 1979), pp. 14–19.

43. L.A. Cook, 'Revolt in Africa', *The Journal of Negro History* 18, no. 4 (1933), pp. 396–413.

44. Cited in Nzongolo-Ntalaja, *Revolution and Counter-revolution in Africa*, p. 117.

45. R. Gott, *Mobutu's Congo* (London: Fabian Society, 1968), p. 44.

46. Dia Mwembu, *Histoire des Conditions*, p. 46.

47. J. Higginson, *A Working Class in the Making: Belgian Colonial Labor Policy, Private Enterprise, and the African Mineworker 1907–1951* (Madison: University of Wisconsin Press, 1989), p. 187.

48. Perrys, *Black Mineworkers*, pp. 225–7; Higginson, *A Working Class in the Making*, p. 193.

49. Dia Mwembu, *Histoire des Conditions*, pp. 52–3.

50. Higginson, *A Working Class in the Making*, p. 206.

51. Young, *Politics in the Congo*, p. 33.

52. H. Winternitz, *East along the Equator: A Congo Journey* (London: Bodley Head, 1988), p. 65.

53. T. Mukenge, *Culture and Customs of the Congo* (Westport CT: Greenwood Press, 2002), p. 174.

54. H.F. Weiss, *Political Protest in the Congo: The Parti Solidaire Africain during the Independence Struggle* (Princeton: Princeton University Press, 1967), p. 191.

55. Young, *Politics in the Congo*, pp. 274–7.

56. Gérard-Libois, 'The New Class and Rebellion in the Congo', p. 270.
57. Nzongolo-Ntalaja, *Revolution and Counter-revolution in Africa*, p. 99.
58. Gibbs, *Political Economy*, p. 57.
59. Ibid., p. 60.
60. Legum, *Congo Disaster*, p. 59.
61. Weiss, *Political Protest in the Congo*, p. 190.
62. P. Lumumba, *Congo My Country* (New York: Frederick A. Praeger, 1962), p. 12.
63. R. Govender, *The Martyrdom of Patrice Lumumba* (London: Neillgo, 1971), p. 35.
64. Weiss, *Political Protest in the Congo*, p. 37.
65. Ibid., pp. 61, 84.
66. Legum, *Congo Disaster*, p. 60.
67. *Guardian*, 1 July 1960.
68. A. Hochschild, *King Leopold's Ghost: A Story of Greed, Terror and Heroism in Colonial Africa* (London: Pan, 1998), p. 301,
69. *Lumumba Speaks: The Speeches and Writings of Patrice Lumumba 1958–1961* (Boston MA: Little, Brown, 1972), pp. 220–21.
70. Belgium's former Prime Minster Mark Eyskens (son of the prime minster at the moment of Patrice Lumumba's death in 1961) during an interview in December 2000 commented: 'Lumumba was considered a Communist, with so many deaths on his conscience that a consensus to eliminate him developed in the West. He may be compared with men such as Milosevic and Saddam Hussein today. Had he remained in power, it would have been a catastrophe for the Congolese people'. E. Bustin 'Remembrance of Sins Past: Unravelling the Murder of Patrice Lumumba' *Review of African Political Economy* 93/94 (2002), p. 539.
71. Ibid., p. 541.
72. A.M. Babu, *The Future that Works* (Trenton NJ: Africa World Press, 2002), p. 66.

three

1. C.D. Young, *Politics in the Congo: Decolonization and Independence* (Princeton NJ: Princeton University Press, 1963), p. 305.
2. *Lumumba Speaks: The Speeches and Writings of Patrice Lumumba 1958–1961* (Boston MA: Little, Brown, 1972, pp. 30–1.
3. A. Gramsci, *Selections from Prison Notebooks* (London: Lawrence & Wishart, 1973), pp. 106–14.
4. Legum, *Congo Disaster* (Harmondsworth, Penguin, 1961), p. 92.
5. Ibid., p. 60.
6. M. Mamdani *Understanding the Crisis in Kivu* (Dakar: CODESRIA, 2001), pp.3–4.
7. *La Relève*, 27 August 1960.
8. L. de Witte, *The Assassination of Lumumba* (London: Verso, 2001), p. 31.
9. R. Govender, *The Martyrdom of Patrice Lumumba* (London: Neillgo, 1971), pp. 66–7.
10. De Witte, *The Assassination of Lumumba* , p. 37.

11. S. Simon, 'The Belgian General Strike', *Revolutionary History* 7, no. 1 (1998), pp. 80–133.
12. *Lumumba Speaks*, p. 293.
13. *Daily Telegraph*, 27 July 1960.
14. Govender, *The Martyrdom of Patrice Lumumba*, p. 81.
15. *Lumumba Speaks*, pp. 42–3.
16. J. Woddis, *Africa: The Lion Awakes* (London: Lawrence & Wishart, 1961), p. 136.
17. J. Higginson, *A Working Class in the Making: Belgian Colonial Labor Policy, Private Enterprise, and the African Mineworker 1907–1951* (Madison: University of Wisconsin Press, 1989), p. 207.
18. Legum, *Congo Disaster*, p. 99.
19. M. Wrong, *In the Footsteps of Mr Kurtz: Living on the Brink of Disaster in the Congo* (London: Fourth Estate, 2000), p. 66.
20. A.M. Babu, *The Future that Works* (Trenton NJ: Africa World Press, 2002), pp. 195–6.
21. B. Berkeley, *The Graves Are Not Yet Full: Race, Tribe and Power in the Heart of Africa* (New York: New Republic, 2001), p. 110.
22. Govender, *The Martyrdom of Patrice Lumumba*, p. 131.
23. A. Hochschild, *King Leopold's Ghost: A Story of Greed, Terror and Heroism in Colonial Africa* (London: Pan, 1998), p. 302.
24. Wrong, *In the Footsteps of Mr Kurtz*, p. 67.
25. Govender, *The Martyrdom of Patrice Lumumba*, pp. 173–4.
26. L. Polman, *We Did Nothing: Why the Truth Always Comes Out When the UN Goes In* (London: Penguin, 2004).
27. De Witte, *The Assassination of Lumumba*, pp. 52–4.
28. *Lumumba Speaks*, pp. 421–2.
29. The conclusions of the report are available online at www.lachambre.be/commissions/lmb.
30. De Witte, *The Assassination of Lumumba*, p. 183.
31. Govender, *The Martyrdom of Patrice Lumumba*, pp. 8–9.
32. Hochschild, *King Leopold's Ghost*, p. 302.
33. De Witte, *The Assassination of Lumumba*, pp. 151–2.
34. R. Segal, *African Profiles* (London: Penguin, 1963), pp. 184–5.
35. Hochschild, *King Leopold's Ghost*, p. 302.
36. A.L. Burns and N. Heathcote, *Peace-keeping by UN Forces: From Suez to the Congo* (London: Pall Mall Press, 1963), pp. 100–131.
37. B. Verhaegen (ed.), *Kisangani 1876–1976: Histoire d'une ville* (Kinshasa: Presses Universitaires du Zaïre, 1975).
38. A. Jones, *Britain and the Congo Crisis 1960–63* (London: Macmillan, 1996), p. 185.
39. Ibid., pp. 199–203.
40. R. Dayal, *Mission for Hammarskjold: The Congo Crisis* (Oxford: Oxford University Press, 1976), p. 258.
41. C. Guevara, *The African Dream* (London: Harvill Panther, 2001), p. xxi.
42. The clearest statement of this analysis is L. Martens, *1958–1966: 10 jarr*

revolutie in Kongo: De strijd van Patrice Lumumba en Pierre Mulele (Berchem: Uitgeverij FPO, 1988).

43. G. Nzongola-Ntalaja, *Revolution and Counter-revolution in Africa: Essays in Contemporary Politics* (London: Zed Books, 1987), p. 110.
44. R. Gott, 'Introduction', in *The African Dream* (London: Harvill Panther, 2001) pp. v–xxi.
45. Galvin and Ferrer are quoted in J. Damu, 'Rebellion in Zaïre – Former Cuban Comrades Cast Doubts on Kabila's Rebel Image', Pacific News Service, 23 April 1997.
46. William Gálvez, *Che in Africa: Che Guevara's Congo Diary* (Melbourne: Ocean Press, 1999), p. 281.
47. Young, *Politics in the Congo*, p. 461.
48. W. J. Samarin, *The Black Man's Burden: African Colonial Labor on the Congo and Ubangi Rivers, 1880–1900* (Boulder CO: Westview Press, 1989); C. Perrings, *Black Mineworkers in Central Africa: Industrial Strategies and the Evolution of an African Proletariat in the Copperbelt 1911–1941* (London: Heinemann, 1979); J. Higginson, *A Working Class in the Making: Belgian Colonial Labour Policy, Private Enterprise, and the African Mineworker 1907–1951* (Madison: University of Wisconsin Press, 1989).
49. Martens, *1958–1966: 10 jarr revolutie in Kongo*, p. 38.
50. D. Northrupp, *Beyond the Bend in the River: African Labor in Eastern Zaïre 1865–1940* (Athens OH: Ohio University Centre for International Studies, 1988).
51. Nzongola-Ntalaja, *Revolution and Counter-revolution in Africa*, p. 105.
52. Higginson, *A Working Class in the Making*, p. 206.
53. M. Malela, *Travail et Travailleurs au Zaïre: essai sur la conscience du proletariat urbain de Lubumbashi* (Kinshasa: Presses Universitaires du Zaïre, 1979), p. 98.
54. Govender, *The Martyrdom of Patrice Lumumba*, p. 8.
55. Wrong, *In the Footsteps of Mr Kurtz*, p. 69.
56. Ibid., p. 72.
57. Ibid., p. 74
58. Ibid., p. 64.
59. Hochschild, *King Leopold's Ghost*, p. 302.
60. Ibid., p. 302.

four

1. M. Wrong, *In the Footsteps of Mr Kurtz* (London: Fourth Estate, 2000), p. 86.
2. Jacques Depelchin, 'The Transformations of the Petty Bourgeoisie and the State in Post-Colonial Zaïre', *Review of African Political Economy* 22 (October–December 1981), pp. 20–41, p. 31.
3. L. Zeilig, 'Students and the Struggle for Democracy in sub-Saharan Africa', Ph.D. thesis, Brunel University, London, 2005.
4. G. Nzongola-Ntalaja, *A People's History of the Congo* (London, Zed Books, 2002), p. 177.

5. Ibid., pp. 173–9.
6. Ibid., p. 179.
7. Later, in 1981, Congolese law relating to nationality was changed, to require the attribution of nationality on an individual, rather than a collective basis, through either paternal or maternal descent. Those who were born thereafter within generally had their Congolese/Zaïrean nationality recorded on their birth certificates and other documents.
8. G. Stewart, *Rumba on the River: A History of the Popular Music of the Two Congos* (London: Verso, 2000), p. 198.
9. Ibid., p. 86.
10. T. Turner, 'Zaïre: Flying High above the Toads: Mobutu and Stalemated Democracy' in J.F. Clark and D.E. Gardinier (eds), *Political Reform in Francophone Africa* (Boulder CO: Westview Press, 1997), p. 250.
11. Wrong, *In the Footsteps of Mr Kurtz*, p. 110.
12. I. Samset, 'Conflict of Interests or Interests in Conflict? Diamonds and the War in the DRC', *Review of African Political Economy* 93/94 (2002), pp. 463–80, 468.
13. M. Barratt Brown, *Africa's Choices: after Thirty Years of the World Bank* (Boulder CO: Westview Press, 1995) p. 37.
14. C. Ake, *Democracy and Development in Africa* (Ibadan: Spectrum Books, 2001), p. 70.
15. M. Larmer, 'Resisting the State: The Trade Union Movement and Working-class Politics in Zambia, 1964–9', in L. Zeilig (ed.), *Class Struggle and Resistance in Africa* (Cheltenham: New Clarion Press, 2002), pp. 98–112.
16. F.O.E. Okafor, 'The Mining Multinationals and the Zambian Economy', *African Review* 17, no. 1/2 (1990).
17. C. Braeckman, *Le Dinosaure: Le Zaïre du Mobutu* (Paris: Fayard, 1992), p. 219.
18. Stewart, *Rumba on the River*, p. 173.
19. E. Hobsbawm, *The Age of Extremes: the Short Twentieth Century 1914–94* (London: Abacus 1995) p. 405.
20. P. Marfleet, 'Globalisation and the Third World', *International Socialism Journal* 81 (1998), pp. 91–130, 104.
21. *Africa Confidential*, 19 January 1996, p. 7.
22. *Africa Confidential*, 7 December 1990, p. 5.
23. Wrong, *In the Footsteps of Mr Kurtz*, p. 110
24. S. Riley and T. Parfitt, 'Economic Adjustment and Democratisation in Africa', in J. Walton and D. Seddon (eds), *Free Markets and Food Riots: The Politics of Global Adjustment* (Oxford: Blackwell, 1994), pp. 158–9.
25. J. Depelchin, 'The Transformations of the Petty Bourgeoisie and the State in Post-Colonial Zaïre', *Review of African Political Economy* 8, no. 22 (1981), p. 33.
26. Ibid., p. 35.
27. Ibid.
28. Stewart, *Rumba on the River*, p. 216.
29. *Salongo*, 26 November 1977.

30. Depelchin, 'The Transformations', p. 36.
31. W. Burchett and D. Roebuck, *The Whores of War: Mercenaries Today* (London: Penguin, 1977), p. 17.
32. Ibid., p. 123.
33. J. MacGaffey (ed.), *The Real Economy of Zaïre* (London: James Currey, 1991), p. 28.
34. Ake, *Democracy and Development in Africa*, p. 77.
35. MacGaffey, *The Real Economy of Zaïre*, p. 28.
36. R. Sandbrook, *The Politics of Africa's Economic Recovery* (Cambridge: Cambridge University Press, 1993), p. 2.
37. Ma Marabundu ye Beda 'The Trade in Food Crops, Manufactured Goods and Mineral Products in the Frontier Zone of the Lvozi, Lower Zaïre', in MacGaffey, *The Real Economy of Zaïre*, pp. 97–123, 122.
38. MacGaffey, *The Real Economy of Zaïre*, p. 33.
39. Barratt Brown, *Africa's Choices,* p. 226.
40. Ibid., p. 227.
41. MacGaffey, *The Real Economy of Zaïre*, pp.13–14.
42. Interview, 12 November 2004, Paris.
43. T.T. Munikengi and W. Bongo-Pasi Mako Sangol, 'The Diploma Paradox' in T. Trefon (ed.) *Reinventing Order in the Congo* (London: Zed Books, 2004), p. 92.
44. J. MacGaffey, *Entrepreneurs and Parasites: The Struggle for Indigenous Capitalism in Zaire* (Cambridge: Cambridge University Press, 1987), p. 33.
45. Barratt Brown, *Africa's Choices*, p. 233.
46. Ibid., p. 235.
47. Ibid., p. 235.
48. Turner, 'Zaïre', p. 253.
49. M. Gaud and L. Porges, 'Dix Biographies', *Afrique Contemporaine*, July–September 1997, pp. 105–6.
50. T.K Biaga, 'Transition et rationalité politiques au Zaïre', in M.C. Diop and M. Diouf (eds), *Les figures du politique en Afrique* (Paris and Dakar: CODESRIA/Karthala, 1999).
51. C. Braeckman, *L'Enjeu Congolais: L'Afrique centrale après Mobutu* (Paris: Fayard, 1999), p. 309.
52. Gaud and Porges, 'Dix Biographies', pp. 105–6.
53. See the website of the UDPS: www.udps.org/Textes-Afrique/tshisekedi-150903.html.
54. Braeckman, *L'Enjeu Congolais*, p. 310.
55. M. Nkongolo, *Le campus martyr* (Paris: L'Harmattan, 2000), pp. 121–2.
56. Munikengi and Sangol, 'The Diploma Paradox', p. 91.

five

1. G. de Villers and J.M. Tshonda, 'When Kinois Take to the Street', in T. Trefon (ed.) *Reinventing Order in the Congo* (London: Zed Books, 2004), pp. 137–154, 144.
2. Ibid., pp. 140–43.

3. M. Bratton and N. van de Walle, *Democratic Experiments in Africa: Regime Transitions in Comparative Perspective* (New York: Cambridge University Press, 1997), p. 5.

4. T. Trefon, S. Van Hoyweghen and S. Smis, 'State Failure in the Congo: Perceptions and Realities', in *Review of African Political Economy* 93, no. 4 (2002), pp. 379–88, 381.

5. M. Nkongolo, *Le campus martyr* (Paris: L'Harmattan, 2000), pp. 96–8.

6. B. Harden, *Africa: Dispatches from a Fragile Continent* (London: Harper Collins, 1993), p. 53.

7. Harden, *Africa*, p. 54.

8. L. Martens, *Kabila et la révolution congolaise: panafricanism or neocolonialisme?* (Anvers: Editions EPO, 2002), p. 115.

9. J. MacGaffey (ed.), *The Real Economy of Zaïre* (London: University of Pennsylvania Press and James Currey, 1991), p. 2.

10. R. Giraudon, 'Un Scandale Géologique?', *Afrique Contemporaine* 183 (1997), pp. 44–54, 50.

11. V. de P. Lunda-Bululu, *Conduire la première transition au Congo–Zaïre* (Paris: L'Harmattan, 2003), pp. 278–284.

12. J. MacGaffey and R. Bazenguissa-Ganga, *Congo–Paris: Transnational Traders on the Margins of the Law* (London, James Currey 2000), p. 30.

13. Ibid., p. 30.

14. C. Sumata, 'Migradollars and Poverty Alleviation Strategy Issues in Congo (DRC)', *Review of African Political Economy* 93 (2002), pp. 619–28, 623.

15. Cited in MacGaffey and Bazenguissa-Ganga, *Congo–Paris*, pp. 48–9.

16. For a radical overview of Zaïre's economic history, see R. Nyembo, 'L'économie Zairoise: une économie consequence d'une-politique', in *Congo (Zaïre) Democratie neo-coloniale ou deuxième independence?* (Paris: L'Harmattan, 1992), pp. 17–29.

17. E. Kennes, 'Footnotes to the Mining Story', *Review of African Political Economy* 93 (2002), pp. 601–7, 606.

18. For a discussion of some of these themes see J. Lea, *Crime and Modernity* (London: Sage, 2002).

19. S. Riley and T. Parfitt, 'Economic Adjustment and Democratisation in Africa', in J. Walton and D. Seddon (eds), *Free Markets and Food Riots: The Politics of Global Adjustment* (Oxford: Blackwell, 1994), pp. 135–70, 136.

20. C. Ake, *Democracy and Development in Africa* (Ibadan: Spectrum Books, 2001), p. 135.

21. N. Mutala, *Troisième République du Zaïre: le round décisif* (Brussels: Éditions de Souverain, 1991), p. 73.

22. Nkongolo, *Le Campus Martyr*, p. 182.

23. G. Nzongola-Ntalaja, *The Congo: From Léopold to Kabila* (London: Zed Books, 2002), pp. 155, 156; note that some commentators repeat the denials of the regime: for example, T.T. Munikengi and W. Bongo-Pasi Mako Sangol, 'The Diploma Paradox', in Trefon (ed.) *Reinventing Order in the Congo*, pp. 82–98, 99.

24. A. Guichaoua and C. Vidal, 'Les Politiques internationales dans la région des grands lacs africains', *Politique Africaine* 68 (1997), pp. 3–10.

25. C. Braeckman, *Le Dinosaure: le Zaïre de Mobutu* (Paris: Fayard, 1992), p. 294.

26. L.L. Djugudjugu, *Troisième République au Zaïre: perestroïka, Démocratie ou Catastroika?* (Kinshasa: Bibliothèque du Scribe, 1991), pp. 178–85; N. Karl-i-Bond, *Un avenir pour le Zaïre* (Bruxelles: Vie Ouvrière, 1985), p. 149.

27. J.P. Kambila-Kankwendie, *Congo: la solution lumumbistes* (Ivry-sur-Seine: Editions Nouvelles du Sud), pp. 78–83.

28. Nzongola-Ntalaja, *The Congo*, p. 188.

29. T.B. Bakajika, *Partis et société civile du Congo/Zaïre: la démocratie en crise: 1956–65 et 1990–97* (Paris: L'Harmattan, 2004), pp. 199–216.

30. Villers and Tshonda, 'When Kinois Take to the Street', p. 142.

31. W. Oyatambwe, *Eglise Catholique et pouvoirs politique au Congo–Zaïre* (Paris: L'Harmattan, 1997), pp. 116–17.

32. Tshisekedi's departure was hastened by his refusal to swear an oath of allegiance to the president, and by his public denunciation of Mobutu.

33. L. Martens, *Kabila et la révolution congolais*, p. 78.

34. Nzongola-Ntalaja, *The Congo*, p. 190.

35. Martens gives a good description of the risks of demonstration, *Kabila et la révolution congolais*, vol. 1, pp. 83–4.

36. W. Oyatambwe, *Eglise Catholique*, pp. 127–33.

37. P. de Dorlodot, *Marche d'espoir: Kinshasa 16 Février 1992. Non-violence pour la Démocratie au Zaïre* (Paris: L'Harmattan, 1994), pp. 100–102.

38. Ibid., pp. 25–6.

39. Ibid., p. 28.

40. Ibid., p. 30.

41. Ibid., p. 36–7.

42. Ibid., p. 50.

43. Ibid., pp. 38–9.

44. De Villers and Tshonda, 'When Kinois Take to the Street', p. 144.

45. See for a good summary of some of the groups active during the 'transition' Bakajika, *Partis et société civile du Congo/Zaïre*, pp. 178–98.

46. Nzongola-Ntalaja, *The Congo*, p. 190.

47. Martens, *Kabila et la révolution congolaise*, p. 84.

48. Parfitt and Riley, 'Economic Adjustment', p. 165

49. S. Riley, *The Politics of Global Debt* (London: Macmillan, 1993), p. 116.

50. P. Decraene, *L'Afrique Centrale* (Paris: CHEAM, 1993), pp. 157–8.

51. Nzongola-Ntalaja, *The Congo*, p. 195.

52. T.K. Biaya, 'Transition et rationalité politiques au Zaïre', in M.C. Diop and M. Diouf (eds), *Les figures du politiques en Afrique* (Paris: Karthala, 1999), pp. 245–91, 280.

53. Nzongola-Ntalaja, *The Congo*, p. 197.

54. Ibid.

55. Kalele-ka-Bila, 'La démocratie a la base: l'expérience des parlementaires-debout au Zaïre', in G. Nzongola-Ntalaja and M.C. Lee (eds), *The State*

and Democracy in Africa (Trenton, NJ: Africa World Press, 1998), pp. 64–73.

56. Nzongola-Ntalaja, *The Congo*, p. 201.
57. I. Samset, 'Conflict of Interests or Interests in Conflict? Diamonds and War in the DRC', *Review of African Political Economy* 29, no. 93/4 (2002), pp. 463–80.
58. Gauthier de Villers and J.O. Tshonda, 'An Intransitive Transition', *Review of African Political Economy* 29, no. 93/4 (2002), pp. 399–410, 403.
59. Martens, *Kabila*, p. 46.
60. Nzongola-Ntalaja, *The Congo*, p. 208.
61. Martens, *Kabila*, p. 71.
62. C. Leys and J. Saul, 'Sub-Saharan Africa in Global Capitalism' in *Monthly Review* 51/2 (1999), pp. 13–30, 26.
63. Martens, *Kabila*, p. 83.
64. Ibid., p. 115.

six

1. C. Braeckman, *Les Nouveaux Prédateurs* (Paris: Fayard, 2003), p. 179.
2. For a general discussion on these themes, see K. Ballentine and J. Sherman (eds), *The Political Economy of Armed Conflict: Beyond Greed and Grievance* (Boulder CO: Lynne Rienner: 2003).
3. M. Mamdani, *Understanding the Crisis in Kivu* (Dakar: CODESRIA, 2001), p. 5.
4. Ibid., pp. 3–4.
5. M. Mamdani, *When Victims Become Killers* (Princeton NJ: Princeton University Press, 2002), p. 240.
6. Ibid., p. 240.
7. Mamdani, *Understanding the Crisis in Kivu*, p. 9.
8. Ibid., p. 9.
9. C. Scherrer, *Genocide and Crisis in Central Africa* (Westport CT: Praeger, 2002).
10. L. Melvern, *A People Betrayed: The Role of the West in Rwanda's Genocide* (London: Zed Books, 2000); also G. Prunier, *The Rwanda Crisis: History of a Genocide* (New York: Columbia University Press, 1997); African Rights, *Rwanda: Death, Despair and Defiance* (London: Africa Rights, 1995).
11. C. Kimber, 'Coming to Terms with Genocide in Rwanda and Burundi', *International Socialism* 2, no. 73 (1996), pp. 127–46.
12. K. Mills, 'Refugee Return from Zaïre to Rwanda: The Role of the UNHCR', in H. Adelman and G.C. Rao, *War and Peace in Zaïre/Congo* (New York: Africa World Press 2004), pp. 163–85, 182.
13. Ibid., p. 169.
14. Mamdani, *Understanding the Crisis in Kivu*, p. 24.
15. M.B. Umutesi, *Fuir ou mourir au Zaïre* (Paris: L'Harmattan, 2000), p. 184.
16. B. Rugumaho, *L'Hecatombe des réfugies rwandais dans l'ex-Zaïre* (Paris: L'Harmattan, 2004); Umutesi, *Fuir ou mourir au Zaïre*.
17. T. Longman, 'The Complex Reasons for Rwanda's Engagement in

Congo', in J.F. Clark (ed.), *The African Stakes of the Congo War* (New York: Palgrave 2002), pp. 129–46, 138.

18. Mamdani, *When Victims Become Killers*, p. 261.
19. Ibid.
20. Kimber, 'Coming to Terms', pp. 143–4.
21. K. Vlassenroot, 'Citizenship, Identity Formation and Conflict in South Kivu: The Case of the Banyamulenge', *Review of African Political Economy* 29, no. 93/4 (September/December 2002), pp. 499–515; see also D.L. Schoenbrun, *A Green Place, a Good Place: Agrarian Change, Gender and Social Identity in the Great Lakes Region to the Fifteenth Century* (Portsmouth NH: Heinemann, 1998), p. 260.
22. L. Zeilig (ed.), *Class Struggle and Resistance in Africa* (Cheltenham: New Clarion Press, 2002); and C. Braeckman, *Le Dinosaure: le Zaïre de Mobutu* (Paris: Fayard, 1992).
23. See B. Collins, 'Rewriting Rwanda', www.spiked-online.com/Articles/0000000CA4BD.htm.
24. W. Madsen, 'How America Ran, and Still Runs, the Congo War', *New African*, September 2001, pp. 18–22, 19.
25. W. Madsen, *Genocide and Covert Operations in Africa 1993–1999* (Lewiston NY: Edwin Mellen Press, 1999).
26. H. Condurier, 'Ce que les services secrets français savaient', *Valeurs Actuelles* 30 August 1997, pp. 26–7.
27. E. Rubin, 'An Army of One's Own', *Harper's Magazine*, February 1997.
28. E. Kennes, 'Footnotes to the Mining Story', *Review of African Political Economy* 29, no. 93/4 (2002), pp. 601–7, 602.
29. C. Breackman, *L'Enjeu Congolais* (Paris: Fayard, 1999), p. 158.
30. A. Huliaras, '(Non)policies and (Mis)perceptions: The United States, France and the Crisis in Zaïre', in Adelman and Rao, *War and Peace in Zaïre/Congo*, pp. 281–305, 282.
31. US Department of Defense, *United States Security Strategy for Sub-Saharan Africa* (Washington DC: Office of International Security Affairs, 1995), p. 3.
32. Huliaras, '(Non)policies and (Mis)perceptions', p. 287.
33. M. Mamdani, 'Why Rwanda Admitted to Its Role in Zaïre', *Mail and Guardian* (South Africa), 8 August 1997.
34. Huliaras, '(Non)policies and (Mis)perceptions', p. 288.
35. G. Prunier, 'Sudan's Regional War', *Le Monde Diplomatique*, February 1997.
36. M.W. Makgoba (ed.), *African Renaissance: The New Struggle* (Cape Town: Mafube, 1999).
37. Huliaras, '(Non)policies and (Mis)perceptions', p. 292.
38. T. Hodges, *Angola: From Afro-Stalinism to Petro-Diamond Capitalism* (Oxford: James Currey, 2001).
39. Huliaras, '(Non)policies and (Mis)perceptions', p. 292.
40. Human Rights Watch, *Ituri: Covered in Blood* (New York: HRW, 2003), p. 55.
41. See, for an overview, L. Zeilig and D. Seddon, 'Marxism, Class and

Resistance in Africa', in Zeilig (ed.), *Class Struggle and Resistance in Africa*, pp. 1–23.

42. J.C. Willame, *L'Odyssee Kabila: trajectoire pour un Congo nouveau* (Paris: Karthala, 1999), p. 22.
43. Braeckman, *L'Enjeu Conglais*, p. 96.
44. Ibid., p. 98.
45. C Wilungula, 'Le Maquis Kabila', *Cahiers Africains* 26 (1997).
46. Willame, *L'Odyssee Kabila*, p. 27–8.
47. L.D. Kabila, *Lettre ouverte de Laurent-Desiré Kabila, Président du Parti Populaire de la Révolution, a Joseph-Desiré Mobutu, Président du MPR*, unpublished.
48. Braeckman, *Nouveaux prédateurs*, p. 183.
49. Ibid., p. 184.
50. Ibid., p. 185.
51. Cited on the Italian antiwar website http://ospiti.peacelink.it/bukavu/rs/CON4_42.html.
52. K. O'Brien, 'Private Military Companies: Licence to Kill', *The World Today* 59, no. 8/9 (2003).
53. Martens, *Kabila et la révolution congolaise* (Anvers: Editions EPO, 2002), p. 423.
54. Ibid., p. 420.
55. M. Nest, 'Ambitions, Profits and Loss: Zimbabwean Economic Involvement in the DRC', *African Affairs* 100 (2001), pp. 469–90. Nest's article is extremely revealing on Zimbabwe's involvement in the war; the argument presented here draws heavily from his evidence.
56. L. Zeilig, 'Crisis in Zimbabwe', *International Socialism* 2, no. 93 (2002), pp. 75–96.
57. United Nations Security Council, *Report of the Panel of Experts on the Illegal Exploitation of Natural Resources and Other Forms of Wealth of the Democratic Republic of the Congo* (New York: UNSC, 2001), pp. 33–5.
58. M. Gwisai, *Revolutionaries, Resistance and Crisis in Zimbabwe* (Harare: ISO, 2002), pp. 11–14.
59. Nest, 'Ambitions, Profits and Loss', p. 476.
60. Ibid., p. 483.
61. Samset, 'Conflict of Interests or Interests in Conflict? Diamonds and War in the DRC', *Review of African Political Economy* 29, no. 93/4 (2002), pp. 463–80, 475–6.
62. S. Perrot, 'Entrepreneurs de l'insécurité: la face cache de l'armée ougandaise', *Politique Africaine*, October 1999.
63. 'Museveni's "Adventure" in the Congo War: Uganda's Vietnam?', in Clark (ed.), *The African Stakes*, pp. 145–65, 161.
64. G. Prunier, 'L'Ouganda et les Guerres Congolaises', *Politique Africaine* 75 (1999), p. 44.
65. Clark, 'Museveni's "Adventure"', p. 152.
66. UNSC, *Report of the Panel of Experts on the Illegal Exploitation of Natural Resources*, p. 8.
67. Ibid., p. 47.

68. Human Rights Watch, *The Curse of Gold* (New York: HRW 2005), p. 16
69. Longman, 'The Complex Reasons', p. 136.
70. D. Montague and F. Berrigan, 'The Business of War in the Democratic Republic of Congo: Who Benefits?' *Dollar and Sense*, July 2001, pp. 15–19.
71. UNSC, *Report of the Panel of Experts on the Illegal Exploitation of Natural Resources*, pp. 6–19.
72. Human Rights Watch, *Ituri*, p. 54.
73. IMF County Report, *Uganda: Fifth Review under the Three-year Arrangement under the Poverty Reduction and Growth Facility* (Washington DC: IMF, 2005), p. 4.
74. G. Monbiot, 'Spin, Lies and Corruption', *Guardian*, 14 June 2005.
75. Clark, 'Museveni's Adventure', p. 153.
76. Human Rights Watch, *Ituri*, p. 53.
77. Longman, 'The Complex Reasons', pp. 156–7.
78. UNSC, *Final Report of the Panel of Experts on the Illegal Exploitation of Natural Resources.*
79. Madsen, 'How America Ran, and Still Runs, the Congo War', p. 21.
80. See UNSC reports: *Report of the Panel of Experts on the Illegal Exploitation of Natural Resources; Interim Report of the Panel of Experts on the Illegal Exploitation of Natural Resources and Other Forms of Wealth of the Democratic Republic of the Congo* (New York: UNSC, May 2002); *Final Report of the Panel of Experts on the Illegal Exploitation of Natural Resources and Other Forms of Wealth of the Democratic Republic of the Congo* (New York: UNSC, October 2002); *Report of the Panel of Experts on the Illegal Exploitation of Natural Resources and Other Forms of Wealth in the Democratic Republic of Congo* (New York: UNSC, October 2003). All these reports are available online: www.globalpolicy.org/security/issues/kingidx.htm.
81. UNSC, *Report of the Panel of Experts on the Illegal Exploitation of Natural Resources*, p.19.
82. Ibid., p. 38.
83. Samset, 'Conflict of Interests', p. 475.
84. Clark, 'Museveni's 'Adventure', p. 156.
85. G. de Villers, J. Omasombo and E. Kennes, *République démocratique du Congo: Guerre et politique, les trente derniers mois de Laurent-Désiré Kabila, août 1998–janvier 2001*, Cahiers Africains 47 (2002).
86. Braeckman, *Nouveaux Prédateurs*, pp. 199–200.
87. Human Rights Watch, *Ituri*, p. 2.
88. Ibid., pp. 6–7.
89. Human Rights Watch, *Uganda in Eastern DRC: Fuelling Political and Ethnic Strife* (New York: HRW, 2001).
90. Human Rights Watch, *Ituri*, p. 11.
91. Human Rights Watch, *Curse*, p. 75.
92. Ibid., pp. p. 71.
93. See Metalor's response to accusation made by HRW: www.metalor. com/fr/advanced-coatings/news.asp?id=1283.
94. Human Rights Watch, *Ituri*, p. 13.
95. Human Rights Watch, *Curse*, p. 24.

96. Human Rights Watch, *Ituri*, p. 24.
97. See Amnesty International Report for 2003: http://web.amnesty.org/report2004/cod-summary-eng.
98. Human Rights Watch, *Ituri*, p. 26.
99. Médecins Sans Frontières, *Ten Years of Conflict, Violence and Human Suffering* (Geneva: MSF, 2002) pp. 48–53.
100. Human Rights Watch, *Curse*, p. 50.
101. United Nations Report, *Special Investigation into Allegations of Summary Execution and Other Violations of Human Rights Committed by FARDC in Kilwa on 15 October 2004* (Kinshasa: MONUC, 2005).
102. UNSC, *Special Report on the Events in Ituri January 2002, December 2003* (New York: UNSC, July 2004).
103. Human Rights Watch, *Curse*, p. 36.
104. Human Rights Watch, 'Democratic Republic of Congo: Civilians at Risk During Disarmament Operations', background briefing, 29 December 2004.
105. Human Rights Watch 'Democratic Republic of Congo: War Crimes in Bukavu', briefing paper, June 2004.
106. Human Rights Watch, *Ituri*, p. 22
107. G. Nzongola-Ntalaja, *The Congo: from Léopold to Kabila* (London: Zed Books, 2002), pp. 234–5.
108. J. F Bayart, J. Ellis and Hibou, *The Criminalisation of the State* (Oxford: James Currey, 2000), p. 19.
109. UNSC, *Report of the Panel of Experts on the Illegal Exploitation of Natural Resources*, p. 19.
110. Samset, 'Conflict of Interests', pp. 463–70.
111. Global Witness and Partnership Africa Canada, 'The Key to Kimberley: Internal Diamond Controls. Seven Case Studies' (Washington: Global Witness, 2004).
112. Braeckman, *Nouveaux Prédateurs*, p. 199.
113. Madsen, 'How America Ran, and Still Runs, the Congo War', p. 22.

conclusion

1. *The Economist*, 13 May 2000.
2. See *Observer*, 1 January 2000
3. M. Wrong, *In the Footsteps of Mr Kurtz* (London: Fourth Estate, 2000), p. 79.
4. Ibid., pp. 11, 57.
5. B. Coghlan et al., *Mortality in the Democratic Republic of Congo: Results from a Nationwide Survey*, Burnet Institute and the International Rescue Committee, April–July 2004.
6. E. Kennes, 'Footnotes to the Mining Story', *Review of African Political Economy* 29, no. 93/4 (2002), pp. 601–7, 602.
7. Ibid., p. 606.
8. Ibid.
9. Human Rights Watch, *The Curse of Gold* (New York: HRW, 2005), p. 80.
10. J. Lea, *Crime and Modernity* (London: Sage, 2002), pp. 112–13.

index